Popular Music
in the Manchester region
since 1950

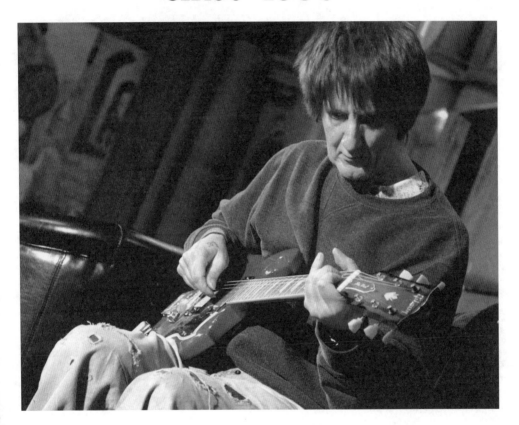

Manchester Region History Review
Volume 25
2014

ISSN 0952-4320

ISBN 978-1-85936-227-3

© Manchester Centre for Regional History, 2014

Typeset by Carnegie Book Production, Lancaster.
Printed and bound by Page Bros Ltd, Norwich, NR6 6SA

Contents

Long reviews

Editorial

Dave
Russell

In 2009 I edited a volume of this journal dedicated to the history of sport. Given the opportunity (gratefully received) to oversee an edition focusing on popular music, I have been forcibly struck by the similarities between the two areas, and, above all, by the intense passion that they both generate amongst their adherents. Interestingly, music probably engenders the greater heat. This is partly because its constituency is significantly bigger: there are simply more music than sports fans at large with opinions to air. However, it also results from the particularly deep and personal meanings that music carries. Sport, of course, is an important embodiment of various individual and collective identities relating to class, locality, nation and gender but music expresses both these and a great deal more. While sporting loyalties are often inherited, musical ones are usually adopted and, therefore, while defending the reputation of a team is often simply about the maintenance of bragging rights, defending a musical choice can involve exposing the absolute essence of an individual's worldview and self-image. For younger people especially this sense that we are what we listen to is particularly acute. As Dave Haslam observes, many people look back on a musical 'Golden Age' which tends to coincide with the 'era when we were young, free and on the town'.[1] In the 1960s and 1970s, the battles, usually symbolic but occasionally physical, between hippies and skinheads, punks and hippies, northern soulites and fans of progressive rock, and lots of people and lovers of disco were about a great deal more than musical taste. Popular music really matters.

'Popular music' is a large and awkward category that has been defined in numerous ways.[2] It has been seen in aesthetic and musicological terms as a collection of musical forms distinguishable by certain features (and modes of dissemination) that mark it out from other genres such as 'art music'; an essentially discursive formation that only takes on a clear existence when consciously set against other genres; the music of 'ordinary' people, or simply music that has been 'popular' in the sense of appealing to many. In the (often Americanized) British context, the first two approaches tend to a concentration on music hall, dance bands and pop and rock music. The latter two are wider ranging, embracing, for example, sacred choral music and Italian opera, both of which were 'popular' in the sense of being well known within working and lower-middle class communities in the nineteenth and earlier twentieth centuries, as a result of the activities of brass bands and choral societies. While no particular definition has been used to shape this collection, the chronological focus on the period from 1950, chosen in order to provide some coherence to the collection, has led to a slight preponderance of articles dealing with music that fits within the narrower field of definitions. These choices are not intended to minimize the importance of earlier ages or other musical forms and institutions. We know a little about Mancunian music hall, the dance bands of the inter-war years and the lives and songs of Rochdale's Gracie Fields and Wigan's George Formby, but we need to know a great deal more. Similarly, the region's brass bands and choirs would stand and benefit from proper scrutiny. The Mossley Temperance Saxhorn Temperance Band won the first ever Belle Vue brass band contest in 1853, Besses o' th' Barn was one of the nations' leading bands between about 1885 and 1905 and Manchester Orpheus was arguably Britain's premier male voice choir immediately before World War One.

The period that has been chosen for study has certainly been extensively written about, and quite rightly so. It is hard to disagree with Dave Haslam's assessment made in 1999 that Manchester had been 'at the heart of English pop music creativity for at least three decades'.[3] Merseyside, above all, and London clearly also exerted major influence but, especially between the late 1970s and the early 1990s, Manchester's music scene attained a striking national and international profile. A rich narrative has coalesced around the city's popular music, usually opening with the 'beat' boom of 1963–5, before moving on, respectively, to Northern Soul at its mid- to late 1970s zenith, the moment of Punk in 1976, Post-Punk, the emergence of Factory Records and its associated institutions, 'Madchester' and, finally, the arrival of Oasis and the flowering of Britpop in the mid-1990s. There are twenty-first century stories to tell as well, not least the rise of Bury band, Elbow, from indie rock band to composer-performers of the BBC's 2012 Olympic theme tune.

Although compelling in many ways, this narrative is somewhat selective. It focuses on music that is deemed to be 'authentic': implicitly, music with strong working-class connotations. It emphasizes particular moments of change and the events that symbolized them, such as the Sex Pistols' two Manchester Free Trade Hall concerts in 1976, the opening of The Haçienda in 1982 and the Stone Roses' performance at Spike Island, Widnes, in 1990. The years immediately preceding these climacterics are often either neglected or presented in decidedly negative terms. The immediate pre-punk period, in particular, is often described as a musical desert. For writer Paul Morley, at that time 'Manchester was a very boring place to be'; for founder of Factory Records, Tony Wilson, in late 1975 'nothing absolutely nothing was happening ... We were in that great dead period one gets at the end of a culture'.[4] Certain genres are similarly marginalized. Songs from the pre-rock 'n' roll era and other musical continuities from earlier periods receive little attention as, indeed, do some forms of music from later ones. Manchester generated some important progressive rock bands (Barclay James Harvest came from Oldham, Van Der Graaf Generator were formed at Manchester University), but they have found little space in existing accounts. As several students of Mark E. Smith and The Fall have noted, the band's failure to fit neatly within certain standard discourses that have structured the writing of the city's modern musical history has limited its place in that history.[5]

This is not in any sense an attempt to deny the importance of the established *dramatis personae* in the existing story or to call for the establishment of a new master narrative. It is, rather, a request that all established narratives be treated with necessary scepticism and a reminder that there are many other stories to be told. 1950s crooners were stranded by rock 'n roll and what followed, but they retained many fans. The regenerative impact of punk on popular music was remarkable but that does not make it necessary to dismiss what came before; 1975 was somebody's 'Golden Age'. Within the limits imposed by a single volume of this journal, the articles here contribute to this process of providing new insights into established topics and offering pathways into new ones.

It has been a great pleasure to work with the authors gathered here, all of whom responded speedily and to great effect when being asked, at relatively short notice, to submit articles. While all of our contributors have a strong interest in history, not all of them are historians. This as it should be for our understanding of popular music, however defined, is always at its richest when shaped by inter-disciplinary perspectives. The essays are organized chronologically and begin with my study of the cabaret clubs of 1960s Manchester and its region. This explores the growth and development of this vigorous element of the city-region's nightlife and discusses the rich variety of popular music available in what is usually dismissively termed the 'middle-of-the-road'. Dennis Bourne and Melanie Tebbutt focus their attention on a rather different form of club, the shebeens (unlicensed drinking places) of Manchester's Moss Side black community in the 1950s and 1960s. They discuss both the role played by discrimination in generating the need for a distinctive Afro-Caribbean cultural institution and the contribution made by black American soldiers to club culture in Second World War Manchester, before examining the role shebeens played in bringing black American and, eventually, Jamaican popular music into the city. CP Lee, both an academic observer of the Manchester music scene and once a professional participant, then explores Bob Dylan's concert at Manchester Free Trade Hall in May 1966 against the context of the contemporary British folk club scene and discusses its impact upon that culture. Lee's work combines a powerful personal involvement in the history he discusses and an academic engagement with it. A similar marriage can be found in the next essay by Manchester-based journalist and radio producer Bob Dickinson, a keen participant in Manchester's punk and post-punk music scene and once a rock critic for a number of local alternative newspapers. Inspired by a walk amongst the ghosts and carcases of Manchester's punk and post-punk venues, Dickinson discusses the audiences that they attracted and analyses the meanings that they attached to the music played there. His essay is attentive to change over time and to the shifting boundaries between those who 'performed' on stage and those who 'watched' from the floor.

The independent record label, Factory Records, and its associated ventures, undoubtedly forms one of the most iconic elements of Manchester's popular musical (and wider cultural) history. Working from within the field of Cultural Studies, James McGrath discusses both the processes through which, from its 1978 beginnings, Factory mythologized itself and the numerous narratives that have grown up around the company since its demise in 1992. While always probing rather than reinforcing myths, McGrath is also anxious to acknowledge Factory's enormously important creative role and distinctive ethos. Bands associated with the label also feature in Georgina Gregory's essay, although, here, they are considered within the wider matrix of relations between the English North and South. Situating the 1980s within a far longer tradition of London-centred deprecation of northern and provincial cultural attainment, Gregory explores contemporary media coverage of the Madchester scene with particular emphasis on the ways in well-honed cultural tropes were used to portray the artists and the city in a negative light. Esperanza Miyake's article is important not least for drawing attention to the fact that modern popular musical life has a large and insufficiently considered amateur, participatory element. Her study of the Manchester Gay and Lesbian Chorus provides a brief history of the choir, a discussion of its and its members place and role within the local, regional and national gay community and a close reading of participants' attitudes to its musical functions and repertoire.

The final essay seeks to provide some guidance to sources and resources that are available to historians of Manchester's popular music: there are so many avenues and opportunities and the field is especially well-suited to interventions by informed 'insiders'. For all the many changes in recent decades, historians have been drawn far less to music than to literature or fine art; a concern that specific technical knowledge might be required is possibly a factor here. In fact, while musical literacy is undeniably a valuable skill for music historians, it is by no means essential. There is no requirement to sing or play, merely to bring curiosity, enthusiasm and an open mind.

Going with the mainstream: Manchester cabaret clubs and popular music in the 1960s

Dave
Russell

'Manchester at Midnight .The verdict ... it's SWINGING!' In February 1964, readers of the *Manchester Evening News* were greeted by this confident verdict on a night-time economy embracing activities that ranged from 'teenagers' disc clubs to luxurious gambling spots'. Singer Emile Ford and comedian Jimmy Tarbuck were amongst those whose expert testimony was used to cast Manchester as the 'club centre of Britain'.[1] Two years later, a BBC television documentary explored the city's casinos and the *Guardian* investigated its blossoming club life, noting *en route* that Manchester had the highest number of clubs per head of population of any other British city. In 1972, the theatrical trade newspaper, *The Stage and Television Today*, offered in its own variation on a theme with a feature entitled 'Manchester, Now Cabaret's Capital City'.[2]

Manchester and, indeed, its wider region was exhibiting a particularly vibrant version of a new pleasure economy that marked British or, at least, English urban culture in the 1960s, typified by casinos, strip clubs, sophisticated restaurants and various styles of night club venue. Strangely, given that these institutions have such potential to illuminate discussion of that decade's so-called 'permissive' culture, they have attracted little historical attention and, beyond a valuable study of the distinctive case of the city's beat clubs, Manchester has shared in this neglect.[3] This study offers partial redress by providing an examination of the region's commercial cabaret clubs that first considers their emergence and function over the period from the mid-1950s to about 1970, before exploring their vital role as centres of popular musical life.

The cabaret club's specific failure to attract historians' attention is undoubtedly rooted in its designation within popular discourse as part of the 'mainstream' or the 'middle-of-the-road', something intrinsically too unchallenging and undemanding to deserve serious consideration. Such a view is seriously limiting, underestimating the opportunities for the expansion of cultural experience that apparently highly orthodox formations can offer. While clubs were hardly transgressive, the opportunities they allowed for eating out, gambling, dressing up, staying out late and enjoying physical proximity to star entertainers provided many ways for patrons to feel 'modern' and to enjoy activities usually associated with privileged social groups. Here, perhaps, was a quiet permissiveness, a broadening of the existing moral consensus from within the culture of 'ordinary' people.[4] Moreover, too easy dismissal of cabaret clubs compounds the neglect of mainstream commercial popular music that was so central to them. While the study of popular music has come of age in the most extraordinarily productive manner in the last quarter of the twentieth century, writers have invariably been attracted to forms that have produced, often from within younger generations, some level of aesthetic or political challenge to the *status quo*. Jazz and rock music, for example, clearly offer rich territories for those anxious to identify and explore new soundscapes or provocations to established moral boundaries. The result has been that musical continuities and many of the traditions that carry them have received scant attention.[5] As long ago as 1992, Dave Harker, identifying the soundtrack album of *South Pacific* as the most popular commercial musical product of the 1960s, argued that 'the musical practices and tastes of most people – the working class – are marginalized or ignored ... The people ... have been left out of "popular" music studies, and it's high time they were included'. Despite this and similar pleas, it was still possible for Derek Scott to acknowledge almost twenty years later that popular musicologists 'have tended to avoid like the plague ... the stratum of taste often labelled "middlebrow" (for example lounge music and easy listening)'.[6] Conservative in its musical languages and far too popular for its own good, such music is deemed unworthy of attention. However, as Michael Brocken has recently argued in a pioneering study, 'distaste for the middle-of-the-road does not justify exclusion from historical narratives'. The Manchester cabaret clubs, with their rich mixtures of mainstream musical genres, provide an ideal location within which to explore a central dimension of 1960s popular culture.[7]

The cabaret club. Definition, description and clientele

Before attempting to construct a chronological narrative of the region's clubs, it seems helpful to describe their function and operation in their sixties' heyday. The approach taken here is to provide a broad discussion but to illustrate it with more narrowly local and regional examples. From the outset, it must be stated that the 'cabaret' club defies precise definition. Indeed, the very name itself, although preferred in this account, is only one of several labels including 'theatre', 'variety' or 'proprietary' through which it was known. It was not a legal or formal administrative category and in many of its functions it merged into adjacent forms such as the casino, country club and restaurant. Further, the broad category of cabaret clubs admitted of many variations between venues. While, for example, a number of Manchester locations made extensive use of striptease, others eschewed it entirely.[8] Whatever the exact nature and balance of programmes, however, it was its emphasis on the extensive provision of live professional entertainment that ultimately distinguished the cabaret club from other elements of the night-time economy in the minds of contemporaries.

Given these definitional problems, exact enumeration is extremely difficult but it is likely that perhaps 150 to 200 clubs existed at the peak of cabaret's popularity in the mid- to late 1960s. They were a national phenomenon, although the vast majority were found in the north midlands, Yorkshire, the north-east and Lancashire, which, as will be seen, was an especially important centre. Most opened six or seven days a week from about 8 p.m. until midnight, although some closed as late as 2.30 a.m. The entertainment, controlled by a compère (a critical role within club culture), consisted typically of between three and six 'turns' per night, with headline acts expected to perform a set of at least forty minutes' duration, approximately double the length demanded in the variety theatre. Most clubs also had resident performers, including house musicians.[9] Although standing was allowed at bars, most of the audience was seated around tables at which were served drinks and food, often taking the form of 'basket' meals involving chicken or scampi. (The clubs have come to be memorialized as the 'chicken-in-a-basket circuit', an association with a now decidedly *passé* form of catering that further squeezes cabaret clubs into an unfashionable and comic space within the nation's collective memory.[10])

Most premises had dance floors, some had separate restaurant facilities and, crucially, many operated casinos. In Manchester, the smallest venues such as the Piccadilly in Major Street and the Cabaret in Oxford Street had seating capacities of only 200 to 250, although 500 to about 800 was probably more typical. A small number of high capacity locations opened in the later 1960s and early 1970s; the Golden Garter in Wythenshawe, opened as 'Britain's first showbar restaurant' in October 1968, could accommodate 1400 patrons, while Blighty's at Farnworth near Bolton, could seat 2,000.[11] All clubs operated a 'smart dress' policy, which effectively translated into a ban on jeans coupled with insistence on a tie for men and fashionable skirts and dresses for women. Although some clubs opted for the most basic decor, many interiors were designed to provide a certain exoticism. In a flourish that referenced a comforting vision of the Edwardian music hall, the Golden Garter sported 'gold and crimson decor' and 'decolette plaster goddesses smiling in pairs on either side of the movable apron stage', while Stockport's Poco-a-Poco, opened in 1967 and modelling its look on the Sands Casino in Las Vegas, offered a more modern ambience via a split-level cabaret room with each level 'furnished in its own rainbow colour'.[12]

Although most undoubtedly had their 'regulars', clubs were always perceived as providing something of a treat or special occasion and were priced accordingly, expensive enough to let people feel that they were enjoying the good life, but not at too high a price. Most charged an annual membership fee of between 10s. (50 pence) and £1 in the early sixties, with half-rates for 'ladies', although by the end of the decade, as the market became highly competitive, such fees became nominal or were waived altogether. Admission prices were then levied for each show, with rates varying according to the standing of the top-of-bill artist and the night of the week. By 1970 weekday prices of between 5s. (25 pence) and 7s. 6d. (37 and a half pence) were reasonably typical, although Mr Smiths in Manchester city centre charged 10s. (50 pence) and Friday and Saturday admission to the Golden Garter stood at £1.[13] Bar prices were higher than in public houses and working men's clubs, while food costs obviously varied accordingly; the ubiquitous 'chicken and scampi meals' were priced at about 6s. (30 pence) while the Golden Garter, on opening in 1968, offered a three-course meal with coffee for 15s. (75 pence).[14]

The result was an entertainment form comfortably beyond the reach of poorer members of society but manageable by those in regular and reasonably well-paid employment. In essence, clubs sought to provide a sophisticated but still recognisable environment for individuals in

The Golden Garter, Wythenshawe, in 1971. One of the country's leading club venues, singer Lulu and comedian Jim Bowen top the bill.

Manchester Archives and Local Studies

their twenties and upwards, drawn largely from the better-paid sections of the working class and the lower-middle class and relatively equally balanced in gender terms. Alcohol licensing regulations effectively set a minimum age of entry at eighteen but some clubs were happy to set the minimum at twenty-one or even higher. The Wishing Well at Swinton tellingly advertised itself as 'The 21 and over club' while the Blackburn Starlight Club initially established twenty-five as its minimum.[15] These rules existed to be broken but the cabaret club ultimately gave entry to an adult world. In class terms, working and lower-middle class patrons predominated although a substantial middle-class element may well have been found in some clubs. Hard evidence is frustratingly thin, but while the contemporary tendency to describe them as the 'working man's nightclub' or similar was too lazy a generalisation, its frequent repetition in the trade press suggests such labels captured an essential truth.[16] Individual clubs undoubtedly had their own social tone. While Manchester's Cromford, at least in its earlier years, was more a nightclub for the region's business men than a cabaret club, it is hard to see clubs located in working-class districts such as the Russell Club in Hulme or the Domino in Openshaw as serving anything beyond a fairly narrow social constituency.[17]

Men had a higher profile than women within the clubs. The men-only 'stag' nights combining striptease acts with comedy of varying shades of blue that were so popular in Manchester were a clear indication that the ideology of the 'breadwinner norm' was still a dynamic element in the gendering of leisure. Men also tended to predominate on weekdays, particularly in the late evening and early morning.[18] Nevertheless, women were a critical element of the audience and much sought after by managements, bringing economic benefits as individual patrons but also conferring a highly desirable respectability. The high emphasis on facilities such as the 'luxurious toilet and powder room' that graced the Poco-a-Poco in Stockport and the popularity of bingo in many clubs attest to significant female attendance levels, while the vast majority of acts were clearly intended to appeal across gender boundaries.[19] An advert in the *Manchester Evening News* in 1963 stated baldly, 'Take Her to Mr Smiths', and it may have been the case that most women went with male partners.[20] However, oral tradition certainly records groups of unaccompanied women attending on Thursday and Friday nights and clubs may well have taken on some of the role previously associated with dance halls in popular courtship.[21] The cabaret club (and, indeed, the working men's club concert room) provided a highly visible site for women's engagement with the modern leisure environment.

The origins and growth of the cabaret club

Although cabaret clubs were a product of the 1960s, like so many of the decade's supposedly novel elements, they were strongly prefigured in the 1950s, and, indeed, earlier. By 1950, there were already some 19,000 registered clubs in England and Wales.[22] Most were voluntarist and associated with such organisations as the Club and Institute Union, the governing body of the working-men's club movement, although a commercial sector ranging from exclusive establishments in London's West End to the most basic of bars certainly also existed. Many clubs of both types had traditions of offering live entertainment, particularly at weekends, that dated back into the late nineteenth century. However, the 1950s offered crucial new opportunities for the expansion and diversification of such activities. The wider economic and social climate was certainly conducive to growth. Post-war desire for entertainment remained strong and low unemployment levels (the rate for the North West Region stood at 2.1% in 1953, 2.7% in 1958 and 1.6% in 1961) and rising real incomes, albeit not on the scale to be experienced in the 1960s, provided a promising environment for the popular consumption of modestly priced pleasures.[23]

There were, too, highly beneficial changes specific to the entertainment industry, and not least the repeal, in 1952, of Defence of the Realm regulations allowing police to object to club registration. A prospective club proprietor now had only to gather a minimum of 25 members, construct a set of rules and pay an annual fee of 5s. to the local council.[24]

The Broadway Club, Failsworth in 1970, unable to disguise its origins as a cinema.

Manchester Archives and Local Studies

More widely, fundamental structural changes resulting from the impact of television on previously dominant forms of public entertainment worked favourably for the club sector. The variety theatre was effectively dead by 1960, while cinema closures accelerated rapidly; the number of cinemas in Manchester fell from 91 in 1951 to 33 by the mid-1960s, with Tameside losing 13, over a third of its number, in just four years from 1957–1961.[25] However, despite the boost that this gave to the long-term privatisation of leisure, appetites for 'going-out' were still powerful and, indeed, were often stimulated by a desire to enjoy live stars seen on television.[26] At the same time, the collapse of variety provided a ready and willing labour supply, while redundant entertainment venues, especially cinemas and dance halls, an institution similarly affected by changing popular tastes, became available to aspiring club owners at 'almost knockdown prices'.[27]

Some 800–1,000 new clubs were estimated to have opened across England and Wales between 1954 and 1958 alone.[28] While many of the commercial venues that emerged were extremely modest in ambition, a small number of managements saw the potential to establish what were effectively proto-cabaret clubs. The Manchester region was at the absolute forefront of this process. The first of its new clubs was probably the Cromford which opened in the ground floor of a warehouse in Cromford Court, Market Street, in October 1954; warehouses added usefully to the region's stock of suitable club premises. It was followed by the Russell Club in Hulme (1955), the Northern Sporting Club (1956), located in the disused Cimitra cinema in Harpurhey, and the Cabaret Club (1957).[29] By 1960, there about ten such clubs within three miles of the Town Hall, while others were also appearing in the wider Manchester region including the Ritz at Ashton-under-Lyne (1957), the Club Majestic and the Ritz Theatre Bar, both opened in Oldham in 1959 and both in converted dance halls, and further afield at the Tudor in Church, near Accrington (1958) and the Empire Cabaret Club in Burnley (1959).[30] The balance of entertainment varied, with striptease, boxing and wrestling more common at some than others and there were marked differences between the levels of facilities offered. While beer and basic snacks were the norm, both the Cromford and Cabaret clubs opened daytime restaurants at which, in the latter case, customers were offered a three-course lunch accompanied by 'A Terrific Glamour Show' featuring 'exotic dancers'; the Cromford , and probably others, may well have offered illicit gambling.[31] At the core, however, were the live entertainers, many of whom enjoyed a high profile nationally; singers Donald Peers, Roberto Cardinali, Josef Locke, Tessie O'Shea and Denis Lotis all appeared in Manchester clubs in 1959.[32] The transition from variety theatre seems to have been almost seamless.

There were also significant developments in the voluntary sector. Throughout the industrial north and midlands, the late 1950s and earlier 1960s saw an increasing focus on entertainment, often featuring star names and expensive new concert rooms, within working-men's clubs.[33] Manchester once again seems to have been a key location. The Manchester Entertainers and Concert Artistes Association [M.E.C.A.A.] was founded as early as 1954 in order to provide local artists with advice on contracts, wage rates and other practical issues; 1,400 performers were members by 1960. Local trade magazines also grew up to advertise the club scene, with at least three, *Clubland Review, Encore* and *Fanfare Review,* in existence at various stages between 1958 and 1960.[34] Although some of the bigger clubs had the potential to rival the commercial sector – the concert room at the New Langley Labour Club, Middleton, which opened in 1961, had a capacity of 1,000 and an ambitious booking policy – synergies were equally apparent. The working men's club circuit generated a further pool of local talent and its venues sometimes shared headline artists with commercial venues, resulting in a helpful spreading of fees for both parties.[35]

It was a change in the national socio-legal environment that allowed for the final transition to the mature cabaret club. Mark Jarvis has demonstrated how the modernising agenda of the Conservative Governments of 1957 to 1964 was critical in establishing the foundations for the 'permissive' social, cultural and moral changes of the 1960s.[36] For the commercial club sector, the 1960 Betting and Gaming Act and the 1961 Licensing Act were the two most important legislative enactments, although neither were remotely intended to serve this purpose. Beyond its central aim of legalising betting shops, the 1960 Act purported to be modest indeed, specifically designed, in the words of one M.P., to prevent Britain becoming 'a casino country'.[37] However, poor drafting of clauses designed to limit the levying of entry charges to small private and/or charitable gatherings, combined with ill-considered regulations relating to specific games such as roulette and *chemin-de-fer* to have precisely the opposite effect. The opportunity for public membership clubs was swiftly spotted and, by 1967, over 1,000 commercial gaming clubs existed nationally.[38] The licensing legislation was similarly far more wide-reaching than expected. Allowing for alcohol to be served into the early hours of the morning if accompanied by food, dancing and entertainment, it was aimed mainly at the 'the tourist trade ... holiday resorts and coastal places'.[39] Once again, other sectors seized their chance.

Taken together, these acts gave the nascent club industry a critical boost. Certainly, not all clubs availed themselves of the new possibilities. Gambling was by no means fully embraced; approximately half of Manchester's clubs offered the facility by the mid-1960s and, with corrective legislation clearly looming, most clubs opening later in the decade did not adopt it. It was, however, almost universal in clubs in the wider region and clearly a significant attraction. The 1961 legislation, however, was taken up with great alacrity. Its newly created Supper Hours Certificates and Special Hours Extensions, allowing, respectively, for one-hour extensions of drinking time beyond normal hours and the sale of drink, if accompanied by food and entertainment, until 2.00 a.m., proved highly popular. The act also allowed clubs to opt for a Justice's licence rather than undertake the registration process and many owners availed themselves of this opportunity which, while opening them up to police scrutiny, gave them far more freedom in setting membership regulations. In a competitive setting where it was now desirable to attract as many people through the doors as quickly as possible, this was a worthwhile trade-off.[40]

The legislation of 1960–61 made what had been, for many, the seedy and illegal worlds of gambling and late night drinking into legitimate consumer activities. Armed with these new attractions and a propitious economic environment in which, nationally, the real income of manufacturing workers increased by 19% within the period 1959 to 1964 alone, the cabaret scene expanded rapidly.[41] New clubs emerged in Manchester city centre, including the College Theatre Club (1961) and The Piccadilly, Mister Smiths and Denos, all in 1963, as well as in the suburbs and, crucially, in towns within the region more widely. Blackburn saw the opening of the Starlight in 1961, Bolton and Burnley their respective Casinos in 1961 and 1963, Preston the Club Royale in 1964, Stockport the Empress in 1962 and Wigan the Sportsman and the Casino in

1960 and 1962. At any one time in 1966–1967 when numbers reached their peak, some 25 clubs focusing mainly on the provision of cabaret entertainment were operating within three or four miles of Manchester Town Hall, including about 4 in Salford. This compares with just 3–4 in Liverpool, 3 in Leeds, and 1 in Bradford, while Sheffield had no major venue at all until 1970. In a wider region bounded by Oldham to the east, Macclesfield to the south, Wigan to the west and Preston and Burnley to the north, approximately another 20 clubs existed at this time. Manchester and its region thus provided perhaps 20–30% of the nations' provision.

When discussing Manchester's booming night life more generally in 1966, *The Guardian*'s Benedict Nightingale could find 'no easy sociological explanation' for its national pre-eminence and it is scarcely easier to do so at a distance of half a century.[42] The area was clearly sharing in the nation's rising real incomes, but it was not especially affluent, with one economist concluding in 1969 that 'the average wage earner is still worse off in the North West than the nation as a whole'.[43] The sheer size of the adjacent urban population and the city's role as a genuine regional capital certainly provided key prerequisites – Nightingale noted coachloads of visitors arriving from Stoke, Preston and Liverpool – but given that many city-regions with not dissimilar advantages failed to capitalize upon them, these may have been necessary but not sufficient causes; the exact structure of the respective regional urban systems would benefit from greater scrutiny.

Several other factors are worth considering. The regular and relatively high family wages of 'textile Lancashire' in particular had placed the county at the absolute vanguard of leisure provision from the late nineteenth century, as illustrated by its role in the growth of profes-sional football, the seaside holiday the fish and chip trade, cinema and much else, including working men's clubs.[44] Along with Durham and Cleveland, the Manchester district had the highest level of CIU-affiliated clubs in the country in 1962 and cabaret club owners were clearly benefitting from offering a new version of a familiar form.[45] The nature of managements must also have played a role, although the exact dynamics are hard to capture. There is simply not space here even to begin the business history that is required, but it is noteworthy that the sector locally and nationally was largely driven not by large leisure combines but by small businessmen running single clubs or small circuits. In the 1950s and early 1960s, a number of such proprietors in Manchester appear to have been drawn from within the worlds of sport and entertainment, notably ex-theatrical agent Syd Elgar, wrestler Bill Benny, and comedian Bernard Manning.[46] In East Lancashire a cluster of clubs were operated by Brian Tattersall, who combined ownership of what was supposedly the world's largest penfriend club with cinema and bingo interests, while in the Wigan and Bolton area, Howcroft's Model Brewery opened several clubs in its 'Casino' chain.[47] It is possible that such individuals and institutions brought a relevant industry expertise at a critical time. Finally, Nightingale was shrewd in his observation that the city may have earned its reputation as club capital 'largely by the default of other places'. The Liverpool Watch Committee, for example, banned striptease in the 1950s and 1960s and this undoubtedly boosted at least one aspect of its rival city's club life.[48] It is perhaps in a detailed comparative study of local planning laws and regimes of civic morality that a full understanding of clubland's distinctive geography might lay.[49]

Music in clubland

The extensive use of comics from the club circuit in TV shows such as *The Comedians* (Granada TV, 1971–1992) has meant that popular memory equates clubs with stand-up comedy. Comedians certainly played a major role, not least in the Manchester region where the circuit proved a training ground for a number of performers who went on to achieve national stardom. As noted above, one of these was also a successful club owner. Bernard Manning opened the Embassy in Harpurhey in 1959, followed by the Palladium, Collyhurst and the city-centre Wilton Club in 1961. (When registering the Palladium with the City Council he mischievously claimed that its formal objective was 'to cultivate rational recreation for members'.[50]) Nevertheless, the role of stand-up has been exaggerated as any random analysis of 'top-of-the-bill' artists demonstrates. Nine of the headline acts identifiable at the Lancastrian Club, Prestwich, in the 12 weeks from 11 February 1965, were singers or musicians, as were 10 of those appearing at the Wigan Casino in the 12 weeks from January 1 1966 and 14 of those at the Talk of the North in the 17 weeks from June 6 in the same year. Of the 21 clubs advertising in the *Manchester Evening News* on 28 March 1970, 14 led with musical acts.[51] Obviously, it would be misleading to reduce club entertainment simply to a matter of stand-up or music, with magicians, fire-eaters, contortionists, hypnotists and other speciality acts diversifying the mix. Moreover, neat division between music and comedy more widely is unhelpful. As will be discussed shortly, comedy was an essential part of many musicians' acts and music featured in many nominally non-musical performances. The essential point, however, is that music was the key currency.

As Brocken has observed, 'no single musical genre, no sound or instrumentation (despite the pervading "keyboard" stereotypes), can be associated with cabaret'.[52] What can be said is that the many genres on offer would normally be placed into such categories as 'mainstream', 'middlebrow' or 'middle-of -the-road'. These are all imprecise and deeply subjective terms, often demonstrating more about labeller than labelled. They undoubtedly have some value in that they capture the lack of experimentation and fundamental challenge to dominant musical languages (and social conventions) that typifies so much popular musical culture, but they all fall a long way short of capturing the realities of that culture.[53] They carry too heavy a connotation of 'blandness' and lack of worth and obscure the fact that audiences could encounter popular music that was largely new to them, beyond the main stream of their experience. While, for example, pedal steel guitar music was known to British audiences from the 1930s and 1940s, a full set from the American-Samoan Tau Moe family at the Wigan Casino in March 1966, would have represented a highly novel encounter for many patrons.

To move beyond potentially inhibiting blanket terminology it is necessary to undertake some basic content analysis. While it is impossible to provide anything resembling a full survey of genres and repertoire, analysis of performance types at one club at one particular time can be highly informative. The method adopted here is to record the headline acts at Mister Smiths, Manchester, between 6 June and 26 September 1966 (musicians or singers topped the bill for all but one of the seventeen weeks in this period), and to use this as the basis for a wider discussion of cabaret's particular blend. Opened in Brazil Street in March 1963 by locally-based concert promoter, Paddy MacKiernan, the club was a prestigious venue: footballers George Best and Mike Summerbee were regulars along with members of the *Coronation Street* cast and the visiting actors who attended after appearing at local theatres.[54] Although star names did appear, at this time it drew largely upon performers who, while often enjoying a high profile, were not of especial national or international eminence. While no club can ever be entirely representative, many of the acts discussed here appeared frequently elsewhere in the region and can be taken as broadly indicative of the range of the musical fare that cabaret audiences encountered.

Even this relatively cursory survey demonstrates, following Brocken, a surprising range of music on offer, from calypso to pop song to operatic-style ballads and perhaps even opera itself. This to some degree resulted from the specific commercial imperatives of the club industry. As already noted, clubs did not serve a settled, regular body of customers; the fact that Mister Smiths had a membership of 7,000 within one year of opening is indicative that it had a reasonable fluid audience.[56] Needing a large pool of 'floating' patrons, managements had to be alert to market opportunity. Although the exact audience composition for individual performances eludes the historical record, it is not difficult to imagine the shifts of demography and taste that would have occurred from week-to-week, as fans of a once-famous Bobby Breen were replaced or augmented by members of a regional Irish community anxious to greet Bridie Gallagher or fans of political satire seeking Cy Grant's take on current news items. Above all, however, the diversity is a demonstration of the innumerable, albeit often overlapping, taste publics that inhabited an extremely wide middle-of-the-road.

Date	Name	Style of Music	Comments
6 June	Bobby Breen	Vocalist. Probably mainly ballads, possibly soul influence	In 1930s, Canadian boy soprano featuring in several Hollywood movies
13 June	Mike Preston	Ballads, light pop	4 UK Top 40 hits in 1959–60
20 June	Freddy Starr	Beat music with comedy	Later, popular national comedy star
27 June	Chris Rayburn	Black American female vocalist. Sang standards with jazz and blues tinge	
4 July	The Modelles	Female trio, but nothing known of style	
11 July	Chas McDevitt and Shirley Douglas	Husband and wife duo, probably then playing light pop, although probably some folk	McDevitt a leading figure in UK skiffle scene of 1950s
18 July	The Rekordites	Music act but content unknown	
25 July	Cy Grant	Calypso and folk	Guyanese actor-singer, 'sang the news' on BBC TV's 'Tonight' from 1957
1 Aug	The Chants	Five-piece Black Liverpudlian close harmony group, with strong Do Wop influences	One of the most highly regarded acts on the cabaret circuit
8 Aug	Frankie Davidson	Singer and dancer, sang rock 'n'roll but also many comic numbers	One of Australia's most popular singers and light entertainers
15 Aug	Bridie Gallagher	Modern Irish ballads	Seen by some as Ireland's first pop singer
22 Aug	Caroline Showband	Showband (see discussion below)	Probably Manchester-based. Also performed as 'The Carolines'
29 Aug	Erica Bax	Female vocalist ranging from music hall, to show tunes and opera	Then contracted to Covent Garden Opera House
5 Sept	Bonnie Lowe and Steve Hamilton	Trinidadian jazz-influenced vocalist backed by husband on guitar	
19 Sept	Margo and The Marvettes	Six-piece Irish showband, fronted by vocalist Margo Burns, with increasingly strong soul influences	Hugely popular club act and later had some Northern Soul following
26 Sept	Steve Martin	Ballad vocalist, including, at this stage, a Mario Lanza tribute. Also some comic impressions	

As stated, a single snapshot cannot capture every aspect of the region's cabaret culture. In terms of personnel, the leading national and international stars absent from this list were drawn by the often lucrative fees that some managements offered. In August 1965, Shirley Bassey, by then one of the world's premier cabaret entertainers, appeared at both the Wigan Casino and the Talk of the North, while Frankie Vaughan, another major draw in this period, made his provincial club debut at the latter venue that same summer.[57] The Golden Garter, in its turn, numbered American cabaret star Eartha Kitt amongst its impressive roster of singing stars in the early 1970s.[58] In a setting that often provided a refuge for many performers once their hit parade days were over, current top twenty artists were also a more frequent presence than might have been expected. Sandie Shaw, then one of the country's leading female vocalists, sung at the Garrick in Leigh, in June 1965 and, perhaps rather more surprisingly, The Kinks, at that stage still a hard-edged rock group, played at Salford's Devonshire and Manchester's New Levenshulme Sporting Clubs in March 1965.[59] This was indicative of the fact that during the 'beat' boom of 1963 to 1965, cabaret clubs and contemporary pop music had forged something of an alliance. A number of the city's clubs, notably The Domino and The Princess, were happy to mix beat groups with other acts in their standard cabaret programme, while others tended to segment audiences by introducing specific beat nights. The Domino and Princess continued to book rock acts beyond this point, including Little Richard in June 1966, but by the late 1960s contemporary pop music had largely disappeared.[60] 'Trad' jazz, another popular element earlier in the decade, also had a much diminished place by this stage. By reducing their any way limited links with contemporary modishness in general and youth culture in particular, cabaret clubs had now settled on the musical policy that eventually defined them rather more distinctly as a cultural form.

Although much of what follows concentrates on identifying and discussing the different styles and genres of music-masking to be found within clubs, it is important to note that a considerable body of repertoire was shared across these genres. While some artists performed at least some of their own material, many were effectively providing cover versions of existing repertoire: this apparent lack of originality was another factor that diminished the credibility of club singers in some circles. At the core of this body of music were the so-called 'standards', a wide and, slightly in contradistinction to that very label, always subtly shifting body of material, drawn mainly from Broadway and West End shows and the back catalogue of American and British commercial popular music from about the 1920s onwards. These were amongst the most frequently performed songs in the clubs and could unite the repertoires of the most unlikely combination of performers. 'The party's over', Jule Styne, Betty Comden and Adolph Green's song of 1956, had become almost synonymous with

Shirley Bassey by the mid-1960s and yet Lonnie Donnegan, father of British skiffle and an enormously popular figure on the club circuit, once finished his set at the Georgian, Salford, with what one member of the audience remembered as 'the most haunting arrangement/version I have ever heard' of the number. 'When he sang the last note, the place just erupted with clapping, stamping, table banging, whistling and shouting his name'.[61] Cabaret could be a surprising place.

As the Mister Smiths listing tends to suggest, the biggest single category of performer in the cabaret clubs of the Manchester region and, indeed, nationally, might best be characterized as the 'ballad singer'. Bridie Gallagher worked largely within a highly distinctive ballad tradition of commercially-produced late-nineteenth and twentieth-century Irish numbers such as 'The girl from Donegal', 'A mother's love a blessing' and 'At the close of an Irish day'. Bobby Breen, Mike Preston, Chris Rayburn, Erica Bax and Steve Martin appear to have worked largely within a more Americanized ballad tradition and several other acts also clearly drew upon this. The exact style of song and performance clearly differed according to individual preference. Chris Rayburn, for example, had recorded an eponymous album in 1966 on which could be found two much-recorded hits from 1941, Duke Ellington and Paul Francis Webster's 'I got it bad and that ain't no good' and Harry Warren and Mack Gordon's 'I know why (and so do you)', along with a further popular Webster number from the 1950s, 'The mood I'm in'.[62] These jazz-influenced numbers were emotionally and musically some way removed from the more pop-flavoured numbers of, for example, Mike Preston. Nevertheless, for all the looseness of the term, many contemporaries would have recognized the ballad label as one which could embrace a large constituency of singers.

Certain elements of Steve Martin and Erika Bax's repertoire point up a significant contemporary enthusiasm for semi-operatic and operatic vocalists, a taste which, although at first sight possibly surprising, grew naturally from pre-existing musical life. As in many northern communities, the serious study and practise of vocal music was deeply rooted in the wider Manchester region from the late eighteenth century.[63] This socially broad-based culture drew many adherents from within working-class communities: an amateur quartet party from Burnley that included two women cotton weavers won the operatic class at the prestigious Blackpool Music Festival in 1911, while Wigan miner, Tom Burke, rose to become principal tenor at La Scala, Milan in the 1920s.[64] Although weakening from the 1920s, popular art music traditions remained significant and were partially met by recordings of emotional ballads featuring operatic or near-operatic tenors. The Italian-American Mario Lanza (1921–1959) represented the apotheosis of this approach and it is unsurprising that singers such as Martin might appropriate his repertoire as both act of homage and demonstration of his own talent.

Britain produced a number of similar performers in the 1950s, most notably David Whitfield, a fixture on the cabaret circuit, and David Hughes, who, in the mid-1960s, combined work in leading opera companies including Glyndebourne with club bookings; he topped the bill for the opening of Burnley Casino Club in 1964.[65] Perhaps the leading British female act of this type was Susan Lane, a soprano from Bolton, who was a clubland favourite both locally, winning the accolade of a Golden Garter booking in 1970, and nationally. Journalist Graham Turner noted how she held an audience 'in awed and appreciative silence' when seeing her perform in south Yorkshire, while a columnist in *The Stage* observed that during her tour of working men's clubs in west Yorkshire, 'the usual rustling sounds were inaudible while she held the stage'.[66] Most singers of this type focused on show tunes and ballads although operatic arias were not unknown. At the time of her Mister Smith's booking, Bax was including a non-specified aria from *Tosca* in her act while Lane had certainly performed 'One fine day' from *Madam Butterfly* and an aria from *La Boheme* in concert and television work in the mid-1960s.[67]

The fact that Steve Martin could mix his Maria Lanza tribute with comedy impressions underlines the ease with which performers crossed categories. Two more Mister Smiths performers, Freddie Star and Frankie Davidson, similarly married comedy and music, although their comedy routines were combined with contemporary pop music. This particular blend formed an important and highly distinctive element of club repertoire. Comedy had long been at the heart of much British popular music, utterly central to the music-hall and variety tradition and featuring extensively in inter-war (and later) dance band culture, where 'novelty' numbers were frequent. Again, from the late 1950s, singers including early rock 'n' roll star, Tommy Steele, often adopted comic numbers, not least to ease their transformation into becoming 'family' entertainers. While cabaret clubs, then, did not inaugurate 'comedy-pop', along with the seaside summer show and pantomime, they did much to cement its place in 1960s and 1970s popular culture. It became almost obligatory for 'straight' pop groups to perform some degree of comic material on the club stage. In the early 1970s, for example, the Bee Gees reluctantly performed a vaudeville medley during an engagement at the Golden Garter.[68] Moreover, a number of acts began to specialize in comic performance often based on humorous dance routines and/or impressions of other pop stars: the familiarity with public figures engendered by television made impersonation a defining feature of 1960s light entertainment. The Manchester region produced some significant acts of this type, and most notably Freddie and the Dreamers, who had six Top Twenty hits during the beat boom of 1963–64, but whose comedy-dance routines, developed partly in local clubs, were central to their longer-term popularity. The Statesmen, although criticized in

The Stage for offering impressions shackled too firmly 'to that favourite hitching post, the tv commercial', the North Stars and, perhaps pushing regional boundaries to their limit, the Black Abbots from Chester, were amongst highly regarded local performers.[69] Comedy-beat acts with national profiles including the Barron Knights, whose 1964 pop parody single 'Call up the Groups' had done much to stimulate the genre, The Rockin' Berries and singer Wee Willie Harris were all powerful draws within the regional circuit.[70]

Comedy was also central to many of showbands that featured so strongly in cabaret clubs from the mid-1960s. Showbands originated in Ireland about 1950, with the Clipper Carlton from County Tyrone, often regarded as the prototype. Mixing Broadway show tunes with skiffle and rock 'n' roll, comedy routines and impressions, they were at their height in Ireland in the 1960s and increasing numbers tried their luck in the United Kingdom, initially during Lent when they were effectively barred from performing in some parts of their own country.[71] Margo and the Marvettes, founded in County Down in 1960, became English cabaret favourites from the middle of the decade, appearing frequently in Manchester and the north-west, as did the Belfast region's Witnesses Showband, which enjoyed an extremely successful residency at the Talk of the North in 1966.[72] Similarly popular were the Maori showbands that had emerged in 1950s New Zealand.[73] The Maori Castaways and the Maori Volcanics were frequent visitors to the Manchester region, the most popular of the five Maori bands that one Manchester agent had on his books in 1968.[74] The Castaways, largely Maori although fronted by a Canadian female vocalist, were described by The *Stage*'s Peter Hepple in 1967 as 'possibly the greatest show in cabaret today, complete with Maori dances and action songs, original arrangements of standards, instrumental dexterity on piano, organ, drums, guitar, bass, bongos and trumpet'.[75] He might also have added, both of this group and the genre more widely, extensive visual comedy routines. As Hepple demonstrates, showbands compressed much of the overall cabaret experience into a single spectacle, serving as both one of its signature acts and its embodiment.

Showbands, like so much else described here, also underscore audiences' love of virtuosity and showmanship. While not all critics will have appreciated such self-conscious forms of display, cabaret clubs were places where vocal range, an ability to thrill with high notes or mastery of an instrument, were much celebrated, a key part of the good night out. Bert Weedon, pioneer electric guitarist virtuoso was a favourite of the regional and national club scene. So, too, were the jazz-influenced close harmony act, the Morgan James Duo; harmonica troupes such as the Harmonica Rascals, The Three Monarchs and the Morton Fraser Harmonica Gang; Shep's Banjo Boys, who became a house band at the Golden Garter, and Manchester's Gina Branelli and the Mario Three, a group that featured Branelli's much admired accordion playing and won the 'best musical act' category in a prestigious national club award ceremony in 1973.[76] While the music played by such artists might sometimes be familiar, the manner of its treatment was often decidedly not, thus giving the mainstream a distinctively novel gloss.

Decline and fall

The 'age' of the cabaret club lasted from about 1963 to 1970; by 1980 the form was almost entirely extinguished. Its decline stemmed from the almost complete reversal of the specific matrix of forces that had generated its initial growth. The legislative context had certainly become ever less propitious from the late 1960s at both national level, as the second Wilson Labour government began to address some of the unintended consequences of the Macmillan liberalisation, and, if not throughout the region, then certainly within Manchester. The introduction of the breathalyser as part of the November 1967 Road Safety Act which reduced bar profitability was swiftly followed by the establishment, under the auspices of the 1968 Gaming Act, of the Gaming Board. This body had soon gathered 'substantial evidence' that the demand for gaming was stimulated by the added attraction of entertainers, food and dancing and recommended a 'complete separation between casino gaming and entertainment' with effect from 1 July 1970.[77] As a result, a number of clubs closed entirely while others abandoned entertainment in favour of gambling; Manchester's Cromford, for example, took the latter course in July 1969.[78]

At local level, 1 January 1966 saw the implementation of the 1965 Manchester Corporation Act which introduced extremely aggressive policing controls over the so-called 'coffee' or 'beat' clubs, a particular preoccupation of the Chief Constable, John McKay.[79] On his retirement in 1966 his successor, W.J. Richards, turned his attention to the city's cabaret circuit. Concerned that organized crime was moving into the industry, convinced that clubs were flouting licensing legislation, especially in regard to drinking after standard hours, and anxious about the apparent cosiness of relationships between owners and individual policemen, he acted.[80] All constables were banned from using clubs, even as customers, on pain of disciplinary action, while, as had been the case with coffee clubs, a specialist squad of under-cover officers was established in order to investigate club practices.[81] By late 1967, legal proceedings were in train. Mister Smiths was one of three clubs to lose its Supper and Special Hours certificates in November 1967 and although an appeal was partially successful, further action was taken against the club and others the following year. Even the Golden Garter, opening with Bruce Forsyth as top-of-the-bill in October 1968 and rapidly becoming one of the country's leading cabaret venues, came under attack; production of catering receipts destroyed the police's case that drink was being served without accompanying food.[82]

Structural factors within the cabaret industry added to this dispiriting and disruptive legislative climate. In particular, artists, encouraged it must be said by some of the more self-aggrandising owners, demanded ever higher fees which were hard to provide in the new climate. Clubs had to scale down their entertainment programmes or even close. There is also some evidence that audiences may have been growing tired of the cabaret format; warnings of growing 'fickleness' were certainly common in the trade press.[83] The declining economic situation from 1973–4 proved a further troubling factor. Initially, these various problems worked through relatively slowly. At any time in 1970 perhaps 20 clubs might still be found to be operating within a five-mile radius of Manchester city centre, a figure not dissimilar to that appertaining in the boom years of 1965–67; several of these, moreover, were new clubs. However, by 1974 the number had fallen to about 8 and by 1978 to 4. Some simply closed, others mutated to greater or lesser degrees into other forms. Mister Smiths is remembered as essentially a strip club by 1972, while the Piccadilly and the Cabaret, the latter now renamed as 'Kloisters', became discotheques. The Golden Garter carried on until 1982, becoming a bingo hall the next year, while the Poco-a-Poco, another very late survivor, eventually became a 'fun pub' in 1982.[84]

One or two of these re-designated venues had their greatest days ahead of them. In 1973, the Wigan Casino, once the Empress Ballroom, returned to its dance hall roots, albeit, in the very different guise as one of the key centres of northern soul. The Russell Club was to be home to the very first 'Factory' nights in 1978.[85] Northern Soul, Factory and Madchester have generated sizeable literatures while cabaret clubs have barely received a mention. In some senses, that is perhaps as it should be. In musical terms, cabaret clubs were essentially spaces in which a variety of pre-existing popular tastes could be enjoyed by adult audiences. They did not stretch musical boundaries or generate new urban cultures and even if popular musical studies had existed in the 1960s, the clubs would not have brought many excited musicologists to their doors. Nevertheless, as an important element of the emergent culture of popular consumption, providers of an image of Manchester as a modern city ('swinging' in the sixties' parlance), a window into musical tastes and, quite simply, a source of pleasure for thousands, they would benefit from being patronized a little less and studied rather more.

Shebeens and black music culture in Moss Side, Manchester, in the 1950s and 1960s

Dennis Bourne and Melanie Tebbutt

Unlicensed shebeens played an important part in the evolving social and music scene among Caribbean and African migrants to Manchester in the 1950s and 1960s, but their development and significance has received relatively little academic attention. Dave Haslam's *Manchester, England* contains a chapter which alludes to the influence that Moss Side had on the Manchester music scene between the 1940s and the 1990s. CP Lee's *Shake, Rattle and Rain* also makes specific reference to how the black music scene based around the Moss Side area influenced white teenagers in the city. More recently, Commonword Writers' Development Agency, a writing development organisation based in Manchester, has pioneered a project on the black music scene in Manchester between the 1950s and 1990s, by collecting oral testimony about the shebeens and clubs of Moss Side and Hulme across this period. Interviews compiled as part of the Commonword project have proved an invaluable source for what follows, which is intended to introduce the reader to the post-war development of black leisure networks in Manchester, and their relevance to the evolution of Manchester's broader entertainment scene.[1]

Before considering the context out of which shebeens emerged in post-war Manchester, it is useful to consider the origins of the term 'shebeen'. Shebeens were originally defined as any unlicensed premise which served alcohol. According to the *Oxford English Dictionary*, the word originates in the Anglo-Irish word síbín, from séibe meaning 'mugful' and can be traced back to the eighteenth century when it referred to an establishment where alcohol was sold without a license.[2] As the origins of the word suggests, shebeens were not a purely West Indian phenomenon, but were to be found in Scotland and Ireland from at least the eighteenth century, from where they may well have travelled to the West Indies. The word was associated with Scottish and Irish immigrant communities in England in the nineteenth century. In more recent times, shebeens have been associated with townships in South Africa, where they developed as a response to the segregation which denied places of entertainment to the country's non-white residents and, as is the case here, were also associated with music and dancing.

From the mid-to-late twentieth century, shebeens were particularly associated with a West Indian tradition of 'exuberant' all-night parties, which immigrants brought with them from the Caribbean.[3] These unlicensed clubs or parties, usually held in rooms or cellars of houses, seem to have first emerged in Manchester in the late-1940s, when they were also known as 'blues'. The development of these unlicensed activities paralleled that of a network of licensed clubs run and or owned by African and Caribbean entrepreneurs in the early 1950s which developed along Oxford Road, Denmark Road and extended into the Moss Side area, along Moss Lane and Princess Road. These continued to thrive until the 1990s, when a large number of both 'illicit' and legal entertainment establishments were closed down by the local police and city council.

Black settlement in Manchester

Manchester and Salford have been home to a black population since the mid-nineteenth century, when mainly African seamen settled in and around the Ordsall and Greengate areas, near the Salford docks, leading the area to become known locally as 'Little Africa'.[4] Bill Williams has suggested that a small population of about 250 Africans, West Indians and black Americans inhabited Greengate in the 1920s. By the 1930s, the threat of slum clearance encouraged many of these to move north east to Broughton and Cheetham, as well as to extend into the southern suburbs of Manchester such as Hulme and Moss Side. This pre-war black population was augmented during the Second World War, with the arrival of many West Indian servicemen. (There were two hostels for African and West Indian seaman in Moss Side during the war, on Carlton Street and Demesne Road.[5]) Holmes highlights the difficulties of distinguishing between these black servicemen and black residents in Britain who also served in the British Armed Forces.[6] The wartime population of servicemen was encouraged to leave after the war, but only a third of the 1,000 civilian recruits accepted government repatriation, while a third of the 10,000 Jamaican servicemen based in Britain chose not to accept demobilisation to their country of origin.[7] Many who remained in Manchester after the war settled in Moss Side; a significant number of West Indians who sailed to take up jobs in Britain after the war were ex-servicemen who had formerly been based in Britain.[8]

The wave of passenger migration from the West Indies commonly associated with post-war immigration is seen as starting with the arrival of the S.S. *Windrush* in June 1948, although most Caribbean migrants did not enter Britain until after 1952, after the American implementation of the Walter-McCarran Act (1952) effectively closed the door

'Yams for all' at the Community Stores on Moss Lane in 1958.

Manchester Archives and Local Studies

on Caribbean migration into the United States. Figures for the number of these settlers in the 1950s are hard to come by, because they were not counted in any official statistics. Those figures which have been collated are at best an estimation. The *Interim Report on the Condition of Jamaicans in the United Kingdom*, published by the British government in 1954, concluded that Jamaicans tended 'to be distributed among the largest cities, with London retaining the lion's share, approximately 15,000'. Of the other cities, some 2,000 Jamaicans were thought to be living in Birmingham (including Coventry, Wolverhampton and Dudley), approximately 1,250 in Liverpool, and about 1,000 in Manchester.[9] In the country as a whole, West Indians arrived at a rate of approximately 1,000 per year between 1950 and 1951, rising to 2,000 in 1952 and 1953, 10.000 in 1954 and 32,850 between 1955 and 1962. By 1961 an estimated 171,000 West Indians were living in Britain.[10]

Accurate figures for the Caribbean and African migrant population living in Manchester during the 1950s and 1960s are similarly hard to come by. Jo Stanley, using Manchester City Planning Department estimations, suggested that only 350 Caribbean people were living in Manchester in 1951, a figure which had grown to 2,502 by 1961.[11] These figures contrast with those provided by Mosley and Ingham, who suggest that by 1951, approximately 2,500 Afro-Caribbeans were living in the Moss Side area.[12]

Moss Side had acquired a reputation for notoriously bad housing by the mid-nineteenth century but by the late-Victorian period its terraced housing had been complemented by larger three-storey houses for a prosperous white, middle-class population. From around 1914, however, many of these wealthier residents began to move further south of the city, into Withington, Didsbury and into Cheshire. This left their large residences to be sub-divided into private rental accommodation for the West Indians who started to move into the area in the 1930s and 1940s, attracted by the district's proximity to the Manchester docks and Trafford Park industrial estate, which offered the possibility of work as skilled and unskilled labour.[13] By 1954, Moss Side's mixed population of 37,000 was densely packed into the district's Victorian housing. Many larger properties vacated by the middle class now provided high density accommodation, although the streets were mostly characterized by 'drab 2-up, 2-down terraces.'[14] In 1954 Manchester's Chief Medical Officer reported that of all Manchester's thirty eight districts, only Beswick (with a population per acre of 79.80) was more crowded than Moss Side (with 67.13 people per acre).[15]

The black leisure scene in Manchester

Mosley and Ingham have suggested that African and West Indian clubs began to surface in the Moss Side area from the late 1930s.[16] Several of these were identified with particular ethnic groups, which reflected the prosperity of some Africans who had accumulated sufficient capital to buy local property. The Palm Beach (later the Reno) was founded by a Nigerian, as was the Merchant Navy. The Cotton Club had Ghanaian origins, while the Kroo Club had links to Sierra Leone and Liberia.[17] The daily lives of black people in Manchester were littered with racist remarks and exclusion from various leisure venues, all of which reinforced the social role of both licensed clubs and unlicensed shebeens which were important social centres and meeting places, part of a broader infrastructure already well-established by the late-1940s.

World War Two had an immense impact on Manchester. Various bombing raids destroyed parts of the city, hundreds of children were evacuated to the countryside for safety, while the arrival in the region of United States servicemen, who were stationed in Britain from 1942, has been described by CP Lee as 'the most culturally important event of the decade'.[18] Approximately three million United States military service personnel remained in Britain throughout the Second World War, mainly concentrated in south-west and eastern England and parts of the North West.[19] Of particular significance for this article, is the fact that 135,000 of these were African-American.[20] In north-west England, black American servicemen were stationed at Bamber Bridge, near Preston in Lancashire, and Burtonwood, a couple of miles to the north west of Warrington. Burtonwood airfield opened in 1940 as a storage and servicing centre for RAF aircraft and was transferred to the United States Army Air Force in June 1942, to become a servicing centre for the United States Eighth, Ninth, Twelfth and Fifteenth Air Forces aircraft.

Burtonwood became the largest airfield in Europe during the Second World War, and it is estimated that some 18,000 service personnel were stationed at the site in 1945.[21] Manchester has been described as a magnet for American servicemen stationed there.[22] Dorothy Jasper, a Moss Side resident, recalled how a great many American servicemen who relaxed in Manchester were stationed at Burtonwood: 'It wasn't just black Americans, white [as well].'[23] For many Black American servicemen, the clubs, bars and shebeens which catered for the city's local black community became a favoured place for spending time away from the airbase. The money they spent proved to be a valuable source of income, as did the alcohol and music they also provided. Many contributors to CP Lee's work commented on the influence of the American G.I.s, seeing it as a significant point in the 'Americanisation' of British popular culture.[24] Lee described Burtonwood as an 'autonomous, independent outpost, serviced by its own P.X., schools, cinemas, and Radio Stations [which] staged massive dances in aircraft hangars, [with] swing and Jump bands', a means by which many local residents and musicians in the North West became exposed to American culture.[25] (The PX, or Post Exchange, was a military retail store which sold provisions and equipment.)

How African-American service personnel spent their leisure time in the region was shaped by the discriminatory policies of US military regulation expectations which also had repercussion for local black populations.[26] In some cases, local people actively opposed attempts by officials from the US armed forces to impose segregation upon leisure activities which involved their servicemen.[27] Nonetheless, whether officially or unofficially, many facilities and leisure spaces in Manchester became segregated or separated, as a result of pressure from white Americans.[28] Dorothy Jasper recalled how 'all the black Americans' loved to go to the Cotton Club, maybe because it was 'hidden' away on Oxford Road and they could party 'until 8 o'clock in the morning.'[29] By the end of the 1950s, an entertainment infrastructure had developed in and around the Moss Side, Oxford Road and Manchester University area which was undoubtedly shaped by the dual effects of the economic influence of black American GI's and US racial segregation:

> The top of Oxford Road, not the bottom, because that was for the white yanks at the bottom. From All Saints down, all that belonged to the white Yanks. From All Saints upwards belonged to black Yanks and black people.[30]

This 'colour bar' not only had an impact on the American servicemen but also had a knock-on effect for the local population, as many of Manchester's pubs, clubs and hotels refused to let black people enter their premises or serve them food or drink.[31] The minutes of the council's General Annual Licensing Meeting (Brewster Session) in June 1954, for example, reveal that some pubs and hotels, in this case the Whitworth

Hotel in Moss Side and the Paragon Inn on Oxford Road in Manchester, had been refusing to serve alcohol to black residents.[32]

Memories of Shebeens

By the mid-1950s shebeens had begun to appear across the country in urban centres like London and Manchester with significant Jamaican populations. What seems to have contributed to their appearance was the ease with which they could be hosted; a room and the required musical equipment were all that were needed to host a 'blues' or 'house party':

> If you have a Blue Spot [a type of radiogram] and some tunes you could push back the furniture and have your own little function every Saturday night. That's where the shebeens come from.[33]

Moss Side became the centre for the shebeens which proliferated in Manchester from the mid-1950s and into the early 1960s, although the illicit and casual nature of these arrangements makes it difficult to provide a fully accurate picture of their number. Some were hosted in former commercial buildings such as old hotels or dance halls; some sprang up in the front rooms and cellars of people's homes; others were located in disused houses. A front room in Meadow Street, for example, was the location of one Moss Side shebeen in the late 1950s.[34] A particularly infamous and much-mentioned location was Monton House, a former hotel on the corner of Lloyd Street and Monton Street, which was home to both a gambling house and a shebeen. As Dorothy Skinner recalled:

> It was gambling upstairs and downstairs. When I say gambling upstairs I meant you had to go upstairs when you went in the front door to gamble, but downstairs – and women were not allowed there. And downstairs in the cellar was the shebeen.[35]

Kenneth Williams, a singer on the Manchester scene in the 1950s, also had fond memories of the place: 'The Monton House, that was our favourite haunt the Monton House, play cards, dice, shebeen – oh all sort.' Monton House continued to be a popular place through the sixties and seventies: 'Anybody that was working down Deansgate where you know clubs were and that, they came to the Reno afterwards, they always did and then they ended up in Monton House.'[36] Several streets in the Moss Side area developed a reputation for housing shebeens within a short walking distance. By the early 1960s, when Sidney Lewis arrived in Moss Side from Jamaica, Cartmel Road had become the location for a number of 'house parties', as had Harpenden Street which housed so many that it became known locally as 'Beat Street'.[37]

> so many beat was on there, you don't have to ax where the party is, if you go

on Harpenden Street there was party der, so you call it beat street. It use to run across and come out to Moss Lane East and there was a scrap yard at the end of it der, some Irish scrap yard and there was a bookie across der.[38]

Many of the shebeens on 'Beat Street' and in other parts of Moss Side were known for their all night opening, and some patrons could find themselves partying for the entire weekend. Sydney Lewis recalled:

I leave the house on a Saturday evening and I went to the gambling cellar and I lose my money, I remember that and I was in a bad mood anyhow I drive to Harpenden Street that was where we use to call Beat Street and I go to a few party and I leave from there and I go to a few more and I finish up at Cecil Street you know where the park is where the Academy is ... It was off Denmark Road anyhow, I finish up there and I leave from there and I don't know where I went too. I lost all track, I got home Sunday morning after 8 o'clock stuff like that because [shebeen] use to carry until 7 o'clock you know half past sevens on a Sunday morning, not all of dem but some of dem. [39]

It is clear that many shebeens not only charged an entry fee, but also sold alcohol to be consumed on or off the premises. 'You know these Blues in the front room and you could only get a certain amount in and they would sell drinks.'[40] Alcohol was always available at the venue and it was customary to buy your crate and take your place or 'hold down' your regular corner.

You bu[y] it from them, they use to sell it. If there is eight of you, you all put two and six together and five bob and that's it, you XX corner, so when your friend walks in you know where you are because say this is a regular beat place you know this corner is your corner you see. Every time he comes down there he doesn't have to look anywhere for you, he know [you is] in this corner or that corner, everybody had their own corner you see. It was the in ting, so you have all your drinks there.[41]

The perception of the shebeens as centres of criminality and vice were apparent even in the early 1950s, and the Caribbean community itself was aware of this perception;

They were what were always called illegal drinking dens, and the press would make out that all sorts went on in them, but they were just ordinary working people's houses or their basement – sometimes it would be in an empty building. And it was only illegal because the guy hosting the gathering have no licence to sell the drink.[42]

Police attitudes towards these illegal establishment were ambivalent. Some local residents recalled relations with the police as quite cordial and reasonable.

Well the police as I said we never had any problem with the police ... in those days if somebody said there was noise at a party da police come politely, we turn it down a bit they would have a drink some of them might and they go, they have something to eat and they go.[43]

Sydney thought these casual exchanges were based on an understanding that no 'fighting nor any cutting up, nor any guns and tings like that' were going to occur in the clubs and shebeens. Relationships between the police, shebeen owners and shebeen patrons emerge as ambiguous and collusive in many interviews. Kenneth Williams recalled of Monton Street, for example, how:

> The police use to come in there and they use to come in there and whoever owned the place, the clubs and all that, the police would come in and they would get free drinks and I don't know probably got a few bob as well. But we knew, all the people, all the informers in Moss Side in them days, the black informers, and they would inform on one another, and inform on one another's clubs and we all knew. Everybody knew who was the informers because they used to come to them specially.[44]

Other shebeen regulars depicted the shadowy ways in which clubs were policed in the 1950s and 1960s, an issue which would clearly benefit from archival research and police oral testimonies.

> Ah, the police were in it as much as we were. The police were paid, there were a lot of back handers going on and we all knew it, but they used to come into The Reno when it was shutting for drinks. There was a lock in, so they could stay open if the police were there because it was a lock in and detectives used to come. I am not talking about police in uniforms, I am talking about detectives, used to come. They frequented the Mayfair, the Cotton Club and the Reno but the Reno wasn't open at the time of The Mayfair. Mayfair was first, but at that time police were always paid.[45]

Although shebeens provided members of the Jamaican community with a familiar cultural form to which they could turn with relative ease, there is no simple explanation as to why they became so widespread during this period. Some West Indians were certainly unhappy with the limitations and restrictions placed on them by British society and wanted to take part in leisure experiences which reminded them of home, allowed them to play loud music, drink freely and stay out as late as they pleased. Some have argued that the traditional phenomenon of the shebeen or house party took on a greater importance among Caribbean migrants who settled in Britain. The deejay Jah Vego, who used to deejay at dances in London during the 1960s, suggests that Jamaicans were more receptive to 'Jamaican-style' dances when they were in England, because the dance had changed from being an everyday, mundane form to become a reminder of home.[46] The type of entertainment culture which Jamaicans were used to, contrasted sharply with the leisure activities that they assumed that British people preferred. Lee, for example, suggests that shebeens were the West Indian and African migrants' response to 'archaic English licensing laws'.[47] The quiet reserve associated with British pub culture was seen as inhibiting and lacking the freedom of expression which many young migrants desired, as Soul Persian indicated. Persian, born in Kingston, Jamaica, in 1943, arrived in Manchester in the early 1960s, when he was eighteen, and blues and shebeens quickly came to play an important part in his new social life, as he and his friends set up their own shebeen in the cellar of the Denmark Café, on Denmark Street in Moss Side.[48] These small beginnings proved to be Persian's stepping-stone to licensed club life, as he was soon invited to become DJ of the Reno Club, in Moss Side. Persian suggests how 'alien' the restricted and reserved character of British leisure culture seemed to him and other West Indians:

> [W]e didn't understand pubs, going sitting in pubs, just sitting there staring at the walls and drinking till 10.30 and then go home. You know, when people work a long week, come the weekend they need to let their hair down, and the British way didn't suit us.[49]

Other interviewees focussed on the shebeens' role in providing a respite from the harsh realities and difficulties of living in England.

> The life here was hard. *Hard.* Everything was so different, from the climate to how people talk to you if you go in a shop. So come the weekend you have to relax, completely, among your own crowd and be able to carry on like you did back home. Not that there was much choice for us, because so many places in London wouldn't let black men in. So we have to do our own thing, keeping dances in houses, in basements, in the shebeens, or in school dinner halls.[50]

For Arthur Culpeper, who came to Manchester in 1954, the shebeen scene was a place to catch up with people 'like you', a welcome respite from the challenges and the threats of violence which many migrants faced.

> You go to a club in Moss Side. You sit on a table and your friends will be there who you saw the week before and it's really something else … Everybody seems to be one great family. You drink … you dance with your partners and you had no fear of a bottle coming across your head and anything like that.[51]

Despite the popularity of licensed clubs in Manchester, such as the Reno, Nile and the Cotton Club, some felt that they did not cater for everyone, and much preferred the atmosphere of the house party:

> The Nile and the Capital were the two main [clubs], because they weren't clubs as such that young people could go too. Even the grown-ups never used to go to these clubs because what they use to have is house parties. On a Saturday everywhere you go there is a house party, a blues as well call it, you know. Just normal people keeping blues.[52]

Music of the shebeens

Shebeens were a product of the 1940s and 1950s, when one of their main functions was to give people the opportunity to 'dance all-night'.[53] Much of the music they played, as well as alcohol and other merchandise, originated with American servicemen from Burtonwood and Bamber Bridge. Servicemen from Burtonwood, which remained the largest military airbase of its kind in Europe, regularly spent their leave in Manchester and Liverpool, where they mixed and exchanged records and musical influences. When largely white youth culture was developing around Manchester's coffee bars and juke boxes in the 1950s, local shebeens became what Lee has described as the 'main influence' on jazz musicians in Manchester.[54] Tosh Ryan, saxophonist in the Victor Brox Blues Train Band, described how the base at Burtonwood became a conduit for live and recorded music in the North West, as American G.I.s brought albums with them from the United States and became part of the local live music scene;

> [Burtonwood] … was a massive camp – that changed dance hall music quite radically I think because you got Americans bringing albums over, you got Americans who were playing in bands at weekends, that includes dance band music, moving from dance bands to Jazz, small groups. From Jazz things developed through the late 1950s into the early 1960s,[55]

The Reno (downstairs) and the Nile (upstairs) on Princess Street, about 1969. These were key venues in the development of the city's black culture.

Local musicians in Liverpool were similarly grateful for the 'regular exchanges of records' between themselves and servicemen who were stationed in the region. Eddie and Chris Amoo, for example, recalled how inspirational the 'music, dance fashions and record collections' of visiting black American servicemen were in the Liverpool club scene between the 1940s and 1960s.[56]

American servicemen were not, however, the only source of recorded music from the United States. The black community's historical links to the docks and Manchester Ship-Canal provided another channel for black American and Caribbean music during the 1950s and 1960s.

> Nat King Cole was coming out then and these black singers from America. They had all this music that we didn't. You wouldn't have heard it on the radio, it was all English singers. You only heard this because the men on the boats used to bring these records from America. They brought all that music with them.[57]

The music of the big band jazz era prevailed from the late 1940s into the early 1950s, changing to the sounds of 'jumping blues' and the 'crooning' black singers in the mid- to late-1950s. In the first half of the 1950s, rhythm & blues, or what was formerly known as 'race music', popular with black urban Americans, was taken up by many in Jamaica, where the development of open-air dances, playing the 'hottest R&B and hot jazz' sowed the seeds for the sound-system culture which was, in turn, passed on to the clubs and shebeens of Manchester.[58] The Eric Deane Orchestra, which played at the Nile nightclub in the 1940s and 50s, comprised West Indians and Africans, including renowned musicians such as Fela Kuti (fourth trumpet) and Lord Kitchener (string bass).[59]

The West Indians who moved and settled in Britain from the mid-1950s, brought with them not only traditions of the dance and the sound system, but a love for American R&B and Jazz. Bradley's *Bass Culture* provides a flavour of the music which was transported from America via the Caribbean, describing how the sounds of 'prolific' artists like Louis Jordan were 'perennial favourite[s]'. Wynonie Harris's US hit 'Blood Shot Eyes 'was virtually stuck to the Jamaican sound men's turntable between 1951 and 1953'. Artists such as Bill 'Mr Honky Tonk' Doggett , Professor Longhair and Jimmy Reed would 'regularly rock crowds'. Jazz was represented by Dizzy Gillespie, Sarah Vaughan and Earl Hines. The 'roots of rock 'n' roll were present in the music of Fats Domino and Lloyd Price while the honey-dripping likes of Nat King Cole, Billy Eckstine, Jesse Belvin or the Moonglows were the lurrve gods of their time.'[60]

By the late 1950s, American artists were not the only musicians to be influencing young visitors to the clubs and shebeens of Moss Side. The West Indians also imported new musical genres, which were partly influenced by the black American music of the era and partly by their own cultural musical roots. After the end of the Second World War more and more young people in Jamaica and other parts of the West Indies began purchasing radios and, as a result, were increasingly exposed to the rhythm and blues of American artists such as Wynonie Harris, Louis Jordan and Fats Domino. As the popularity of this music grew on the islands during the early 1950s, some local artists attempted to recreate its sounds and pulsating rhythms, playing them at the open dances which were also very popular. This music intermingled with the styles and sounds of the islands' indigenous musical genre, Mento, as well as Calypso, the carnival music of the islands of Trinidad and Tobago, to give rise to a distinctly new form, Ska. Ska was produced by studio owners such as Prince Buster (whose first record 'Carolina', in 1961, became a timeless classic), Duke Reid, owner of the now legendary 'Trojan Sound system, and Clement 'Coxsone' Dodd, owner of 'Studio One' studios. This was also the period when the sound system emerged as an important part of Jamaican musical history, as DJs competed fiercely with each other to provide the largest and loudest systems. As Ska began to replace R & B as the 'number one sound' during the late 1950s and early 1960s, it was brought to Britain by many Jamaican immigrants, when its spread was greatly helped by the 'Barcelona' Blue Spot (Blaupunkt) radiogram, noted earlier. For the Blue Spot was not only a combined radio and record player, with a drinks cabinet for entertaining, but it could receive signals direct from Jamaican radio stations, bringing both music and news direct from 'home' on its built-in radio receiver. It is from this music system that many people claim the term 'Blues', another term for shebeens or parties, originates.

The music played in the shebeens and clubs gave Caribbean migrants the opportunity to listen to the music they most liked and which they felt was not being played, either on the BBC or commercial radio stations, because as Dorothy Jasper recalled, 'on the radio all you heard was English music at that time which was very boring you know. There was no jazz.'[61] Kenneth Williams's 'favourites were black "crooners" like Nat King Cole, Billy Eckstine Sammy Davies and Ray Charles'.[62] Jasper described the music played at the Reno as 'more or less all Calypso and Nat King Cole', although the music played at venues such as the Nile, Reno and Monton Street was also 'a bit of a mixture'.[63] Interestingly, Tab Hunter, a white singer and teen heartthrob, whose ballad 'Red Sails in the Sunset' was released in 1957, was popular by the mid- to late 1950s, as was Shirley Bassey:

> [She] was just coming to focus – she started to get well known, Shirley, with her very first new numbers what she had. I can't remember what it was called but Shirley was singing. You [also] got Lou Armstrong records.[64]

By the late 1950s several newly established record shops in Manchester were providing those fortunate enough to own record players such as a Dansette or a Bluespot the opportunity to purchase the 78s and 45s, which were beginning to be imported from the United States. Places such as 'Penny's Record Corner' on Princess Street, and 'Paul Marsh Records', at 24 Alexandra Road, which stocked the latest R & B, jazz and various other types of music, were soon joined by record shops in the city centre, which included Barry's Record Rendezvous on Blackfriars Street and Robinsons Records, also on Blackfriars, whose owner, Arthur Robinson, used to visit the United States to import 45s.[65]

Conclusion

Initially, the opening, and development, of clubs and shebeens catering to a black clientele was driven by the racial discrimination which many African and Caribbean migrants experienced in and around Manchester in all aspects of their daily lives. Leisure and entertainment were important areas in which such prejudice manifested itself, as black people found themselves barred from or refused service in pubs and clubs around the city. Their response was to open and run their own pubs, clubs and shebeens, which gave them the freedom to listen to the sort of music unavailable in the city's mainstream clubs or on mainstream radio stations. Much of the prejudice and discrimination which the black community faced could be traced back to the pre-World War One period, but there is plenty of evidence to suggest that by the early 1940s this was also being driven by the stationing of United States servicemen at bases like Bamber Bridge and Burtonwood. The United States military was a segregated institution, and segregation was practiced on and off base in Britain, mostly at the insistence of high ranking US military officials. The imposition of segregation undoubtedly consolidated a 'colour bar' in Manchester's pubs, bars and hotels, effectively creating separate cultural spaces divided along racial lines. As a consequence, money from relatively well-paid black-American servicemen helped sustain a network of shebeens and licensed clubs from the mid to late 1940s, whose appeal for those on leave included their extended opening hours. The impact that American servicemen had on Manchester leisure culture both during and after the war role is a potentially rich area for further research.

Shebeens in Moss Side developed alongside the infrastructure of 'licensed' clubs, welfare centres and cafes which emerged between the late 1940s and the late 1960s to the south of Manchester city centre, down Oxford Road, along Denmark Road, and around Moss Lane and Princess Road. Many of these 'blues' were hosted in the homes of Caribbean migrants, especially from Jamaica, whose numbers grew with the closure of Caribbean migration to the United States. American GI's, and black workers on the transatlantic shipping routes to North America were important channels for the music, clothes and alcohol which became culturally desirable in the 1950s and 1960s, as levels of disposable income rose and youth culture expanded. Of particular cultural value were the jazz, blues and R&B records then being released in the United States by artists like Nat King Cole, Louis Jordan and Fats Domino.

The early rhythm and blues played in venues like the Nile and the Capital and in many shebeens brought musicians together from both sides of the Atlantic and across racial barriers.[66] White teens, some of whom had begun to recognize that the 'white' dance music to which they were exposed had rather different roots, started to seek out the black artists who had inspired the sanitized swing of white band leaders such as Benny Goodman and Glen Miller, and in the process came into contact with West Indian musical traditions.[67] Lee argues that it was this desire to understand 'beyond the mainstream', mixed with the influences of 'USAAF personnel, African and West Indian immigration', which gave a particular 'richness' of talent to the Manchester jazz scene. As Victor Brox, a local white blues musician in the 1950s observed:

> At the time they were actually increasing the size of the school [William Hulme Grammar School] and we had a lot of Jamaican and Trinidadian people ... and some of these guys were great musicians and they came in and joined the band. You'd have like a West Indian bass player, and a West Indian guitarist, so the music, although it was ostensibly a traditional jazz band, its parabola was very, very, very wide.[68]

Lee has argued that during the 1950s, coffee bar and youth club culture combined with the influences of the Moss Side music scene to give birth to the 'beat boom' which became massively popular from the mid to late 1960s, not only in the North West but throughout Britain and in the United States. Although it is impossible, without further evidence, to quantify the impact which shebeens made in this melding of racial, social and musical influences, it seems inevitable that they had some impact, as Dave Haslam has suggested, in describing Moss Side's importance as a focal point and melting pot for less mainstream forms of music.[69]

> Moss Side ... provides graphic evidence of the centrality of music in Mancunian lives, and also the key part played by black music in shaping popular culture, from jazz, blues and soul: the Moss Side jazz clubs of the 1950s ... brought fresh rhythms to the dance floor, featuring far rawer sounds than the mainstream jazz dominating the rest of the Manchester circuit; the sound system, moveable feasts of bluebeat and blues, ... sustained the roots of the black community in the 1960s.[70]

This short survey of shebeens has only touched the surface of their role and significance. It is, however, a reminder of how much research remains to be done on the origins and development of these local music cultures, and on their role in reinforcing a sense of community against a frequently hostile society. What has been highlighted here is intended as a small contribution to a wider project of exploration, as local groups and individuals embark on the task of unearthing the complex hidden histories of black music and the Manchester music scene.

Bob Dylan, folk music and Manchester

CP Lee

Introduction

My first foray into the world of Manchester folk music was attending a club (The Ladybarn Folk Club) in 1964. I first saw Bob Dylan live at Manchester's Free Trade Hall in May 1966. It was this gig that several decades later ended up being the subject of my book *Like the night – Bob Dylan and the road to Manchester's Free Trade Hall*.[1] The book told the story of Dylan's artistic journey to that legendary evening and something of the background as to how events combined that night to create such an incendiary moment in modern musical history. The book mainly concentrated on oral histories of that night and now I'm pleased to have the opportunity to present a broader contextualization of Manchester's place in the folk revival along with an account (some of which may be familiar to some, *mea culpa*), of Dylan's three visits to Manchester in the 1960s. I have drawn information for this essay from three sources – one, my own interviews with participants; two, contemporary folk magazines of the time and three, books which have dealt with the folk revival. The historical account of Dylan's visits to Manchester are presented and juxtaposed with the proponents and development of the 1960s folk movement in order to show how his influence on music and effect on his audiences led to the winding down of the folk revival and reveals how its roots were coalesced into modern-day rock music.

The Folk Revival Part One

Importantly, the 1960s folk revival was not the first; this actually occurred around the turn of the nineteenth and twentieth centuries when there was an upsurge of interest in the traditional, indigenous music and dance of the British Isles.[2] This was aided in no small way by the boundless enthusiasm and work of collector Cecil Sharp (1859–1924). An early member of the Folk-Song Society (founded 1898), Sharp went on to found the English Folk Dance Society in 1911 which in 1932 merged with the Folk-Song Society to become the English Folk, Dance and Song Society. Thanks to Sharp and his colleagues a large number of such songs and dances were saved and not lost to successive waves of popular entertainment with its new technology and inherent promotional power to replace the traditional ballads and songs in the public's consciousness. He laboured tirelessly, roaming the countryside, recording and notating the songs and customs of mainly agricultural workers. Later collectors would begin to preserve material from the urban songscape and add these to the banks of knowledge that were being built up in Cecil Sharp House (home of the EFDSS) and elsewhere.[3]

Sharp believed strongly that schoolchildren should be educated in folk music and he published a series of music books that were added to state school curriculums over the ensuing decades. Although it was his fine intention to inculcate appreciation of musical heritage, the piano and vocal arrangements divorced the tunes from the raw vibrancy of the originals and with such hindsight we know also that imposing Morris dancing on children is perhaps not the best way to promote a love of the tradition. Classical conductor Sir Thomas Beecham, Oscar Wilde and Sir Winston Churchill are amongst those who purportedly said, that people should try everything once 'except incest and folk dancing' goes some way to summing up people's attitudes to Sharp's crusade.[4] That there was a revival though, is undeniable despite this apparent lack of general enthusiasm.

Up until the 1950s folk music was more or less controlled by a number of middle class 'experts', to the extent that a number of 'authentic', traditional singers were actually treated like exotic, performing animals. For instance, Fred Jordan, a farm labourer from Ludlow in Shropshire, sang in his local pubs, entertaining the regulars who drank there. He performed from a large repertoire of traditional and non-traditional ballads and tunes. In 1952, according to Bill Leader in conversation with the author at Salford University in 2000, Jordan was invited by the BBC to appear at a folk song festival to be broadcast from the Royal Festival Hall and when he turned up in his usual attire of suit and tie, he was duly dragged off by the producer Peter Kennedy to be 'made over' into something more 'rustic'. His collar, tie and jacket were removed, his sleeves rolled up and a cloth cap found for his head. Now he was a 'proper' folk singer and this scene describes very well the situation at the beginning of the second revival.[5]

The 1960s Folk Revival

The second folk revival was the result of a combination of factors; a general dissatisfaction with the state of 1960s 'Pop' music and a quest for something more 'real' and 'authentic'; a movement away from the codes and conventions that had brought the country into two world wars and with that a concomitant change in fashions, music and morals that came hand-in-hand with the newly emerging world of 'Youth'. This was the start of the generation wars, of moral panics in the mass media about young people who were active for nuclear disarmament and through the birth control pill, sexual liberation. Political and social change was in its infancy, yet it was becoming evident in the writings of the so-called 'Angry Young Men', a term used by the British media to describe novelists and playwrights disillusioned with traditional English society. To paraphrase Bob Dylan, the times were indeed 'a-changing'. Another major factor in the second revival was the publication in 1951 by the Communist Party of Great Britain (CPGB) of a pamphlet entitled *The American threat to British culture.*

Written by the National Cultural Committee of the CPGB the 65-page pamphlet criticized the dominance of American cultural products on mainstream British popular culture and included critiques of American mass cultural products such as film and pulp novels. It also tackled what it called 'the plight of the British songwriter' highlighting a formal protest that had been made to the BBC by the Song Writer's Guild of Great Britain about anti-British bias in the choice of material then broadcast on the BBC. This led to a statement in support of indigenous Folk culture and a plea for a re-education of the masses into the values and importance of Traditional music. This was the clarion call for a fight back against commercialization and Americanization. Two members of the CPGB took notice.

A.L. (Bert) Lloyd (1908–1982) was born in London and at fifteen he was given an assisted passage to Australia and whilst working on sheep stations there, he began to collect folk songs from the shearers.[6] This was the start of what became his lifelong fascination with folk music and folklore. An autodidact, he spent as many hours as he could educating himself through mail order books. When he returned to Britain and was jobless in the early 1930s Lloyd found himself with even more time on his hands to spend studying because the country was in the depths of the great depression. He said that there is 'nothing like unemployment for educating oneself' and he went on to develop other interests, in economic history and languages.[7] In 1937 he signed on to a whaling ship and sailed for the Antarctic. Back in Britain once again he joined the Communist Party and began writing articles for the *Daily Worker* and translating the plays of Federico Garcia Lorca from Spanish into English.

In 1938 he got his first commission from the BBC to make a documentary and in 1944 his first book *The singing Englishman: an introduction to folksong* was published. By the 1950s Bert Lloyd was an established expert on Folk song and folklore 'in a field of one!' and he set about trying to persuade the Trade Union movement to fund some sort of folk revival.[8] It was inevitable that he would meet up with Ewan MacColl and in 1953, he did.

Ewan MacColl (1915–1989) was born in Broughton in Salford, though as his biographer Ben Harker points out, his name then and until 1945, was Jimmie Miller.[9] Brought up by his Scottish parents in a staunchly radical working class home he was another autodidact, who after leaving school at 14 educated himself at the Workers' Arts Club in Weaste and at Manchester Central Library. He became a member of the Young Communist League and supported himself through a series of jobs and by street singing before joining a local socialist theatre company The Clarion Players. This introduction to the world of the dramatic arts would become the main arena for his talents for the next fifteen years. Looking for inspiration to the Soviet Union and Berlin he created the Red Megaphones street theatre group who performed topical, radical short pieces on the back of a truck outside football matches and political meetings.

In the mid 1930s a young actress called Joan Littlewood hitchhiked from London to Manchester, found work at the Rusholme Rep and ended up at the BBC in Piccadilly where she met Jimmie Miller. He had been taken on to do various voice overs and script work for documentaries. They hit it off immediately and with their shared visionary outlook for *avant-garde* drama became inseparable; they worked steadily together and went on to found the Manchester-based Unity Theatre, a platform for Miller to cut his teeth on and begin building the construction and theory of a 'true', 'people's' theatre. With success came their decision to move the Unity Theatre to London and by 1950 they had done so; Jimmie Miller changed his name to Ewan MacColl and tunes such as 'Dirty old town' had already been written under Miller's newfound Scottish name.

MacColl went on to meet American political refugee, Alan Lomax who had relocated to Europe at the height of the McCarthy 'witch hunts' in the States. Lomax had brought his song collecting knowledge and enthusiasm with him and MacColl soon moved radically away from theatre after this introduction and they worked together to collect the authentic folk music of the British Isles with a view to producing a set of 30 LPs of *Music from around the world* for Columbia Records. MacColl was fired up with a genuine fervor for folk and the tradition and it was Lomax who brought about a meeting with like-minded crusader Bert Lloyd in 1953.

MacColl was fascinated by a book Lloyd had just published called *Come all ye bold miners*, a clarion call to the workers of the coal mines of Britain. It was a revolutionary volume inasmuch as it encouraged contemporary song writing and featured not just traditional tunes but fresh ones written through the inspiration of Lloyd; this was the old meeting up with the new and becoming reinvigorated. Having met them individually Lomax had activated the three of them into an incendiary mix, presaging the second revival in folk music.

According to Cox, its beginning came in 1953 when the BBC

commissioned six radio documentaries from the trio called *Ballads and blues* which explored the roots of British and American music.[10] This led to the starting up of musical evenings in a variety of London venues under the banner title, 'The Ballads and Blues Club'. Lomax, Lloyd and MacColl gathered around them a disparate group of performers, including West Indian Calypso singer Cy Grant, Irish piper Seamus Ennis, Humphrey Lyttelton (a fellow member of the CPGB) and Scottish singer Isla Cameron, the musicians entertained singly and as an ensemble. At this time, MacColl had no ideological problems singing American tunes in what would be Britain's first Skiffle group, The Ramblers; these tautological ramifications would come later. 'The Ballads and Blues' ensemble performed to a sell-out crowd at The Royal Festival Hall in 1954 and at this time the revival was well under way.

Interestingly, at around the same time as this was happening in London, in Manchester, Harry Boardman had started off a musical evening. He tells Mike Brocken:

> 'There was a classical guitar session in a Manchester pub called the Guitar Circle, so Lesley (Boardman) and I thought of starting a 'folk circle' ... I was not even aware of MacColl's Ballads and Blues Clubs until 1957'[11]

Back in London, MacColl with all possible energy and enthusiasm, was working with radio producer Charles Parker on a series of documentaries for the BBC that combined reportage with music and vivid, drama-documentary recreations of contemporary events, such as a train crash (*The ballad of John Axon*, broadcast 1958), or the trawler industry (*Singing the fishing*, broadcast 1960). In 2001 the contemporary BBC Radio producer Bob Dickinson explained to the author how these programmes were so influential on the format of radio programming that they remained for decades as commendable examples in documentary making for BBC trainee producers and were a main part of BBC scheduling until the early 1960s. The programmes also initiated a new audience to the possibilities of an alternative to what many saw as the monotony and blandness of mid twentieth century popular music.

It was not just folk music that appealed to people tired of the supposed inanities of the top twenty 'pop' charts. Jazz, in particular, traditional 'trad' jazz grew from being an underground phenomenon into an overground success, with artists such as Kenny Ball and Acker Bilk consistently scoring top ten chart hits. Also, through the pioneering musical work of jazz musicians Ken Colyer and Chris Barber, British audiences were presented with the opportunity to see and hear original American Blues artists such as Muddy Waters and Sister Rosetta Tharpe, both guests on UK concert tours for the two respective British players. Their appearances in Manchester in the 1950s were promoted by Paddy McKiernan at the Free Trade Hall. It was through trad jazz that skiffle, another British hybrid musical form emerged. Skiffle was a kind of approximation of American jugband music played on simple instruments like a tea-chest bass and washboard. It was its simplicity that made it attractive to amateur musicians and it wasn't long before the country was swamped with home-grown skiffle bands. Many of these, such as those founded by Bert Jansch from Scotland, Martin Carthy from Hatfield, and Pete Smith and Lee Nicholson from the Manchester region, took inspiration from the roots music they were discovering and in turn this led many young musicians into the world of folk in a search for more authentic material.

Recording became another successful way of promoting folk music. Both Lloyd and MacColl were popular artists from the outset of the revival and MacColl already had a proven track record as a songwriter, with tunes such as 'The Manchester rambler' celebrating the mass trespass on Kinder Scout in 1932, and 'Dirty old town', written in 1948 (back in Manchester when Miller – MacColl – wrote in his spare time in stage production). Both he and Lloyd could now indulge their passion for traditional songs by releasing their versions on record and they were distributed through the auspices of the Workers' Music Association and Topic Records, jokingly referred to by aficionados as the 'world's first smallest record label!' Originally available only in limited outlets such as Dobell's music shop and Collett's record shop in London, or through mail-order, as folk music grew in popularity an increasing number of shops began to stock the burgeoning folk releases that were appearing by 1960. In Manchester the best place for 'specialist' music such as folk was the musical instrument shop Hime and Addison on John Dalton Street where the basement was given over to selling records. It had sections for every genre of music which at that time numbered just four: pop, folk, classical and jazz.

The rising popularity of folk music records was reflected in the increased attendance at folk clubs around the country. According to Denselow, Ewan MacColl claimed that in 1960 there were 1,500 Singers Clubs around Britain with a combined 11,000 membership. These figures have been disputed by Mike Brocken in his book *The British folk revival*, but even as an approximation the numbers are impressive.[12] What is undeniable is that more and more young people were beginning to attend folk clubs, not just simply as members of the audience but as player participants, and this was true in Manchester as well as elsewhere.

The Singers Clubs were a kind of MacColl-operated 'franchise' and maintained strict 'Policy Rules' on what sort of songs could be sung, how they were to be sung and by whom. One of the more authoritarian edicts was that a singer could only sing a tune from the area they came from; for example, English singers could only sing English songs. The inner circle of the Singers Clubs debated long and hard as to what kind of instrumentation, if any, was allowed. Certainly any form of amplification was forbidden in the clubs and MacColl was known to dictate to female performers how they should dress and what kind of make-up was permissible. This Stalinist style of organization was justified by the argument that it was preserving and encouraging a home-grown folk movement.

Outside London, however, the clubs were less rigorous in enforcing the letter of the Singers Clubs' guidelines and also alternative clubs to the MacColl/Lloyd axis sprang up where there were no particular restrictions at all. In Manchester a more liberal attitude prevailed although, even here, core traditionalists continued to hold on to the public perception of folk and they held onto their puritanical fervor in the early 1960s right through until 1966 when Bob Dylan, with his popularity and his musical actions and reactions, changed it all in one electrifying fell swoop.

The Folk Scene in Manchester

The popularity of jazz, evident in Manchester throughout the 1950s, and the desire for a more authentic form of musical entertainment, led to a variety of new venues opening up. Two of these venues in particular promoted blues as well as jazz and provided a welcome to original American performers whenever possible: Paddy McKiernan's Bodega Club on Cross Street, which opened in the city centre in 1957 and John Mayall's Bamboo Club above The Black Lion which began a year later, in 1958. Harry Boardman and his wife Lesley had moved on from the Guitar Circle and by 1960 were singing in various city pubs. The nascent folk scene in Manchester was in no small way encouraged in its development by the presence of Paul Graney, a collector and raconteur who spent the best part of three decades proselytizing the ballads and songs of the industrial north of England. Without his ardour and input things may have been markedly different in Manchester. He provided the newly emerging musicians with a steady stream of source material for their repertoires.[13]

In 1961 The Manchester Sports Guild (MSG) on Long Millgate opened its doors as a jazz club but very quickly offered space for the rapidly growing folk movement. Originally the smaller upstairs room accommodation was used for folk music and jazz was in the basement. The proprietor Frank Duffy ran a singers' night on Mondays and admission was one shilling and threepence whether you were singing or not! Later, as folk became the more popular, jazz was moved upstairs and folk went into the basement. Friday and Saturday events at the club attracted capacity crowds to watch artists like Paul Simon, who was living in England at the time, guitarist/singer Martin Carthy, who was to be a major influence on Bob Dylan's song writing, and home-grown talent included Harry Ogden, The Beggarmen and Mike Harding among many others. Thus it was the thriving folk scene at the MSG incorporated traditionalist performers such as Ewan MacColl and Peggy Seeger, whilst facilitating leeway for younger, more blues-influenced players to bring a revitalizing approach into folk music.

By 1964 folk was established as part and parcel of popular entertainment. Peter, Paul and Mary had entered the UK charts with Bob Dylan's 'Blowin' in the wind' in 1963 and many other folk-oriented acts were to follow. Groups like Liverpool's The Spinners and Birmingham's Ian Campbell Folk Group were appearing regularly on TV. One of the most popular TV/Folk tie-ins was a programme that came from ATV's Didsbury studios called *Hallelujah*. Broadcast on Sunday evenings and hosted by Sydney Carter who wrote 'Lord of the dance', *Hallelujah* was filling the slot usually occupied by religious broadcasting and in that sense, Carter and the show's producer Ben Churchill chose songs and artists who 'had something to say'. Fronted by the Johnny Scott Trio (a jazz band) resident artists were Isla Cameron, Martin Carthy and Nadia Cattouse. During its run, *Hallelujah* hosted performances by some of the top folk artists of the time including Bob Davenport, Alex Campbell, Bert Jansch and Leon Rosselson and they all performed songs by such writers as Ewan MacColl, Tom Paxton and Bob Dylan as well as their own. On one occasion, Dylan himself made his way to the studio in Didsbury in south Manchester and recorded a session (see below).

Meanwhile the continuing success of the folk scene in Manchester went beyond the MSG venue with many and varied clubs opening their doors to folk fans. On Fridays and Saturdays for those not inclined to travel into town, there was The Unicorn with Harry Boardman, Paul Brown's Old Moat and Ladybarn Folk Clubs. On Thursdays, Seftons on Corporation Street featured The Manchester Ramblers, while The Waggoners welcomed you to The Pack Horse on Bridge Street on Wednesday nights. Further afield The Stockport Folk Club met every Thursday at The Navigation, and there were clubs at The Black Lion in Salford, The Two Brewers, Salford, Poynton Folk Club, Altrincham, Cheshire Folk met in Sale, The Pennine Folk Club was at the Bush in Hyde and there were also regular nights at The Fishermans at Hollingworth Lake and Heaton Moor Rugby Club. Visiting American singers like Pete Seeger and Odetta were now performing sell-out concerts at the Free Trade Hall (1964 and 1965 respectively). Folk music was embedded, settled in its way in popular music and in danger of becoming moribund, which is how the importance and relevance of Bob Dylan to this seemingly healthy scene is relevant to pop music history.

Bob Dylan in the UK

Bob Dylan first visited England in December 1962, having been hired to appear in a BBC TV drama entitled *Madhouse on Castle Street*. He stayed at the Mayfair Hotel and set about immersing himself in the London folk music world, starting straight away with singer Pete Seeger's recommendation to visit The Troubador Folk Club. There the organizer, Anthea Joseph immediately recognized Dylan from his photo on the cover of his recently released LP and she invited him to perform there that night. That evening, an early encounter with the English folk music revivalist Martin Carthy signalled a new direction in Dylan's career development and over the next few weeks he was introduced by Carthy to a wide number of British singers and, more importantly, to a wide range of British ballads such as 'Lord Franklin's Dream' and 'Scarborough Fair'.

Just before this event, Dylan had finished recording his second LP *The freewheelin' Bob Dylan*, but after his return from England he postponed the release of the album and went back into the studio to lay down a number of new songs that were derived and or inspired by British traditional ballads for inclusion on the new album and subsequent releases. These included 'Masters of war', 'Bob Dylan's dream', 'A hard rain's a gonna fall', 'Boots of Spanish leather' and 'Girl from the North Country'. One of Carthy's adaptations in particular was a favourite of Dylan's, 'Scarborough Fair', which the young musician utilized the melody of twice, on *Freewheelin'*s 'Girl from the north country' and 'Boots of Spanish leather' on his *Times they are-a changin'* album.

As well as becoming immersed in British balladry through the influence of Martin Carthy, one more event took place during Dylan's first visit and that was an appearance before the 'king and queen' of the folk revival, Ewan MacColl and Peggy Seeger on the 22nd December 1962 at a Singers Club held at the Pindar of Wakefield pub on Grays Inn Road in London. Appearing in *North West Labour History* in 2001 is a photograph of Dylan singing to a packed room, though as Bill Leader, present that night, told me, 'the audience probably had no idea that Dylan was on, nor even less of who he was'.[14] Behind Dylan on the right of the picture, on a raised dais, sit Bert Lloyd, Ewan MacColl and Peggy Seeger. Lloyd seems to be enjoying himself, but the looks on MacColl and Seeger's faces appear stony. According to Bruce Dunnett, the doorman that night, Peggy Seeger had got wind that Dylan might show up and ordered him to 'not let that shit in!'. From then on MacColl would bristle every time Dylan's name came up and he constantly referred to his music as 'puerile' and 'third rate'.[15]

MacColl's attitude towards Dylan arguably amounted to a virtual prohibition of his music for his crime against the folk revivalist movement, that of commercializing his talent. Over the next eighteen months, Dylan's popularity spread among young music fans in Britain as more people became aware of him. This came about through the chart hits of Peter, Paul and Mary, the American folk trio who popularized his songwriting abilities thereby making him better known to a wider public and through a word of mouth buzz that passed around the folk clubs and folk scene. By the time Dylan returned to Britain in 1964 his star was on the rise, and the controversy over his success and his folk roots was aflame.

Folk aficionados who had heard his next album, *The times they are a-changin'*, released in early 1964, would probably have found little to indicate the coming furore, containing as it does such 'classic' protest songs as the title track itself as well as 'Only a pawn in their game' and 'The ballad of Hollis Brown', both startling song portraits of desperation and social injustice. In between the album's completion and its release Dylan, it would appear, had undergone something of a transformation in his song-writing style and approach, branching out into a more cerebral and transcendental use of imagery and narrative. His move away from social protest song-writing towards a more surreal and expressionistic style would be the cause of an admonishing editorial written by *Sing Out* magazine's editor Irwin Silber in November 1964. The editorial was written as a result of Dylan's appearance at the Newport Folk Festival where he premiered much of the material that was to appear on his second 1964 album release, the aptly named, *Another side of Bob Dylan*. I can recall the album creating quite a stir in Manchester folk circles when it was released and the arguments that ensued about 'commerciality' and 'selling out'. The album's most outstanding track, the visionary, apocalyptic hymn to the dispossessed and abandoned, 'Chimes of freedom', was performed by Dylan for the first time in this country in March 1964 in Didsbury.

Bob Dylan in Didsbury

Dylan came to Didsbury unannounced in March 1964 to make an appearance on the *Hallelujah* TV show. Accompanied by his manager Albert Grossman, the two of them shut themselves quietly in Dylan's dressing room until he was called into the studio to record his set. A young gopher called Neville Kellett had been put in charge of looking after Dylan and the two had got on reasonably well, probably owing to Neville's knowledge of blues music. Dylan had asked him what he would like him to play and naturally, Neville was astounded when the American sat on his stool in front of the cameras and, as requested by him, launched into 'Honey just allow me one more chance' from his second album. Dylan's delivery of what for him was now quite a dated part of his repertoire was solid and vibrant. Next came the world premiere (for TV) of 'Chimes of freedom'.

Introduced by Dylan as 'An halluc-in-a-tory song', the tune unreeled and rolled around the hushed studio. At the end of it Dylan coughed and slid off his stool. Neville helped him back on it and the show's director Ben Churchill came down to the studio floor to talk to Albert Grossman. After some heated discussion, Albert explained to Bob that 'Chimes of Freedom' was not what they had in mind at all and would Dylan now play something the audience would recognize, say, perhaps 'Blowin' in the wind'? Dylan duly obliged, went back to the dressing room, collected his jacket and together the two Americans went back to the Midland Hotel and then off to London where Dylan played to a packed out Royal Festival Hall. No-one other than Kellett had got anywhere close to him, and seemingly no-one in the folk fraternity even knew that Dylan had made another visit to Manchester. For them, they would have to wait a year.

Bob Dylan Dont Look Back (sic, no hyphen!)

In contrast to his unheralded 1964 visit, Dylan's return to Manchester in 1965 was a major event. An estimated 45,000 people attended Dylan's live performances on his eight-date UK tour and a further countless number watched him on television; BBC TV had outbid Granada in their efforts to have Dylan play two concerts broadcast later in the year. The American singer had become successful on an international scale and in Britain alone he was the subject of numerous articles in tabloid and broadsheet newspapers alike, one example from the *Guardian* on the 6th April 1965 describing him as 'Homer in blue jeans'.

Dylan's popularity played a significant part in attracting more people into the 'folk movement' despite the folk fans' concern about his credentials as an 'authentic' folk singer as described in Irwin Silber's *Open Letter to Bob Dylan*.[16] Through 1964 and early 1965, the folk fans' long and resounding debate continued as Dylan released more albums, each one revealing a more contemplative, thoughtful and symbolist style of song writing. The progressive content of the songs was no longer overtly political but was becoming much more introspective. To the tradition-alists in the folk scene this was viewed as anathema, a betrayal, a sell-out, of what is uncertain. Perhaps commercial success itself was enough to signify this betrayal. Ewan MacColl felt compelled to write a set of diktats in *Folk Music Magazine* explaining the terminology of words such as 'professional', 'traditional' and 'commercial' which he maintained was 'not a term of abuse, although 'commercialization' can be'.[17]

The Manchester audience remained very much on Dylan's side, however. His concert of 7 May 1965 at the Free Trade Hall was a sell out within two days. With publicity consisting only of one advert in the *Manchester Evening News* and a typed sheet in their shop window, just over 2,000 tickets were sold, mainly through Hime and Addisons. Footage of the concert exists and can be seen in DA Pennebaker's classic documentary *Dont look back*. As was typical on this tour at all his British (and American concerts) Dylan came on and, accompanied by his harmonica and acoustic guitar, played two sets of 45 minutes each with a 15 minute interval. With ticket prices ranging from one shilling and sixpence to just over a pound audiences were getting their money's worth. They also got a serious cross section of Dylan's music ranging from the anthemic 'Times they are a changin', 'Don't think twice it's alright' (which thrilled Nev Kellett who was in the audience that night, as he would be a year later), the jokey 'If you gotta go, go now', all the way to the surreal 'Mister tambourine man', and the final, vaguely prophetic 'It's all over now baby blue', an indicator of things to come perhaps. The audience response was rapturous, hushed, almost reverential; several people there including photographer Mark Makin described the first half as like being at a church service.[18] They had come to listen to Dylan's words and they fed on them like manna from heaven.

Bob Dylan at the Midland Hotel

There was an after show party at the Midland Hotel, a rowdy affair and the duty manager had to ask for the noise to be kept down. In researching for my book *Like the night* I interviewed the hotel's trainee manager at that time, a young man named Walter. His story highlights the other-worldliness of Dylan, rather as Neville Kellett's has done. Working through that night at the Midland Hotel, instructions were given that Dylan's entourage had specifically requested fresh orange juice be served at breakfast. It was Walter's task to go across town to Smithfield Market to buy oranges for the kitchen staff to squeeze ready for Dylan's breakfast. Apparently, screens were put around for the Dylan crew in the dining room so as not to disturb the other guests at their breakfast table. Walter remembers when he came down to breakfast, Dylan, accompanied by Pennebaker's film crew, his manager Albert Grossman, his personal roadie, Bob Neuwirth and several other hangers on ordered everything on the menu, kippers, eggs, toast, cereal, etc, plus coffee and orange juice and then to everyone's surprise all the food was ignored and Dylan and his team basically just drank coffee and smoked cigarettes. Eventually Albert Grossman stood up and ordered everyone to leave the hotel and head for the limousines waiting at the front. Relieved that breakfast had passed without incident, Walter began clearing up when he noticed that Dylan had left behind a large notebook containing writings and drawings. He grabbed it and ran as fast as he could to reception and dashed through the door to see Dylan's Austin Princess pulled up and waiting at the traffic lights. He reached Dylan's window and knocked on it. Dylan rolled down the window and Walter said, 'You left this!'. Without a word Dylan took it and the car drove off. I asked Walter what he thought about Dylan's lack of gratitude. 'It could have been worse,' he told me, 'It could have been Donovan'.[19]

Bob Dylan and a Town Called Malice

Manchester would have to wait another year before Dylan's return to perform again and the concert would not go so smoothly. Over the course of those twelve months Dylan's world changed dramatically. There was an indication of the direction the mercurial artist was heading in with his first 'electric' single 'Subterranean homesick blues' appearing in the charts in May 1964. Then followed not one but two more albums, *Bringing it all back home*, and *Highway 61 revisited*. The first of these could be described as designed to gently ease people into the idea of Dylan playing with a backing band as one side featured Dylan on electric guitar with other musicians playing drums, bass, keyboards and guitars, while on the other side of the album he stuck to more familiar territory (for the folk listener) using acoustic guitar with a minimal backing. The next album to be released in 1965 was out and out electric backing, crashing drums, swirling organs weaving around jangling electric guitars and wailing harmonicas. To those fans in Manchester used to going to the Beat clubs, this wasn't too unusual, but to traditionalists it was perceived as a deliberate slap in the face, an abandonment of all that they held dear.

When news of the 1966 tour broke in the music press a debate was raging within Manchester's folk clubs with the question, had Dylan 'sold out'? In much the same way as the Modernists fought with the Classicists at the premiere of *The rites of spring* Dylan's electric set represented a turning point that did not sit well with the traditionalists, many of whom refused to hear his new music. It's hard to understand these days what all the fuss was about, but folk fans were really taking Dylan's new musical direction deadly seriously. When the date for Dylan's concert was announced via the usual means of a typewritten sheet of paper in the window of Hime and Addisons, word was filtering in of the reaction that Dylan was getting from audiences on the first leg of his world tour. There had been reports in the British music press in late 1965 about his electric debut at the Newport Folk Festival where he had been booed by a section of the crowd, but not much more than that. With seemingly no comment about it in the mainstream press, something was beginning to bubble up. Student members of Manchester University Folk Society held an emergency meeting where they voted to stay away from the concert as a protest at the direction Dylan's music had taken.[20] Beer fuelled bravado led to a few people explaining what they would do if they could get face to face with Dylan and give him a piece of their mind, but overall there was more of an atmosphere of disbelief that he would bring his travelling circus of musicians to town with him. Somehow, some way or another it was believed that Dylan would see the error of his ways and revert to performing solo.

Outside the Free Trade Hall that evening of the 17 May the crowd waited expectant, nervous and above all chattering. In those days the wait outside the building until the porters opened the doors was always around thirty minutes before the concert was due to start, at which time the audience could all politely file in. The conversations were mainly about Dylan's reception in Dublin the week before. Pieces in the *Melody Maker* and *New Musical Express* had reported Dylan being booed when he came on with his backing band and these reports were not being viewed as encouraging. The concerts had been tense they said and it was confrontational and unsettling so everyone there outside waiting was wondering what the night was going to bring.

Being in the audience that night, I can see now the audience alongside and all around me taking our seats in the auditorium, giving Dylan rapturous applause when he appeared on stage at 7.30 pm and all the while knowing as we could see an organ, amplifiers and a drum kit on the stage that he was not going to remain alone, he was going to use a band! And so it was. Dylan played a forty-five minute set consisting of some old standards like 'Mister tambourine man', but new numbers also that were a complete mystery to us being prior to their appearance on the *Blonde on blonde* album which Dylan had recorded (with backing) in Nashville a few months before and was scheduled for release in July. Among them were 'Just like a woman' and the sublime 'Visions of Johanna'. As Dylan bowed and left the stage for the intermission it seemed the crowd breathed a sigh of relief; satisfied with the performance, any confrontation that might have taken place in Manchester had been defused. I actually heard somebody say that Dylan had 'seen sense' but when Dylan came back on after the break there was no question that he and the rest of the deniers would be very quickly disabused of this notion.

The group who would become known as The Band launched with Dylan into his second, quite contrasting 45-minute set. The audience punctuated it throughout with slow handclapping, catcalls and booing. After the penultimate number 'Ballad of a thin man' a voice from the gallery shouted out the immortal 'Judas!' cry, the heckle which would go down in history as one of the defining moments of twentieth century popular culture. It is the significance of the remark that struck through. Judas betrayed Christ, Dylan had betrayed Folk music; what Dylan was doing was an act of monumental treachery. On reflection, I'd say there were only a few dozen people that night who felt moved to show their anger and annoyance by becoming involved in heckling. It perhaps appeared more as pockets of them were spread throughout the hall, a few maybe were in groups, for example Mike Bowden, a heckling confessor, had come along with friends from the MSG. In *Like the night* it is reported two people claiming to have shouted 'Judas' at Dylan. Keith Butler, who came over from Canada to take part in BBC Radio 1 documentary *Ghost of electricity* was the first contender before several months later, another claimant, John Cordwell, was interviewed by the author and Andy Kershaw. Cordwell's story was that he had arrived with a group of friends from one of Manchester's folk clubs and shouted 'Judas'. Both Butler and Cordwell are no longer living but have passed into the mythology of Dylan.[21] One most likely candidate for having shouted 'Judas', John Cordwell, had arrived with a group of friends from one of town's folk clubs. Such die-hard traditionalists felt that Dylan had abandoned the political potential of protest songs in exchange cash for

Clockwise from top left: Dylan tuning up
early in the 1966 Free Trade Hall concert.

The warning 'handle with care' on the
amplifier's packing case perhaps takes on a
wider meaning here.

Dylan as some of his more traditionalist
admirers would have liked him to remain.

Mark Makin

the trappings of fame. By the end of the year, they had changed their
minds and became avid fans, but as that evening ended and everyone
drifted out into the night there hung an air of shocked bewilderment
like a cloud of mustard gas. For me, I soon began the process of putting
the events of the gig into some kind of context, but for others, no kind of
appeasement was on the agenda.

Manchester Post-Dylan

In Manchester generally, folk music had always been a bit of a broad
church, accepting of both worlds; there was no major schism between the
traditionalists and the modernists after Dylan's concert. Unaccompanied
ballad singers were as welcome doing a floor spot as were budding blues
players. American artists such as Paul Simon had built a steady following
in the North West, as had Minneapolis blues man and friend of Dylan,
Spider John Koerner who spent many months in this country in the
mid 1960s. What does appear to have happened and would probably
have happened anyway is that those who had a foot in both the folk and

the beat camp inevitably drifted more into the electric underworld of proto-rock music and R 'n' B, already established in clubs like the Twisted Wheel and The Oasis. Proto-rock was what Dylan and the Band had created, not pop music, not rock and roll, but something new, perhaps folk rock. As Bruce Springsteen said of Dylan at his induction into the Rock and Roll Hall of Fame in America, 'Elvis freed our bodies, Dylan freed our minds'.

Nationally, folk rock, arguably begun by Dylan and the Band, became increasingly popular through the 1960s. However, in Manchester, folk's fiery brightness as a potent force in popular music waned but the flame wasn't extinguished altogether. After the closure of MSG as part of Manchester's urban redevelopment programme in 1970, audience numbers in pub folk clubs went into decline as the fans moved away, got married, or simply stopped going out, attendance at singular events such as concerts at the Free Trade Hall of bigger named artists, such as Joan Baez, Tom Paxton or Al Stewart continued unabated. The folk club as an entity eventually shrank until only a handful remained to usher in the new decade. It was time of consolidation and retrenchment. In 1968, Harry Boardman brought out a collection called *Deep Lancashire* involving many of the best performers from that period. It was a celebration of the Industrial song and ballad heritage of the north west and marked a turning point in the folk revival's history. It was not dominated by the politburo-style thinking of the Singers Club but was homage paid to regionalism and perseverance.

Though folk carried with it a stereotypical image of men singing with their fingers in their ears, the folk music scene here nurtured a group of talented people who believed in a kind of 'people's music'. They performed their music in rooms where audience and singer were interchangeable, performed with little fuss and with a stoic belief in authenticity. The venues that survived post-Dylan, allowed for the emergence of what would eventually become known as alternative performance; artists who could not and did not fit in to established genres were embraced for their differences in style and content from the cliché of the folk entertainer. For example, Mike Harding became 'the Rochdale Cowboy', having evolved from straight singer of ballads into a witty raconteur and singer of comical and topical songs. Another figure who began his career as an entertainer in Manchester's folk clubs was poet John Cooper Clark, who stalked through the scene as a lanky, long-haired hippy in search of an audience for his savvy, street wise rhymes and his manic, rapid-fire delivery and biting wit. Dylan's no-surrender attitude and commitment offers a route also to punk and its ethos.

The similarities between the folk and punk movements are quite interesting and instructive. Putting aside for a moment the strict 'puritanicalism' of the MacColl faction and researching the clubs that flourished in the regions, we can argue that both grew from a grass-roots support base made up of adherents, devotees and enthusiasts, and both demanded a token fealty to certain dogmas in order to separate themselves from other, more mainstreams of music. These dogmas consisted of a strict allegiance to core values such as 'authenticity' and 'informality'. Both movements encouraged 'amateurism' in as much as they believed in a 'have a go!' attitude; anybody was welcome to get up and perform and this interchangeability between audience and entertainer is one of the strongest links between the two forms. To a degree, at the inception of both movements, promotion and presentation was an *ad-hoc* affair with publicity consisting of as much by word-of-mouth as by paid advertising; venues were small scale, folk clubs often in rooms above pubs, punk gigs in low-key music bars.

Both genres had their own print media outlets, very often small-scale, *samizdat* type publications that utilized the latest in new technology, Gestetner and Xerox being the technology of the folk magazine until a more formal access to off set-litho could be commandeered. Punk text, of course, found its way into the hands of its fans through the newly available photo-copying machines that were being installed in offices and colleges.

Another similarity between punk and folk was the use of independent music labels through which to sell records. There has been a kind of revisionist tendency in cultural studies that regards the Buzzcocks' E.P. *Time's up*, released on their own New Hormones label, as being the first of the independent records available in the UK, and being the one that lead to the explosion of DIY recording during and after the punk era. Although the latter part of the above is true the idea that they were the first is misleading, Topic Records, Transatlantic and Folkways and others were operating from before the 1960s. In Britain Bill Leader, pioneering folk record producer led the way in field recording and home studio recording in the 1950s. A microphone, a Revox reel-to-reel tape recorder and a wall covered in hanging blankets to act as sound baffles was all Bill needed to create an album.[22] Again, both groups shared a tendency towards left-wing politics, CND and anarchy in particular. Both allowed for an extremism in dress, punk certainly being the more *outré*, but at one time folk's jeans and beards were considered almost as *avant garde*. Ultimately what both groups shared in common was a devout belief in the 'righteousness' of their belief and that belief was in the music that the group held in common.

At a time when there was a vibrant revival of folk music in Great Britain, when folk music, particularly in Manchester, was in an extremely healthy state, American musician Bob Dylan paid three visits to the city and upended the entire music scene not least locally but also globally. This historical account, juxtaposing Dylan's first three visits to Manchester with the proponents and development of the 1960s folk movement, shows how his influence on music and effect on his audiences led to the winding down of the folk revival and reveals how the roots of that revival were coalesced into modern-day rock music.

Audiences in punk and post-punk Manchester

Bob
Dickinson

February, 2012. Afternoon darkness advancing quickly indicates the inevitable early arrival of a winter night accelerated by impending rain. I'm alone, I want to get under cover and get warm. But in Manchester, you can't avoid the void.

On my left, yawning away down several stone steps, and impossible to miss, an open doorway glows an almost obscene shade of pink. It reveals a basement shop selling takeaway kebabs from a metal counter, overlooked right and left by glowing illustrations – photos perhaps, but almost certainly photoshopped – of the dishes you can order. The meat is red or white or brown with scorched edges, the salad mystically green. There are no customers. A solitary employee stares upwards at me. But I'm not hungry, I keep walking along the cold pavement, thinking not about kebabs but a memory, the memory of an audience.

They got together down there, in the space now occupied by the kebab shop. In the early 1980s it was called the Cyprus Tavern. You felt the clingy, underfoot pull of sticky carpets, the warm touch of bodies, and the din in your ears of loud live music. Possible perpetrators might well have been The Spurtz, a band performing on a small stage at the back of the room. Their lead singer, Corky, around eighteen years old, has a voice like a child and ties up her hair in a bun, a post-punk Gracie Fields. She wails out a song called 'I Won't', to a deliberately naïve riff played on an electric keyboard tuned to sound like a toy piano.

The audience probably doesn't exceed fifty people, and you know half of them, because you have either shared accommodation with them or they have visited your shared accommodation, and they would include Corky. Near the doorway, a balding, bearded man, Alan Wise, who is likely to have been promoting the event, is standing, smiling, in his stained and straining, colourless suit, perhaps talking to a younger man, Andy Zero, who has wild innocent eyes staring out of a face covered in greasy, oily dirt. He wears an old coat that may have been waterproof once, and was motorcycle gear but has gone beyond dirty into some other phase preceding decomposition, and from inside this he pulls out a wad of fanzines, offering one to Alan, who takes it, and lets Andy inside.

But how clean this place seems in 2012, how above-board.

In the February drizzle, I walk round the corner, to Oxford Road, where a Tesco supermarket is stacked full with brightly lit, colourful products awaiting attention from zombielike consumers, happily wandering round, selecting their stuff. Here, at one time, there were nightclubs on two floors. Upstairs, a chicken in the basket cabaret establishment called Fagins, good for a night out getting smashed on lager watching Tony Christie taking you down the avenues and alleyways of his back catalogue: Is this the way to Amarillo? But downstairs, Rafters. Another music in a different kitchen. More images unfold in my mind, of more staircases and wrecked carpets connecting a succession of rooms drawing all visitors eventually towards a sort of tomb for the living. In this final chamber, the crowd circulated, yelling at itself above the volume of the music, played from records by a DJ. On stage, various persons, road crew or engineers, would perhaps be positioning instruments, and carrying out last-minute checks on cables and microphones. The space shaped the crowd, defined the boundaries, and interacted with several other basic conditions, including the nature and quality of the band soon to take the stage, and the mood or moods within the packs and grouplets constituting the arriving public. And who knows what band or which performer they'd have come to watch – perhaps the Fall, or Joy Division, or Pere Ubu, or X Ray Spex, or John Cooper Clarke, or any number of others, individually and in combinations, famous or infamous or obscure, signed or unsigned. The crowd was like a volatile mixture of chemicals in a test tube, about to be shaken up.

Many in this crowd had subtle lines beginning to advance across parts of their faces – evidence, perhaps, of drug aided enhancement or physical neglect. And some were courting fame: band members, managers, journalists, photographers – posing, deal making, winding one another up, a lot of egos in competition with one another. But it didn't matter how important they were, or thought they were, for in the end there was always shutdown, and everyone had to disperse, and from this thing that they had been, an audience, they had to go back to being lonely individuals again, wandering creatures, a little deaf from all the noise. 'Haven't you got homes to go to? Get the fuck out, clear off', the penguin-suited doormen would shout, offering little solace. And after the movement, there would be a stillness, and one thing you would notice especially would be the glitter on the floor from all the shards of shattered glass mixed up with cigarette ends and slicks of spilt fluids, excretions of experience.

Hardly any of these cellar dives exist anymore. Manchester is still full of clubs, or rather, expensive discos, but their predecessors have been well and truly done away with. In many places the buildings above them were derelict or out of use, soot-encrusted, grey-gold Victorian sandstone warehouses, where the only life behind the fly-posted windows went on underground. Like the Second World War air raid shelters a few of them had actually once been, these places were teeming again at night, with groups of people who, as previously indicated, knew one another, to the extent that after a while, over the months, they became casts of characters, in a sort of soap opera about the life of a huge, out-of-control problem family. Carol Morley in her fur coat, Liz Naylor and Cath Carroll in their immaculate suits, Dick Witts behind his smiling mask, Martin X slagging off Andy Zero, Andy still flogging fanzines, all with their talk, talking up one thing and putting down another, to each other, or against one another, a big, bickering life-form.

Further away, in suburbs where Soviet-style, brutalist, slab concrete flattened and fattened the landscape, or where older redbrick terraced houses were coming down and becoming endless heaps of dusty rubble, there were other gathering places for audiences. Landmarks such as the Mayflower, an old cinema, still displaying crumbling details of ageing gaudy paintwork, or secretive, multi-roomed, round-the-bend establishments like the Russell Club, Hulme, where reggae bass lines shook you physically to the stomach, would all be penetrated on certain, regular nights of the week, by a similar crew, at the end of the bus route, at the end of their tether.

From the suburbs as well as the centre of Manchester, these less than salubrious meeting places for audiences have disappeared. The landscape is different, cleaned up in many residential areas like Ancoats or Hulme, where substandard public housing has been removed to make way for the safe and nice, red, yellow or pink-brick houses with little gardens, and low-rise, pastel coloured apartment blocks, made possible by public-private partnerships encouraged by the City Council from the 1990s onwards. And hermetically sealed off from the past is Manchester' shiny city centre, where a new kind of consumption has taken over from the north west's old killer, consumption of the lungs. Somehow to walk through this place it all feels oddly flat and two-dimensional, a bit like a film set. For during the final years of the twentieth century, Manchester experienced a miniaturized version of what Naomi Klein calls economic 'shock therapy' thanks to an IRA bomb, and although some of the changes the city has experienced were already under way before the blast, and others are still happening, the lorry full of explosives that was detonated that morning, 15 June 1996, accelerated a whole series of processes and reorientations.[1] Now, here, the past is not history. It is heritage, and therefore it is not personal. The dreams suggested by this new city, and its privately owned elements, have little time for any intimate knowledge of the past.

The real and the unreal coexist, cheek by jowl, in this city centre, like never before. On the way to Piccadilly railway station, on my February walk, I went up Shudehill, past the Printworks, where each night, the northern editions of several daily newspapers used to roll off the presses. At one point, when the *Daily Mirror* was based here, the building was actually named Maxwell House, after its owner, the man who ripped off his workers' pension fund and then jumped off his own yacht, to be swallowed up by the void. Now, however, it is a themed location for shopping, eating, and watching blockbuster movies, its great hollow centre which used to contain printing presses now echoing to the chattering of people at leisure.

I am not really sure what 'leisure' is for. Perhaps me, walking around Manchester, constitutes a leisure activity. After all, I was not being paid to do it. But thinking about those audiences I had been a part of in the late 1970s and early 1980s, I am not sure they could be described as people simply 'at leisure', either. The experience was more important than simply lapping up some entertainment. Being in those audiences mattered, for reasons I will try to explain. I will also examine the way audiences changed during the period, and the way certain aspects of audience behaviour could be viewed as creative. But it is important, first, to emphasize that the years to which I am referring were the starting point for the musical and subcultural movements commonly referred to as punk and post-punk. The importance of Manchester and Liverpool from early on in this period has been well established, notably by Jon Savage, in his book *England's dreaming*, in which he states that by early 1977, 'Manchester started to develop as England's second Punk city after London and, as the capital quickly became Punk-saturated, its most creative site.'[2] The starting point for this development is well-known: the appearance of the Sex Pistols at the Lesser Free Trade Hall, in June, and again in July, 1976, when members of the audiences included key personnel who would afterward form several important future Manchester bands, including Mark E. Smith of The Fall, Peter Hook, Bernard Sumner and Ian Curtis of Joy Division, Steven Patrick Morrissey, and Howard Devoto and Pete Shelley of the Buzzcocks. Also present, on the first night, was Granada TV presenter, Tony Wilson.

Savage argues that it was thanks to the groundwork of the Buzzcocks (who, in January, 1977 released the first truly independent record, 'Spiral Scratch', on their own label, New Hormones), that Manchester's nascent punk scene became truly creative, forming bands, performing, recording, and making fanzines. Quoting their singer, Pete Shelley, and manager, Richard Boon, Savage links the band's rapid development to their use of two small, cheap venues where they, and other emerging local punk bands, could play: the Electric Circus, a former cinema in Collyhurst, in east Manchester, and the Ranch, a gay bar in Dale Street, attached to the Palace Nightclub, owned by the local drag comedian, Frank 'Foo Foo' Lammar. As Dave Haslam notes in *Manchester, England*, the places where punk took off in the city were frequently 'unlikely'.[3] Other locations where new bands found a footing included The Squat, an old building owned by Manchester University on Oxford Road, and The Oaks, a pub in Chorlton.

The look of the audiences attending punk gigs in some of these venues is captured vividly in Kevin Cummins' photographic book, *Manchester: looking for the light through the pouring rain*. Most telling is a shot of the front row of the audience watching Wythenshawe punk band, Slaughter and the Dogs, at The Oaks, taken on 22 February 1977.[4] Most of those visible are young girls in pageboy haircuts, and displaying lots of eyeliner, some wearing jeans, one in a rather odd fur coat, all looking more like fans of glam rock bands like T Rex than punks. Another photo shows an audience waiting outside the Electric Circus, in August, 1977, with a more equal gender balance, many of the young men wearing flared jeans, and several children who are making v-signs at the camera.[5] From inside the Electric Circus, Cummins includes one photograph he titles 'Riot at Wayne County gig' taken on 24 July 1977, in which the American band are entirely obscured by people, all male, who have invaded the stage, and all, seemingly, good natured – there is no obvious aggression in anyone's facial expression, no fighting going on.[6] Generally, again, this audience seems to have paid no attention to, or had no funds available to afford, the clothing commonly associated with punk at the time – the sort of gear worn by bands and fans from London, particularly the Sex Pistols, and obtained from or inspired by Vivienne Westwood's shop 'Sex' (in King's Road, Chelsea), later renamed 'Seditionaries'. A couple of exceptions captured by Cummins' camera are in close-up shots taken in the Circus in June 1977 of girls dressed up to the nines: Denise in black leather top, fishnet tights, black vinyl thigh-high boots with a paper flyer tucked into the top, and Joan, with big staring eyes, lots of eye makeup, leather biker jacket, badges, striped miniskirt, padlock and chains and a school scarf.[7] In both cases, the look is decidedly home-made. And in the background of both shots, there stand the inevitable young males in flares, and dirty trainers.

In early 1977, then, the independently-minded punk scene in Manchester was busy and buzzing, in its out-of-the-way little venues. 'Things are looking up for us in Manchester now', stated the lead column in the Moss Side-based punk fanzine, *Shy Talk*, in April 1977.[8] Fanzines were another illustration of the extent to which the early punk audience was at the centre of its own creative development. *Shy Talk* was run by Steve Shy, who worked at The Ranch and managed a local punk band, The Worst. Another early punk fanzine was also linked to a notable 'unlikely' venue, *Ghast Up*, and published (on an old duplicating machine) at the Electric Circus building. It was partly run by the young Mick Middles, who would later become a full-time music writer. Talking about *Ghast Up* in 1992, for my book *Imprinting the sticks*, Middles said, 'It was ugly. It had green ink, which was quite celebrated by people like Richard

Boon, who thought this was a wonderful innovation. But we went and actually bought, for twenty pounds, we bought a printing press from a junk shop in Ashton and we couldn't get the green ink out of it ... and as it printed the ink got darker and darker so you could barely read the last ones that were printed.'[9]

The most important rising writing talent, though, was Paul Morley, who produced *Girl Trouble*, a fast-moving series of single-sheet photocopies with text on one side and, on the other, a photographic collage, usually the work of Linder Sterling or Jon Savage (the latter having moved to Manchester after founding a fanzine there, *London's Outrage*). These collages usually commented on sexual politics, often utilising visuals from corny romantic magazines, pornography, or manuals of gadgets and utensils. *Girl Trouble* 8, for instance,

featured various 1950s photos of couples kissing, with a title 'Illustrated Love Album', but above, the typewritten words 'FOOLS PARADISE ... MINIMALISM MEANS NEVER HAVING TO SAY YOU'RE SORRY.' Each issue had a print run of about 50 copies only. Sterling, acclaimed shortly afterwards for her collaged design for the cover of the Buzzcocks' single of November, 1977, 'Orgasm Addict'- the design featuring a naked woman with nipples replaced by grinning female mouths, and her head replaced by an electric iron – also produced with Savage a pictorial, one-off fanzine for New Hormones, called *Secret Public*.[10] As I noted, it was in Manchester 'more than anywhere else that any kind of debate on notions of sexuality' was opening up in the punk press, and this was significantly influenced by the graphic design input of artists like Sterling and Savage, plus the lyrical outlook of bands like the Buzzcocks, plus the 'unlikely' spaces in which punk audiences gathered.[11] But this first wave of fanzines did not last long. 'There was no point after you got into 1977,' Middles said.' The punk thing took off and got national exposure. Sunday nights would be punk nights at the Circus, and there were a thousand people at a time, so once it became that big, it ... it lost the impetus then. By the time you got to April '77 there'd be twelve or thirteen fanzines on

The cover of *Shy Talk*, April 1977.

Author's collection

sale from all over the north, everybody was doing a fanzine, and it just became ridiculous.'[12]

The accelerating demand for punk music in Manchester, and the consequential increase in audience numbers at venues like the Electric Circus, was, in part, due to the persuasive power of the weekly television programme, 'So it goes', presented by Tony Wilson, and produced in Manchester by Granada. Broadcast locally at first, it was televized across many (but not all) other ITV regions in 1977, each edition including material filmed by experienced documentary film-crews, at local venues, including the Electric Circus, shortly before it closed in October 1977. These sequences capture very effectively the number of people crowded into the venue, with hardly any sign of a security presence or crash barriers to hold the packed crowd back from the stage. On the other hand, there is a real relationship established between audiences and artists. As a result, the films sometimes show how explosive the overcrowded conditions, caused by an ever-growing intake of fans, could be. A notable clip of the Middlesbrough band, Penetration, performing at the Circus, in August, 1977, focuses on their lead singer, Pauline Murray, bellowing out their first single 'Don't dictate', which was becoming an anthem even before its release in November. Almost as soon as she opens her mouth, she has a torrent of beer thrown and spat at her by two young men very near the front of the audience, preventing her from seeing properly, although she is able to keep singing. Bearing in mind the title of the song, the incident so far is already highly ironic. But, at the end of the first verse, Pauline is close enough to reach out and grab one bottle that has been used to throw beer, and she then jumps back to centre of the stage, just in time to take up the song again at the chorus. The hand-held camera pans around to catch a fight breaking out around the perpetrators with beer bottle number two. Behind Pauline, the band keeps going, despite the fact that the guitarist is momentarily put off and miss-plays a chord or two. As an example of confrontation between band and audience, it is exciting and grubby and full of life.

Seeing that Penetration film clip (which is easy enough to find on You Tube nowadays) brings to mind instantly the time, only a year later, when I saw the same group perform at one of the clubs that, in Manchester, sprang up in 1978 to contain those larger audiences and the charged and changing nature of punk music as it mutated: the Russell Club, in Hulme.

The audience that night was sizeable – over five hundred, in my estimation – and a high proportion of them were skinheads, and therefore almost exclusively male. As I watched from the back, they rapidly got aggressive and a big fight broke out in front of the stage, dividing the crowd into two opposing halves. Pauline Murray tried to cease the scrapping, by shouting, 'Stop!' over and over again into her microphone. But it didn't have any effect. Instead, it was the band that came to a grinding halt. 'Stop!' Pauline kept yelling at the two contesting armies of testosterone-fuelled, punch-throwing, young and hairfreemen. I remember thinking that it would have been better if the band had just kept on playing.

The revival of the skinhead subculture did not in itself reflect a move to the political ultra- right among punk audiences. But the threat of politically ultra-right views becoming influential in the wider field of pop and rock music had given rise to the formation of Rock Against Racism in 1976, as a response to comments made that year by ageing blues guitar superstar Eric Clapton, which revealed him to be an admirer of ageing Tory, Enoch Powell's views on the repatriation of non-white immigrants.[13] The expanding punk underworld also, eventually, bred its own ultra-right element, and a succession of none-too-pleasant bands and followers, although they would always be in a minority. But locally, the National Front made an impact in Autumn 1977 when leader Martin Webster staged a one man march in Hyde (protected by 2,500 police), to distract attention from a sizeable march by NF members and hangers-on, between Longsight and Belle Vue, which led to brick-throwing and fighting with anti-fascist demonstrators.

Simon Reynolds argues that it was the 'dislocation' caused by Britain's move to the right under the new Thatcher government that partly caused the 'dread' underlying the bleak, post-punk aesthetic which, in Manchester, was to become so strongly associated with bands like Joy Division.[14] But it is often forgotten that Joy Division actually played gigs for Rock Against Racism prior to Thatcher's election in 1979, and the RAR and Anti-Nazi League also did much to bring audiences together in a defiant spirit, reminding everyone who was there how strong and how positive music could be, especially on the occasion of the Northern Carnival against Racism, over two days in July 1978. The event was timed to coincide with a by-election in Moss Side, for which the National Front had put up a candidate. Police interference and general disorganisation resulted in a much-reduced show at Alexandra Park with only Graham Parker and local post-punks The Smirks allowed to play on July 13, but on July 15, a march from Strangeways Prison to Alexandra Park, Moss Side, resulted in a crowd of 35,000, which stood peacefully and watched Steel Pulse, the Buzzcocks, local reggae band Exodus, and Lancaster band, China Street.

But police raids on dubiously-licensed venues filled with oddly-dressed, frequently under-age youngsters also contributed to a rise in tension for audiences. In the second issue of a new Manchester fanzine, *City Fun*, late in 1978, Martin X reported on one such raid at the (briefly relaunched, in a different location) Electric Circus, thus:

> Witnessed the disgraceful spectacle at the ELECTRIC CIRCUS the other Sunday. License difficulties or not, this does not give the police cart blanche [sic] to resort to their now standard animal behaviour. Three people were actually assaulted for attempting to note the officers' numbers. What are the

City Fun number 1, October, 1978, featuring drawing of Distractions bass player Pip Nicholls.

numbers THERE for, then? What have they got to HIDE? We still have another list, Anderton, and it's available as evidence ...[15]

City Fun turned out to be a longer-running publication than any of its predecessors, only stuttering to a halt (after numerous internal arguments) in 1983. Its writers were regular gig-goers, and many of them joined, formed, or were already part of their own bands, which included the Passage, Glass Animals, the Kabal, and others. The fanzine was largely sold at gigs, and always contained many live reviews, sometimes reviewing the same gig more than once, by different writers, in the same issue. When I first met the loose collective behind *City Fun*, in a pub near the flat in Bonsall Street, Hulme, where the fanzine was at that time co-ordinated, co-founder Andy Zero told me, 'We don't edit. We don't cut anything out'.[16] *City Fun* could therefore look at times like a bit of a rag-bag of commentary and points of view. But it reflected accurately the downside of life in post-punk Manchester, frequently complaining about the lack of places to go for under-age music fans, and openly voicing discontent in relation to sexual politics. Liz Naylor's article, 'No city fun', which took up a whole page in the first issue, confessed and demanded: 'it's about time we (including myself) stopped judging people and hating them because they are soul fans, because they like disco. I am a soul fan; i am a punk; i am a disco kid; i am gay; i am straight; i am black; i am white AND i am me.'[17] On the cover of that first issue was a stylized image of an androgynous bass player, whose face was covered by a question mark. It was based on a real musician, Pip Nicholls, of the new local band the Distractions, whom the fanzine championed, and who appeared on stage wearing T-shirts bearing the motto, 'Distractions Fail the Sex Test'.

In parallel with the publication of this collectively written and run fanzine, the democratic side of the post-punk Manchester audience had been finding other ways to rekindle its creativity. In late 1977, the Manchester Musicians' Collective was established by Louise Alderman and Dick Witts, and others, who approached Steve Morris of the Band on

The Wall, a pub in Swan Street, then a jazz and blues venue, for a regular Sunday slot for new bands to meet and play. The Collective attracted beginners, amateurs, poseurs and people with talent, with a regular weekly evening to showcase several of its bands. In the audience you could meet new people and perhaps recruit them into whatever musical experiment you had in mind. The Band on the Wall became a kind of musical melting pot, where the concept of 'band' and 'audience' merged into one. Out of this melting pot, various new groups emerged, including The Fall, The Distractions, The Passage, A Certain Ratio, Bee Vamp, Bathroom Renovations, Fast Cars, Frantic Elevators (lead singer, Mick Hucknall), Gods Gift, the Liggers, Manchester Mekon, Not Sensibles, Slight Seconds, the Spurtz, Property Of?, Vibrant Thigh, and Warsaw (later known as Joy Division).

Through 1978, larger clubs such as Rafters frequently exceeded their fire limit of 500, by booking successful punk-related pop acts like Elvis Costello, or the talent-spotting one-off show known as the Stiff-Chiswick Challenge in which Joy Division made a dramatic late-night appearance, delighting their future manager, Rob Gretton, and future label co-founder, Tony Wilson. Meanwhile the Russell Club also attracted regular big audiences, particularly for the weekly Factory night, which began in May 1978, highlighting some of the future notables to appear on the label of the same name. But smaller venues, reminiscent of the 'unlikely' ones linked with the early days of punk in Manchester, were also explored by promoters. These included Kelly's and Oozit's, basement spaces just off Shudehill, the Osbourne Club, an old cinema on Oldham Road, and The Cyprus Tavern, on Princess Street.

Someone who became increasingly significant as a club promoter during this post-punk period, was Alan Wise, later the manager of Nico, and fictionalized as Dr Demetrius in James Young's book, *Songs they never play on the radio*, about the German-born chanteuse and former member of the Velvet Underground, and her drug-addled later life in Manchester. Sitting in the back room of the Ox, a pub on Liverpool Road, off Deansgate, in 2012, Alan Wise uses a straw to stir his lime juice and tonic, thoughtfully.

> Cellar clubs', he says, 'Yeah, they were dark and mysterious and slightly gangsterish, actually. It was the underground for underground people. As much as in the '50s the beatniks and the beats had lived in underground venues, our natural habitat was underground, dark venues. In fact, when I hired one, some years ago, the Cyprus Tavern, I rather liked it. Now they're quite out of date. These cellar clubs had an attraction. Cause you could hide in them, couldn't you. They were all warehouses, originally. But we used them as places we could hide and relax. You'd usually know everybody there. Although you'd come to watch the group, you'd know everybody there. They weren't clubs per se, because if you put nobody on, nobody would come.[18]

For an audience, these venues were frequently unheated, unhygienic and uncomfortable. But Alan Wise argues that this kind of space was exactly right, not just for experiencing the music that was emerging at that time in Manchester, but for many other vitally important styles that had been influential earlier in the twentieth century:

> Certain shows demand the immediacy of the audience, for instance jazz does ... blues, some pop, some arty pop requires that you remain close to the audience. Stadium rock becomes a thing in its own right. It's sound and lights, sound and lights, sound and lights. If you have an intimate form of music, you can't go above a thousand or two thousand venue. I mean, the music halls and the theatres knew this and were built at a two thousand capacity. There's a reason for that. But for some kinds of music, jazz and blues, smaller still ... You need to be in a club-type setting. So it's small. And that's because the amplification isn't great (it is now of course, it's horrible). And they play at a low volume so you can hear it. You don't get that at a stadium ... the audience is just watching.

In that pre-stadium era in Manchester, even the larger venues like the Apollo or the University Student Union were still small enough to allow some interaction between audiences and acts. As punk became chart music, and therefore mainstream, some bands, like the Clash, the Jam, or Siouxsie and the Banshees began to graduate to this size of venue. The do-it-yourself ethic that had fuelled early punk creativity was, however, able to go on flourishing in the smaller clubs, aided in Manchester by what Jon Savage, quoting Malcolm Garrett, observes as the emergence of a local 'professional infrastructure' – a coming-together of musicians, designers, promoters, writers, photographers, and more – resulting, among other things, in the first release on the new Factory record label, the double EP 'An ideal for living', in December, 1978.[19] This 'professional infrastructure' had also made connections with Liverpool, thanks to the work of Roger Eagle, band-booker at Eric's, the city's leading punk and post-punk club, and 'laboratory for Liverpool's future stars', as Simon Reynolds calls it.[20] Eagle was influential in the formation of a string of important new Merseyside bands including Big In Japan, Wah! Heat, Teardrop Explodes and Echo &The Bunnymen, all of which contained personnel who had met in the audience at Eric's. Eagle began to book acts for venues in Manchester including Rafters and the Russell Club (and later, in the mid-1980s, he became closely associated with the success of the International Club, in Anson Road, Rusholme). But oddly, he was not responsible for Echo & the Bunnymen's first appearance in Manchester. This was partly my doing, and what happened is perhaps worth describing.

Recently, I transferred to CD a cassette tape I made in 1979 on my mum's old recorder, a black Sony model spattered with magnolia emulsion paint from one of her decorating frenzies. Play the CD or the tape and you hear Echo and the Bunnymen performing that first gig in Manchester, in an old, cheap basement café in Back Piccadilly, owned by an Italian, we knew as Mr Gaetano. There are no drums, just the staccato pattering of a drum machine, the original Echo referred to in the band's name. The songs are short, and so is the Bunnymen's repertoire – they have to play their set twice to fill thirty minutes. The gaps in between the songs are filled with the noise of the audience, a mixture of locals and Liverpudlians, a big crowd having shown up thanks to the show being favourably mentioned earlier that night by Tony Wilson on 'Granada Reports', the north west regional ITV news programme. And in the sonic foreground I can hear my friends' voices. There's Teresa's shrill laughter in several places, and, when the Bunnymen ask what they should play during the encore, you hear Fiona shouting, 'Anything! Anything!'

We were running our own club, or we thought that was what we were doing. We called it Tingletangle, after a German cabaret of the Weimar era. We did nearly everything – from designing, printing and pasting up our own posters, to selling tickets on the night and dealing with the management of the bands and the owner of the venue. We hired a PA system, and someone else to do the lighting. We were doing what hundreds of others were doing at that time, as if the fans, the audience behind the whole movement started by punk, were dissolving the difference between performing and eyewitnessing, and moving into a new cultural phase. But it didn't last long. Why?

Perhaps the energy generated by that closeness was too disorganized, or too threatening, for some. Significantly, at the end of that evening there was a police raid. The boys in blue came down the stairs and told us cash had been taken out of the till at the bar. This was the first we had heard about it. Then one brave officer checked the toilets and came back with a used hypodermic syringe in his delicate paw. Obviously, serious drug abuse had also been going on, and none of us had noticed. The gentle Italian proprietor was given a good ticking off, and told he would never be able to put on live music again. Given the fact that he never had a music licence in the first place, I am sure he was happy to see everyone leave. So we had to start looking for a new venue. When we found it, we never had trouble from the police again, because the club in question was owned by local gangsters.

But something happened to audiences, in the wider sense, at around that time, that drained the energy out of things. With the commercial success of punk, and the increasing size of audiences for those bands that were successful, a sizeable proportion of every audience seemed to want the music to stay the same. Audiences were often divided, and their appearance became more tribal. In their frequently shabby, neglected and sometimes unsafe venues, these audiences were almost a perfect embodiment of what the twentieth century philosopher, novelist, and writer of Crowds and Power, Elias Canetti, called 'closed crowds'– crowds which cannot expand beyond a certain limit.[21] As a result the closed crowd 'gains in staying power' because it knows that after dispersal at the end of the night it can reassemble again the next. This crowd 'sets its hope on repetition', Canetti says. And yet, during the time I'm discussing, perhaps partially because of the informality (and cheapness and unsightliness) of the venues and spaces available to create and experience live music, there was also space, mental and physical, for musical and artistic innovation to continue. While some of the music, like some of the audience, remained a cliché, a significant part of it stretched or broke conventions.

Gradually, between late 1977 and 1982, a see-sawing balance of expression between audiences and acts began to break down. Punk had allowed room for argument, or outright rowing, with the public. It may not have been profound or useful – listen, for instance, to Mark Perry (the man behind the first punk fanzine, from London, *Sniffin' Glue*) fronting his band, ATV, and engaging with members of an audience at the 100 Club, London, on February 7, 1978, featured on the album *The Image Has Cracked*.[22] Given the opportunity to occupy a 'soapbox' on which to say what they like within three minutes, audience members' edited comments include one (male) complaining about the need for action against 'the people running this country', then another (male) appeals for someone to join his band, one (female) never stops annoyingly shouting 'Defiant!', someone else (male) accuses the audience of being scared of skinheads … and then mayhem. Perry ends up yelling, 'Right! You stupid bastards, off the stage! One of you people gets the chance to say something and what happens? There's a fight! … I love all you people but I hate you when you act like stupid idiots because that's when they grind you DOWN!'

But by 1981, the conservatism within elements of some audiences was becoming obvious, strange, and even rather dangerous to witness. On October 16 that year, the California hard-core punk band The Dead Kennedys, led by their charismatic frontman Jello Biafra, headlined at the Mayflower, by then possibly Manchester's seediest venue, situated near Belle Vue. The support bands included one called The Crash (not to be confused with the Clash) and Manchester Musicians Collective stalwarts, Gods Gift. What followed when Gods Gift took to the stage was witnessed by *City Fun* fanzine.[23]

Apparently Gods Gift vocalist Steve Edwards had informed the audience that they were all 'media punks' while Gods Gift were the real punks. He had told the audience that they were getting £40 but the Dead Kennedys were getting £1,500 (in fact they got £2000 plus hotel bills). At this point Steve Edwards was dragged/pushed into the audience by 'The Crash's manager and a member of the Dead Kennedys' road crew (Jello Biafra later apologized). He escaped with bruises after being chased by a gang of skinheads. … "More punks here than there ever was at the Circus in '77" says an old friend. But don't EVER EVER think it's the same as it was then. Friends'.

I was also a witness, and remember thinking, when Edwards was pushed into the angry crowd that he might not survive. This was an audience (of around 1,800) that outwardly displayed punk's (by now) most clichéd credentials – leather jackets, Mohican haircuts, Doc Marten boots and so forth. In contrast, Edwards was wearing a snorkel parka (which in itself was enough to draw expressions of ridicule before the band had even started playing). But circumstances such as the discomfort of the venue didn't help. We are talking, after all, about events that were, as all too often, badly amplified, and crudely played, in cramped, horrible holes.

Quite a different spirit of optimism, plus good weather, had dominated another big outdoor festival in Manchester not long

before, on August 8, 1981, when 35,000 people again gathered at Alexandra Park for an ambitious anti-nuclear protest, the Northern Carnival Against the Missiles, featuring John Cooper Clarke, The Damned, Harlem Spirit, and Chris Sievey and the Freshies. But the summer had been dominated by riots in July, when many districts of Manchester, especially Moss Side, had seen open conflict between youth and police. *City Fun* reported on the disturbances – I remember working on that issue in the office the fanzine had by that time moved to, in Salford, in rooms underneath The Fall's rehearsal space, and hearing all night the sound of windows being smashed outside, and footfalls, and police vans roaring past.[24]

City Fun links the urban riots of 1981 with the Peasants' Revolt, six hundred years earlier.

Author's collection

Tribalisation, meanwhile, carried on becoming more obvious in audiences at gig level. Punk loyalists divided into a series of second-generation micro-groupings during the early 1980s. Partly they revolved around a glut of new bands like Blitz, Discharge, and the Exploited, championed for the crudeness and directness of their expression by journalist Garry Bushell (then writing for *Sounds*), who came up with the collective term Oi! to describe them. A widespread Mod revival and 2-Tone scene surrounded the success of bands like the Specials, Madness, and the Selecter. Even in Manchester, where the success of the Factory record label led to the opening of the Hacienda club in 1982, post-punk audiences frequently took on the appearance of what Simon Reynolds calls 'clone armies' of 'overcoat clad boys'.[25]

It was reminiscent of the direction taken by earlier tribal subcultures, such as 1960s mods, or 1950s teddy boys. And the unifying importance of this conservatism was impressed on me especially in 1983 when I went to Farnworth, on the outskirts of Bolton, to see American rock and roller Jerry Lee Lewis, performing in a working mens' club. Down at the front, facing the stage, the tables had been taken over and surrounded by a small army of teds – survivors from that original British subculture of the 1950s. Teddy boys had hit the headlines for their style – their drape jackets, crepe soled shoes and quiffed, greased-up hair – but also for their violence. And there was a hint of that violence, or at least the threat of it, in the air that night in the audience reaction, which you could almost cut with a (flick) knife. Lewis, who was in his late forties at the time, around the same average age of the teds and many others in that club, was highly professional, and his energy was steely. But he was not only a rock and roll artist. In the late 1960s his career in America developed in the country music field. But this the puritanical British teddy boy could never abide. And so it was, with the opening bars of 'What's made Milwaukee famous', his country hit from 1968, that the teds in the audience that night in Farnworth stood up as one and walked out of the building, in a solemn procession. And of this ritualistic act Jerry Lee Lewis took absolutely no notice whatsoever.

In all probability, it had happened to him before. But I had never witnessed anything like it. Instead of ruining the moment, however, or of causing embarrassment, or of rupturing the atmosphere, the walkout actually added something. It was rough and ready and strangely and conservatively British, but in its scruffy solemnity it was oddly beautiful.

At another gig in the late twentieth century, a procession appeared that represented the audience, the fans, and on their behalf it became the artists, the band. At least that seemed to be the idea behind the way Dexy's Midnight Runners made their entrance on their Intense Emotions tour of 1980. When the lights came up on their show at Manchester Polytechnic Students Union, we witnessed the group making their way from the back of the hall, through the middle of the crowd, walking in a line, one after the other, towards the stage. Famously, they wore dark, woollen headgear, black reefer jackets with black plastic yolks and collars upturned, and as well as instruments, they carried duffle bags. These especially referred to – directly quoted – the accessories toted by teenagers at big railway stations on Friday and Saturday nights throughout the 70s and early 80s, as they waited to catch trains taking them to all-night Northern Soul club sessions. In one fell swoop Dexy's merged subcultural signs with performance practicalities and, with all the familiar solemnity with which we recognize the ritualistic, they took over the stage. And their passion as performers seemed subsequently to come in some ways from the self-conscious, thought-out nature of that opening ritual procession.

The element of procession is at the heart of performance. The theatre director Richard Schechner in his 1977 book, *Performance theory*, traces processions back to the earliest forms of theatre, including medieval carnival parades and miracle plays staged on travelling wagons, ritual chorus processions that featured in the theatre of Ancient Athens, and, even earlier, prehistoric hunting bands.[26] Processions are examples of what he calls 'natural theatre', that of everyday life, where the performance simply erupts, you can say quite accurately 'out of the ordinary', and there is little separation between performance and audience. It is not difficult to see how the queue to enter a performance space can easily become a kind of procession, at times – as the queues to enter the Hacienda in Manchester became during the heyday of Madchester in the early 1990s, or the queue for the Roxy was in London in the New Romantic era ten years before. These seemed to be times when the audience became, for a time, the star, sharing the attention of onlookers with the people making the music.

I have argued that audience behaviour in Manchester in the early 1980s became, in some significant ways, conservative, because of tribalism and factionalism, but what is interesting about these fragmentations is the way they enabled audiences to theatricalize their experience, for instance by an increasing emphasis on uniform dress codes, rituals and acts of procession. However, this was in direct contrast to the behaviour and experience of those numerically smaller audiences between 1976 and 1980, when the division between audience and artist seemed occasionally to disappear, and audiences were able to have a direct creative impact on cultural production. I would link the experience and the actions of those earlier punk and post-punk audiences to what Josephine Machon calls the visceral (syn)aesthetic performance style. Importantly, it was a live experience that had 'the ability to communicate that which is intangible in a live(d) and sensate manner, enabling an encounter with ideas as much as actual presence.'[27]

A real audience can be big or small, but no matter how much space it occupies, inside or out of doors, that audience will fill it with its own mixture of emotions, creating its own character. But the formative punk and post-punk audiences I have been writing about had another side to them: sometimes they became aware that they had a role in the proceedings. It may not have been a pretty sight, and, the effect those audiences had on whatever was being performed may not have been aesthetically wonderful to hear, but these audiences were not consuming entertainment passively. Can I say they discovered another dimension to the experience they were living through, and they were aware of this? I am not sure. Different theorists have, indeed, come up with names for this kind of experience – the left-wing, twentieth-century German playwright, Bertolt Brecht, for instance, strove to 'alienate' or 'defamiliarize' his audiences which to read about it, sounds rather unpleasant, all too self-conscious and not at all enjoyable.[28] It just means the audience is being made aware of the artificiality of its experience, which has been deliberately organized to undermine key theatrical illusions, such as the happy ending, the hero and heroine, justice and providence, which were derived from bourgeois theatre of the nineteenth century. The audience could carry this awareness outside a theatre and therefore understand its own wider relevance, politically. To get to this point, what the audience sees often plunges them into darkness, sadness or tragedy, instantly undercut by laughter and absurdity. Of course, none of the scenes I have referred to, in Manchester's punk and post-punk performance spaces, were connected with authored plays or dramas. But they were certainly dramatic, and laced with the indiscipline and spontaneity, or chaos, of popular culture at the time.

Later that February afternoon in 2012, I found myself on Dale Street, in an area that seems to have been missed, so far, in Manchester city centre's unrelenting regeneration. Here the old brick buildings are unchanged and decaying. Some of them are still functioning factories. But the network of streets has only remained this way because it has been so busy earning its keep, representing every-city, anywhere, for audiences everywhere, particularly the ones that watch blockbuster movies at places like the Printworks. This is where you can film, without need for much additional scenery, the b-movie, film noir version of the twentieth-century shadow city, for TV, for Hollywood, or for the fashion pages. It's perfect for a gritty British cop show night-time exterior. But, partly because many of the buildings still bristle with old external fire escapes, jagged and rusting, it's also ideal for the 1930s New York dockside setting of a movie like *Captain America*. During the location filming, in 2010, the old brickwork was plastered with facsimiles of posters from the '30s, some of which are still there, while on street corners a small army of locally-recruited extras hung around wearing the kind of costumes their great grandparents might have been seen in during the Great Depression. A weird reminder of the kind of economic times we are facing again.

Unmarked at the corner of Mangle Street, where technicians often set up lights and makeup assistants gently dab actors' faces with powder, I found a shuttered doorway, behind which lies another disused basement. There used to be a club down there, but the space has somehow escaped upgrading or refurbishment or conversion into a kebab shop or supermarket. Once, it pulled in regular crowds, rowdy as you like, shrieking to have the piss taken out of them. As the man who made this place famous, drag comic Frank 'Foo Foo' Lammar said in his 2002 autobiography, *I am what I am*, describing the night his father threw a bar stool at him during his act: 'Somebody told my dad that I was singing in the Ancoats Arms, but what they did not tell him was that I was stretched across a piano in a frock'. Finding success, Foo Foo moved on, from pubs and established several notable venues in the city centre, but the most famous was here, the Palace. Linked to it, behind this doorway, was the Ranch Bar, one of those 'unlikely' spaces where an important creative phase began, thanks to an audience that did not know its place.

'Closer from a distance': the auras of Factory Records in music, place, film, and historiography

James
McGrath

On Monday 23 November 1992, as independent Manchester label Factory Records was declared bankrupt, co-director Rob Gretton was filmed leaving the company's latter-day Charles Street headquarters. Asked to comment, he buoyantly replied: 'This isn't the final chapter. There's a whole new book to be written. Whole new film to be made.'[1] Gretton has been proven right; repeatedly. Subjected to dozens of books, documentaries and films since 1992, Factory and its artists have received mainstream media attention far surpassing the independent label's profile during its fourteen-year existence. This article discusses how Factory, from its 1978 beginnings, mythologized itself and its artists through notions of distance and absence. Screens of mystique were created. Post-1992 narratives concerning Factory implicitly offer to penetrate these screens, taking audiences somehow closer to the artists, texts and events themselves. Exploring these processes, I adapt and expand on Walter Benjamin's 1936 terms of 'aura', 'cult value' and 'exhibition value'. I apply these to key Factory albums, designs and videos, as well as its celebrated Manchester nightclub, The Haçienda. I critique how Joy Division's media presence gradually transformed after their catalogue was subsumed by a major label, London, in 1992, and how this both developed and contradicted Factory's initially very different approach to promoting (or not promoting) artists. I also want to emphasize Factory's loyalty to lesser-known artists, for this demonstrates how the label remained true to some of its original ideals. Therefore, alongside Joy Division, I periodically discuss The Durutti Column. The article aims to promote new ways of approaching Factory itself as a text, as well as offering new angles on a selection of individual albums, songs and videos, including the key retrospective narratives. Owing to numerous careers and crises simultaneously occurring throughout Factory's duration, the article, although loosely chronological, is sequenced primarily according to theme and theory.

Factory's origins, ethos and mediation

In early 1978, 'Factory' was the name chosen for an experimental, Manchester-based enterprise in popular music by its co-founder, Alan Erasmus. Unemployed after working as an actor and a band-manager, Erasmus decided the name after noticing a sign announcing a local factory's closure: 'I thought, "Factory, that's the name", because a factory was a place where people work and create things'.[2] An idealistic definition, perhaps, yet, a charismatic optimism towards art, audiences and enterprise would undeniably characterize the project that became Factory Records. Most radically, Factory planned to offer artists 50% of sales profits, and would not confine them to contracts, with artists retaining legal ownership of their recordings.[3]

Factory's other co-founder was Granada television personality Tony Wilson, whose show *So it goes* (1976–77) had featured many leading Anglo-American recording artists. Factory operated from Erasmus's flat at 86 Palatine Road, Didsbury, until 1990, when its headquarters moved to Charles Street. From November 1980, the enterprise traded as Factory Communications Ltd, 'Factory Records' having been registered elsewhere. For convenience, however, I refer to 'Factory Records', complying with the term favoured by the co-directors and artists, as well as other authors.

The first band approached by Erasmus and Wilson was The Durutti Column, whom the duo began managing. In May 1978, this band inaugurated The Factory club, where and when Erasmus and Wilson showcased musicians at Hulme's Russell Club on Fridays. However, not until 1979, with several vocalists passing through, would The Durutti Column's leader become fully apparent: guitarist Vini Reilly. Meanwhile, The Factory's first four-week itinerary concluded with Joy Division, a band whose direction, managed by Rob Gretton, was much clearer. In spring 1978, a third Factory partner, designer Peter Saville, joined Wilson and Erasmus. Gretton became a partner that autumn, and producer Martin Hannett in mid-1979. The five co-directors' pooled talents enabled something approaching self-sufficient communality. Moreover, Gretton brought Joy Division, who soon distinguished themselves as Factory's most prolific and acclaimed act, both as live performers and recording artists. Three additional individuals would distinctively shape mediations of Factory, and particularly Joy Division. The band received considerable music press coverage during their 1977–80 career, but mostly from three journalists who, unlike most reporters, were Manchester-based. Paul Morley (*NME*) influentially demonstrated music journalism as an art-form in its own right, particularly when writing about Joy Division. Morley's impressionistic responses powerfully flattered the music's creation of space for listeners' imaginations. Mick Middles (*Sounds*) favoured more lucid reportage: many of the most revealing comments from Joy Division and Factory emerged in interviews with him. Jon

Flier for Durutti
Column, Lesser
Free Trade Hall
December 1981.
Artwork by
Jon Savage

Jon Savage and
Manchester
District Music
Archive.

Savage (*Melody Maker*), more academic in tone, honed an allusively philosophical style, with close analysis yielding sociological commentary. Savage, a Cambridge graduate who moved to Manchester in 1979, promptly emphasized Joy Division's sonic relationship to the Northern city's physical environment. While another key reporter was the more established Max Bell (*NME*), Morley, Middles and Savage became and remain trusted affiliates of Factory's inner-circle, thereby assuming potentially problematic authority.

Asked by Middles to comment on Joy Division's songs in November 1978, the band's singer and lyricist Ian Curtis replied: 'I don't write about anything in particular [...] I leave it open to interpretation.'[4] Although Joy Division had recorded two tracks for Factory's first release, double-EP *A Factory sample* (December 1978), Factory itself is unmentioned in Middles' profile of Joy Division. Nonetheless, Curtis's quoted comment effectively encapsulates an aesthetic shared between the band and Factory. The leaving of statements provocatively 'open to interpretation' would be key to the label's ethos, and relates importantly to Wilson's often-espoused practical and philosophical ideal, praxis.

Wilson's praxis-themed rhetoric helped to promote Factory as a metonym for both intellectual credibility and spontaneous action. Influenced by Christopher Gray's *Leaving the 20th century: The incomplete work of the Situationist International* (1974), Wilson related praxis to Factory (in 1984) as follows: 'you do something because you want to do it, and after you've done it, you find out all the reasons why'.[5] It is apt, then, that since the label's 1992 collapse, it has been subjected to dozens of commentaries. Yet scholarly discussions specifically addressing Factory remain scarce. Howard Slater's learned *Factory Records scrapbook* (1998) critically evaluates Wilson's relationship to Situationist principles, citing the contradictions of Factory being, however experimental, a business.[6] Yet, discussing Factory via Wilson's own terms risks following his implicit instructions on how to perceive the label's history. Doing so is not especially constructive towards opening up wider historical and theoretical debates. Thus, I will also suggest ways in which further, yet still connected ideas, can be applied to the history, historiography and mythology of Factory Records. To this end, I periodically consider Walter Benjamin's 'The work of art in the age of mechanical reproduction' (1936).

Factory, mechanical-reproduction, and aura

A member of the Marxist-influenced Frankfurt School, Benjamin critiques mass-production as alienating the masses from the very notion of a unique, original artwork. Benjamin's 1936 essay concerns the decline of the unique object's cultural value as technology accelerates its mass production. No reproduction can capture the original artwork's 'aura': its unique 'presence in time and space'.[7] Benjamin considers how technological reproduction 'enables the original to meet the beholder halfway', for example through photographs and phonograph records; however, he stresses the 'decay' of aura as a cultural property within this process.[8]

Focusing on technology, Benjamin's essay has, inevitably, dated. In critiquing mediations (and commodifications) of aura in Factory releases and also in later, related texts, I adopt an opposing but still parallel variation on Benjamin's contention. I consider how the allure of unique aura, rather than diminishing in an age of mass-distributed images, actually grows *more* compelling. Reproductions may, as Benjamin suggests, dilute the cultural appeal of aura; but they may also celebrate, reinforce and in effect advertise notions of an original. This process is, in hindsight, discernible in Factory's promotion of its early artists. Joy Division's image was absent from all Factory sleeve designs, enhancing the allure of their aura, and indeed their identity, as a live act. I later reflect on how, once witnessing Joy Division's aura became impossible after Ian Curtis's death, the band's image gradually became an intensely-reproduced commodity. To begin outlining this trajectory, it is insightful to consider the band's first releases, and how Factory established notions of distance around Joy Division.

Although retrospective documentaries extensively acclaim Factory co-director Peter Saville's design for Joy Division's first album *Unknown pleasures* (June 1979), the sleeve went unmentioned in *NME* and *Melody Maker*'s reviews.[9] Befitting the title, *Unknown pleasures* solidifies Factory's aesthetic trademark of giving room and respect to the consumer's imagination and interpretation. Daringly, this debut album from both a band and an independent label left the title and the artists' identity off the front-sleeve. Factory refused to advertise the release, reasoning that, partly through the design, the album could promote itself.[10] An important event towards Factory's formation was The Sex Pistols' first Manchester gig at the Lesser Free Trade Hall (1976), attended by fewer than fifty, but attracting members of Joy Division and numerous other soon-to-be-successful local musicians. Factory's principle seems to have been to similarly inspire small numbers of interested people who could promote the album in their own ways, the audience thus becoming part of the dissemination.

The name 'Factory Records' implies mass-production: something compounded by the label's ostentatious catalogue-system. 'FAC' prefaced singles and other artefacts; 'FACT', albums and long-playing videos.[11] Yet Factory's catalogue-system did not differ drastically from those of multi-national corporations such as EMI. What *was* distinctive about Factory's approach was the prominence of FAC/FACT numbers on designs.

Unknown pleasures' rear-sleeve declares 'FACT 10 – A Factory Records Product' as centrally as 'JOY DIVISION – UNKNOWN PLEASURES'. Mechanical-reproduction is not merely acknowledged, but part of the artwork. Moreover, *Unknown pleasures* openly utilized mechanical-reproduction itself as a musical instrument. Producer Martin Hannett determined to expand this post-punk band's sound via his own expertise with studio technology, endowing their album with a semi-futuristic ambience.

Hannett's production on *Unknown pleasures* persistently uses digital delay, particularly on Steve Morris's drums, creating echo, and thus invoking physical space. While Hannett's acoustic imagery across the songs carries mechanical resonances, the foregrounding of Curtis's baritone vocals establishes a defiantly expressive human presence. Hannett's production of folk-singer Pete Farrow's 'Trouble in A-major' (1977) featured sounds of an industrial lift closing; Hannett repeats this on *Unknown pleasures*' 'Insight'. He explained in 1980: 'I like deserted public spaces, empty office blocks; they give me a rush'.[12] Against image-laden lines such as 'On the tenth floor, down the back-stairs, it's a no-man's land' (on the track 'Disorder'), Hannett's producing sensibilities complement Curtis's lyrics (and *vice versa*) extraordinarily, enhancing the singer as a flaneur of deserted spaces. Yet, amidst the desolation, lyrics vary on notions of imagined meeting points; 'To the centre of the city in the night, waiting for you' ('Shadowplay'); 'Me in my own world, yeah you there beside' ('I remember nothing').

Factory's records were mass-produced, but this does not preclude each one from having an aura of its own. Factory's idea as 'post-rationalized' by Wilson in 2007 was to make sleeves 'glossier, more expensive and more beautiful than those of the multinationals.'[13] Factory created records that were, to adapt Benjamin's terms, *worthy* of the unique presence in time, space and contemplation that they occupied. *Unknown pleasures,* Factory's first album, enticingly played with the distance between artists and audience, creating audacious space for interpretation. Factory's second album, by The Durutti Column, was more extreme. With all information confined to the vinyl's centre-label, preventing the titles' identification while the record played, *The Return of the Durutti Column* (January 1980) appeared in a sandpaper sleeve, after Guy Debord and Sager Jon's sandpaper-jacketed Situationist book *Memoires* (1959). Former Durutti Column guitarist Dave Rowbotham suggested the sleeve. The sandpaper furthers another Situationist reference: '*Sous les paves la plage*' ('Beneath the paving stones, the beach'); and beneath the sand, music.[14]

Benjamin considered how mechanical-reproduction enabled the original artwork and the beholder to meet halfway. However, for mass-produced recorded music, the reproduction *is* the original artwork: a culmination of processes including composing, rehearsing, performing, recording, engineering, producing, overdubbing, mixing, and mastering, as well as designing and printing. The record becomes a meeting-point not between the beholder and the art, but the beholder and the artist. This sense memorably defines Joy Division's single 'Transmission' (November 1979). Invoking the experience of dancing to the radio, Curtis sings of 'touching from a distance'. In subsequent decades, comparable notions of the mass-produced artefact as a point of contact between audience and artist would mark Joy Division's transformed commodification. The separation would no longer be one of distance, but absence. Yet once Curtis's aura – and thus that of Joy Division – could no longer be met, the aesthetics of distance established through Factory's designs would wither away from the band's mediation. In this process, the notion of 'touching' would become suggested less through listening than through watching.

Factory Post-Curtis

Ian Curtis hanged himself aged 23 on 18 May 1980. As well as suffering with depression, he had been diagnosed with epilepsy eighteen months earlier: a condition not helped by Joy Division's intense work schedule. Curtis committed suicide the day before Joy Division had been due to embark on their first American tour. Their single 'Love will tear us apart', released on schedule weeks later, became Factory's first mainstream UK chart entry, reaching No. 13. *Closer*, signifying finality and/or proximity according to pronunciation, was the title of Joy Division's second album (July 1980), completed weeks before Curtis's suicide. Saville's sleeve, showing a tomb, prompted accusations of Factory exploiting Curtis's death, although reportedly, the design had already been agreed with the band, including the singer.[15] Certainly, Saville's sleeve reflects the songs, particularly the funereal pace and imagery of penultimate track 'The Eternal', and the closing, similarly-phrased 'Decades', evoking young men in the afterlife.

In 1981, Greater Mancunian musician Mark E. Smith satirized Factory's 'liv[ing] off the back of a dead man'.[16] Factory had issued two 12-inch Joy Division singles, 'Atmosphere' and 'Transmission', in autumn 1980. Although a double-album of previously unreleased material and live recordings was less sustaining than two strategically-timed single albums might have been, Factory chose the former option for Joy Division's posthumous *Still* (October 1981). However, the label was also embracing a relatively new popular music format: home video. In 1981, Factory established a film-making partnership, IKON/FCL. The debut release, *Here are the young men* (1982), compiling live Joy Division performances, was the first Factory product advertised in the music press.[17] Yet Factory retained an ostensible, if ostentatious, refusal to treat art as an orthodox commodity, stating:

'Normal copyright is held on this video. Anyone however who wishes to reproduce material contained within it on a non-profit making basis is free to do so, in whole or part, in any way they see fit.'[18]

NME had published photographs of Joy Division by Manchester-based Kevin Cummins, and later, Dutch photographer Anton Corbijn. But although Wilson had enabled the band to appear (twice) on Granada TV (1978–79) and BBC2's *Something else* (1979), their visual image remained absent from Factory releases.

Stills from 'Here are the Young men', Factory's 1982 debut video production, featuring Joy Division

Leaving things open to interpretation had been key not just to Joy Division's music, but their identity. *Here are the young men* was Factory's first mass-distributed reproduction of the band's image. The 1982 video repositioned audiences towards a notion of the band's aura; it was the label's last new Joy Division product for six years.

Benjamin emphasizes how aura is, by definition, irreproducible; yet still 'the urge grows stronger to get hold of an object at very close range by way of its likeness, its reproduction'.[19] Aura can never be encountered through a reproduction; the urge to which Benjamin refers is doomed to continue, and this is advantageous to agents of mass-production. But before turning to later representations of Joy Division, it is instructive to consider another Factory project, enabled largely through this band's sales.

The Haçienda

Factory's 1980–82 artists included A Certain Ratio, Section 25, Kevin Hewick, Crispy Ambulance, ESG and Stockholm Monsters, all Hannett-produced. However, it was Joy Division's surviving members who established Factory as an independent label with mainstream presence. Bernard Sumner, Peter Hook and Steve Morris determined to continue after Curtis's death. In September 1980, they became New Order and started touring. Gillian Gilbert joined on keyboards, and guitarist Sumner became lead vocalist. Factory issued three New Order singles in 1981, and in November, a month after *Still*, *Movement*, their debut album. All were Hannett-produced. However, his dominance as Factory's producer broke with The Durutti Column's *LC* (1981), recorded at home by Vini Reilly (with co-producer Stew Pickering) and drummer Bruce Mitchell, thereon the band's second key member.

By 1982, Factory had considerable money at its disposal and was able to borrow more. Hannett wanted to purchase recording equipment to enable Factory (indeed, Manchester) to establish Britain's leading studio. Gretton favoured opening a club. When Gretton's plan prevailed, Hannett legally petitioned for Factory's dissolution. In 1984, he accepted £25,000 for withdrawing his company stake.[20] His departure brought significant changes. Hannett had always insisted that Factory refuse the standard industry practice of hiring professional pluggers to promote releases to radio stations. In 1983, the label's stance on this began changing.[21] Hannett's career, meanwhile, became derailed as he endured drug-dependency. He died on 10 April 1991.

Gretton reportedly conceived the Haçienda club (FAC 51) after reading proto-Situationist Ivan Chtcheglov's proclamation 'The Haçienda must be built' in his 'Formula for a new city' (1953).[22] The club, designed by Ben Kelly and occupying a Whitworth Street former-warehouse, ran from 1982–97. Jointly owned by Factory with Gainwest (the Gretton/New Order partnership), the Haçienda was predominantly Gretton's interest, but Wilson remained its public face. Wilson's speech at the 21 May 1982 opening declared: 'Praxis is embodied in the following statement: we spent the last year building the Haçienda, FAC 51. We have the next year to decide why [...] I hope you all assist us in that'.[23] Thus, the Haçienda opened for interpretation.

Unlike Factory's mass-produced records, the Hacienda embodied unique aura as an immediately shareable presence in space and time. But though little research exists on Haçienda club-goer demographics, it is important not to overestimate the venue's inclusivity. Disconcertingly, the opening night's compère hired by Gretton and Wilson was Bernard Manning, a comedian notorious for racist and homophobic jokes. *NME* (initially) depicted the 'strutting and VERY dashing' clientele as aloof.[24] In the 1990s, the club became a meeting-place for several infamous groups of Manchester gangsters, some members of whom later supervised security.[25] When, after thirteen years of the club losing money, Factory sought branded sponsorship for the Haçienda, prospective clients were informed that customers were 'style conscious' and wanted 'to be associated with the club and its musical philosophy'.[26]

By 1988, the club was (at least, culturally) flourishing. Though the venue had hosted crucial performances by The Smiths and Madonna, its popularity expanded steadily after weekly DJs, instead of one-off gigs, began characterizing the itinerary in 1986. DJs including Dave Haslam and Mike Pickering helped diversify the Haçienda's clientele, Pickering in particular drawing larger black audiences.[27] Haslam's weekly Temperance Club at the Haçienda showcased British indie guitar recordings alongside new American dance releases. Similar fusions would mark a new style amongst Manchester groups, particularly Factory's third major band, Happy Mondays.

In 1990, America's *Newsweek* declared Manchester the capital of youth culture; the journalist proclaimed 'It all started at the Haçienda' (though alongside this assertion, it is noteworthy that Wilson was a main interviewee for the feature).[28] Nevertheless, Happy Mondays' *Madchester rave on* EP (1989) had nominally affirmed an imagined community. 'Madchester' became a metonym for new Manchester bands (also including The Stone Roses and The Inspiral Carpets) as well as for dance-culture and the drug that enhanced it, Ecstasy. The period 1988–89 marked the Haçienda's peak; yet though the club was regularly full, Ecstasy depleted alcohol sales, and thus income. The Haçienda's association with drugs also led to legal opposition. Historical perceptions of this club's centrality to Manchester culture can be complicated by the fact that Wilson and licensee Paul Mason were forced publically to defend the Hacienda against threats of closure by Greater Manchester Police. In a 1990 *NME* spread defending the club, Mason emphasized the Haçienda as a central reason behind Manchester tourism, adding: 'applications to the University and Poly are up a quarter on last year'.[29] The Haçienda temporarily shut in 1991 after several gun-related incidents. It reopened in 1992 but closed forever (without ceremony) on 28 June 1997, preceding voluntary liquidation.

The Haçienda's closure sealed its functioning years as an historical entity. When, in 1998, Manchester Civic Society opposed the building's demolition, Wilson objected: 'The Haçienda's memory will be preserved forever, but it shouldn't be turned into a museum'.[30] With this notion, the Haçienda's demise, like its conception, honoured a Chtcheglov formula: 'through a transformation in time, *the absence of the object becomes a presence one can feel*' (original emphasis).[31]

'Atmosphere': Cult value into exhibition value

Benjamin relates 'cult value' to the aura of unique, hidden objects, accessible to an elite few. However, mechanical-reproduction, primarily through photography and film, enables an object's 'exhibition value' (and thus, commercial value).[32] Wilson's comment that the Haçienda should be preserved in memory, rather than museum form, raises temporal cult value above spatial exhibition value. Yet, before Factory's own 1992 collapse, Wilson had already shown something of how cult value *creates* exhibition value. *Here are the young men* (1982) demonstrated this commercially, but also aesthetically, through the haunting video spectacle of a singer performing months before his death. In 1988, Factory's next (and last) audio-visual representation of Joy Division provocatively foregrounded the fact of Curtis's absence while dramatically exhibiting his image.

Wilson asked Anton Corbijn (who photographed Joy Division) to direct the video for the band's reissued single 'Atmosphere' (1988).[33] Music-video critic Saul Austerlitz (2007) observes how the prolific Cobijn expertly emphasizes his clients' 'mythic qualities'.[34] Corbijn's work specializes in black-and-white aesthetics. One effect is to recall early Hollywood photographs, which, by the 1980s, signified enduring fame. Corbijn's 'Atmosphere' also utilizes contemporary visual associations in popular music. The black-and-white shots of mountains, bare trees and desert-like plains recall his photography for U2's transat-lantically successful *Joshua Tree* album (1987). Factory was seemingly repackaging Joy Division towards mass commercial appeal. Via Corbijn's video, notions of posthumous fame became key to the campaign.

First, the song's history is significant. Before Curtis's death, 'Atmosphere' was already part of an aggrandizement of the band's mythology, prompting a wry March 1980 *NME* report.[35] Affirming Factory's ethos of artists remaining free from contractual restriction, 'Atmosphere' (plus 'Dead Souls') was released by French independent label Sordide Sentimental (March 1980), run by Jean-Pierre Turmel. Gretton commented: 'it's interesting to see how different people handle different aspects. There are no restrictions from Factory on this sort of thing.'[36] Sordide Sentimental's release, 'Licht und blindheit', packaged the single in a magazine-like folder, reproducing a painting by Jean-Francois Jamoul in parody of Caspar David Friedrich's *Wanderer above the mist* (1818). However, Jamoul depicted not a well-dressed gentleman gazing from a precipice, but a shrouded, reaper-like figure. The package also carried Tummel's sleevenotes, alluding to Debord's Situationist *Society of the spectacle* and quoting St John of the Cross and Pascal before appraising Joy Division. Unlike Factory's releases, this additionally reproduced the band's image: Corbijn's photograph of Joy Division descending into an underground station. This, along with scenes of mountains and shrouded figures, returns in Corbijn's video.

To analyse Corbijn's Wilson-commissioned 'Atmosphere' video is to obey a transparent motivation behind its grandiose yet evasive symbolism. However, from a decade when MTV was presenting hit singles in visual form in a repetitive stream, 'Atmosphere' also exemplifies a mass-produced cultural form designed to endure, as well as demand, attention. Thirteen shrouded figures gather praying beside a spire-like obelisk. Seven wear white, six wear black. The scene is thus loaded with ambiguous Biblical imagery. The white and black figures separate in opposite directions. Suggesting the subject of their search, Corbijn's photographs of Curtis appear in mock-animation. Two black-shrouded figures, like pall-bearers, carry a rectangular object. This is later unveiled as the image of Joy Division descending into the underground. A black-shrouded figure carries, like a cross, a replica of the obelisk on his or her shoulder, but collapses. Mythologizing Joy Division's never-to-happen American tour, a shot is shown of Curtis and Sumner lugging a case stamped 'U.S.'. The figures are shown in procession on a beach, carrying Curtis's gigantic image (not unlike a billboard). Curtis is effectively heralded a cult icon. Alongside implications of martyrdom and worship, the video implies resurrection. The song 'Atmosphere' would become the most elevated text in Factory iconography, closing both Corbijn's 2007 film *Control* and Grant Gee's 2007 documentary *Joy Division* (see below).

'Atmosphere' was re-released alongside a Joy Division compilation,

Substance (1988), collecting singles and other recordings not on the 1979–81 albums, including this song (ending the pattern of Joy Division singles not being replicated on albums). *Substance* was also the title of New Order's 1987 compilation: Factory's biggest-selling album yet. In a mini-documentary promoting *Substance* (1988), Gretton insisted on discussing 'the video', remarking: 'I don't like it. I was never really consulted'.[37] Although Factory's 1988 mythologizing of Curtis is transparent to near-ironic proportions, the label's silence on Joy Division since 1982 had honoured the label's original aesthetics of distance. Moreover, 1988 saw Joy Division promoted on the back of New Order's success. Impressively, New Order had resisted allowing the opposite. Only in 1984, around the fourth anniversary of Curtis's death, with their own status indisputable, had they begun (occasionally) performing Joy Division songs live.

Wilson said of the 1988 re-promotion: 'there's a whole world out there for whom Ian Curtis's mythic role can provide a level of feeling' which 'people deserve to have'.[38] Although the evolution of Joy Division's legacy hereon would not always be steered by Wilson, the stage for its ambitious development has remained set by Factory.

Factory's aftermath, 1992–2002: History into historiography

The fact of bankruptcy as the manner of Factory's conclusion in 1992 enhances notions of the label's ethos of praxis persisting unrepentantly. Wilson became fond of saying 'Some people make money and some make history'.[39] Yet Factory's historiography has appeared far more controlled than its actual history. The following discussions critically review key texts in Factory's historiography, reflecting on how these respond to and frequently (sometimes problematically) reinforce established mythologies.

Factory's November 1992 bankruptcy partly reflected dwindling interest in the label, as grunge replaced Madchester in the critical mainstream. Happy Mondays' long-delayed … *Yes please* cost £500,000 to make but was released to critical contempt in September, peaking at 14 in the UK. New Order, meanwhile, had yet to deliver the follow-up to their 1989 No. 1 album, *Technique*. Their sixth, *Republic* (May 1993), appeared on London Records, who also acquired the Joy Division and New Order back catalogues. This coincided with increased, official emphasis on both bands' histories.

Kevin Hewitt's 1993 documentary *NewOrderStory*, written by Paul Morley, marked the first extended focus on Joy Division and New Order as a linear entity. Broadcast on ITV following *Republic*'s release and issued on VHS, *NewOrderStory* was first in a long sequence of retrospectives concerning both bands. Although parts of Corbijn's 'Atmosphere' video are shown at the start, New Order's appearances refuse solemnity. Band interviews consist partly of a mock game-show. The question 'Who is the laziest member of the group?' prompts the reply 'Ian Curtis'. The documentary proceeds to recount New Order's career, including Factory's recent calamity. Gretton, 'too pissed', declines to answer questions on this; Erasmus refused to appear; Wilson comments: 'It's been one long, *wonderful* nightmare'. Asked whether 'this is really Rob Gretton's story', Wilson replies 'Yeah. But he isn't on TV'.

The next major narrative was contrastingly sombre. Deborah Curtis's 1995 memoir of life with her late husband Ian, *Touching from a distance*, remains a key event in unveiling, as well as enhancing, the singer's mythology. The degree to which his commitments to Joy Division coincided with distance from his family means that there is relatively little attention to the band's music; the emphasis is more on personal, domestic life, contrasting with previous representations of Ian Curtis. The memoir, however, created potentially more intimate listening experiences: for the first time, Curtis's complete lyrics were published, never having appeared on Joy Division releases. The narrative details the couple's daily lifestyle and protracted separation, due to Joy Division's touring plus the couple's strained relationship. The antithesis of Corbijn's (literally) flat 1988 portrayal of an icon, the widow's memoir is uncompromisingly rounded, depicting a troubled musician, equally capable of selfishness and empathy. There is also unprecedented, if fragmented, detail regarding Curtis's employment before becoming a full-time musician in 1979. Overall, the book reveals, to exceptional levels in popular music biography, that the subject's lifestyle was, until his final months, conceivably similar to that of many readers. New possibilities for fans to identify with Curtis were thus created; 'touching from a distance', indeed.

Mick Middles *'From Joy Division to New Order: The Factory story* (1996) provided the first major print retrospective on Factory. As well as presenting old and new interviews with central Factory figures, the book contains Middles' recollections of observing Joy Division. Despite discussing the label as a whole, the 1996 book's title reflects how, in the 1990s, Factory's exhibition value remained subordinate to that of its most celebrated bands. Tellingly, Middles' book was later reissued with minor expansions as *From Joy Division to New Order: The true story of Anthony H. Wilson and Factory Records* (2002), and *Factory: The story of the record label* (2009).

Rob Gretton died of a heart attack on 15 May 1999. In 1998, he donated extensive Factory-related papers, artwork, audio-visual materials and correspondence to Manchester's Museum of Science and Industry. The archive mainly concerns the Haçienda. The thirty-plus box-files evidence the vital roles and personalities of lesser-known Factory workers, as well as Gretton's own centrality to the Haçienda.

An early retrospective on the Haçienda appears in Dave Haslam's

Manchester, England: The story of the pop cult city (1999). As well as providing far-reaching discussions of Manchester's historical and musical heritage, Haslam draws on his experiences as a Haçienda DJ. Similarly valuable is CP Lee's academic monograph *Shake, rattle and rain* (2002). Chronicling Manchester music from 1955–95, Lee locates Factory in various historical, geographical, and cultural contexts. He interviews numerous key figures and also offers scholarly reflection on his own involvement with Factory as (amongst other things) co-producer of *A Factory sample* (1978). Lee also provides tactful, non-sensationalized discussion of Nazi connotations surrounding the names 'Joy Division' and 'New Order' in the context of punk shock-value.[40]

The informative Factory-related narratives reviewed above have a common quality which persists in many further retrospectives: they are written by individuals who, in different ways, had first-hand experience of Factory. In terms of authorship, Factory retained its own cult value in the decade after its demise. As a topic, it remained the historiographic preserve of individuals who personally witnessed and participated in aspects of its history. However, this pattern also reflected limited interest from wider media. In 2002, Factory's own exhibition value as an historical narrative transformed.

2002–07: Factory on screen and in history

Film, not music, would prove the medium to most vitally reinvigorate interest in Factory, gradually bringing mainstream media attention unparalleled in the label's 1978–92 lifespan. The years 2002–07 saw several films and television documentaries capitalize on Factory's mythologies by offering audiences (encompassing a generation not born when the label started) a level of insight which, while sometimes appearing to undo the earlier mystique, also managed to fuel further intrigue. An effect, however, was to make the focal point less the music than the personalities involved.

A catalyst for the twenty-first century appetite (indeed, market) for Factory-related texts was Michael Winterbottom's film *24 hour party people* (2002), written by Frank Cottrell Boyce. Wilson, played by comedian Steve Coogan, is depicted as hapless, lovable and pretentious. He is also portrayed as Factory's central director. Erasmus and Gretton, though represented, are problematically marginalized, their main lines being responses to Wilson. Similarly, Factory's first band, The Durutti Column, are drastically sidelined.

Winterbottom became acquainted with Wilson while working for Granada. In 2000, with producer Andrew Eaton, Winterbottom began meeting Wilson to discuss a film chronicling Factory Records.[41] Although Wilson's input remains ambiguous, the film was branded 'FAC 401', and he authored the film's novelization, titled *24 hour party people: What the sleeve notes never tell you* (2002). The latter gives much greater acknowledgement to Erasmus and Gretton, but the film and the book together expanded, twisted, preserved and established myths with which many subsequent narratives would concern themselves with settling. Coogan's soliloquies as Wilson self-referentially acknowledge the film's dalliances with fiction, though paradoxically, the shambolic narrative of a chaotic history ends with incongruous neatness, conflating Factory's bankruptcy with the Haçienda's closure, though these were five years apart. Nevertheless, Winterbottom's film, whatever its problems for historians, identifies and fulfils Factory as a thrilling parable of anarchic creativity. Produced in association with Film Four, it was promoted by David Robertson's Channel 4 documentary *The Factory Records saga* (2002), bringing Factory's mythologies to further popular audiences.

A potentially instructive effect of Winterbottom's film was to establish, then embrace, the impossibility of master narratives concerning Factory. A more ambiguous way in which it honours Factory's history is its process of (re-)establishing mystique that may later be unravelled. An example is the film's celebration of Factory prioritizing art over profit by the suggestion, expanded by Wilson's novelization, that Factory lost money with every copy sold of New Order's 'Blue Monday' (1983) – one of the bestselling 12-inch singles ever – owing to the cost of Saville's multi-dimensional sleeve.[42] This story is scrutinized by Nolan (2009) and Nice (2010) in their emphatically fact-led accounts (see below), the consensus being that once the financial implications were noticed, Saville redesigned a less expensive format.[43]

Mythologizing Factory at large, both narratives of *24 hour party people* adopt a conversely less aggrandizing focus on Curtis, whose portrayal is ample but not central. Coogan's narrative as Wilson emphasizes the latter's 'wonderful memories' of lesser-known, often jubilant aspects of the late singer's personality. Recreations of Curtis's funeral then introduce Corbijn's 'Atmosphere' video. The emphasis thus divides between Curtis the private individual and cultural icon. Subsequent portrayals of Curtis, as we shall see, continue to stage these as mutually-intensifying. However, as though Winterbottom and Wilson exhausted the possibilities of postmodernist Factory histories, later accounts would attempt grand narratives.

Although Winterbottom's film prompted unprecedented mainstream media interest in Factory's legacy, it was, unsurprisingly, on Joy Division that most attention landed. Archive news-site Nexis records how in 2005, the 25th anniversary of Curtis's death prompted media attention in America and Australia, as well as Britain.[44] A public memorial event on 18 May in Manchester's Exchange Square reportedly attracted 1,500 (a larger audience than most Joy Division gigs), as *Here are the young men* was shown on the BBC's public 'Big Screen'.[45] Most footage of Joy Division was filmed for television or video. The transference to a cinema-sized screen symbolized how the band's appeal had expanded since Curtis's death; it was also portentous of imminent developments.

January 2005 brought the announcement of an Ian Curtis biopic.[46] Based on Deborah Curtis's memoir, with Corbijn as director and Wilson as executive-producer, the title, *Control*, seemed unwittingly fitting; a rival film, written by Michael Stock, had been proposed in 2004. The commodification surrounding Curtis was wryly satirized in Wirral-based band Half Man Half Biscuit's song 'Joy Division oven gloves' (2005), whose lyrics, after invoking 'a post-punk postcard fair', announced (parodying 'Transmission') 'Dance, dance, dance in your Joy Division ovengloves'.[47] Meanwhile, the cult value of Curtis's life, if not that of his elusive aura, continued to prove alluring in print. Middles, with Wilson's ex-wife Lindsay Reade (who spent much time with the singer), co-authored *Torn apart: The life of Ian Curtis* (2006), informatively balancing its focus between his musical career and personal life. It includes exclusive commentaries from Belgian music journalist Annik Honoré, with whom Curtis maintained a loving (previously somewhat misunderstood) relationship.

The Haçienda's twenty-fifth anniversary was celebrated with an exhibition in Manchester's Urbis Centre in July 2007. However, while appreciative attention to Factory's legacy reached new heights, the sense of this organization as something irresolutely past was to be profoundly and prematurely affirmed. On 10 August, Tony Wilson, at 57, died from a heart attack while suffering from terminal cancer. The Durutti Column's 'Sketch for summer' played at the start of his funeral; 'Atmosphere' was chosen for the end.[48]

In his last two years, while also pursuing new projects in broadcasting, local politics and music, Wilson acted (with Deborah Curtis) as co-producer of Corbijn's *Control*. In 1988 Corbijn had glorified Curtis as icon. In 1995, Deborah Curtis had grounded her late husband's story in more human terms. *Control*, released in October 2007, powerfully fuses these approaches, establishing an increasingly tense balance between professional and domestic identity. Corbijn's black-and-white aesthetics establish a social realist ambience, evoking the singer as a determined working-class youngster, whose talent led him into extraordinary circumstances. Yet *Control* conveys how, while Joy Division were successful, they were never wealthy. Closing scenes were filmed on location at Ian and Deborah Curtis's small terraced house in Macclesfield. It is less the film's content that further ionizes Curtis than the form, a major cinematic release. It testifies to Wilson's dignity as co-producer that, countering Winterbottom's work, *Control* establishes Gretton, not Wilson, as Joy Division's chief mentor. Wilson's last overtly retrospective interview was for Chris Rodley's BBC4 documentary *Factory: Manchester from Joy Division to Happy Mondays*, broadcast September 2007. Again, cinematic releases synergetically coincided with broader media attention.

Control risked enhancing already disproportionate attention to Curtis at the expense of Joy Division. Grant Gee's cinematic documentary *Joy Division* (2007) revolves around interviews with the band's surviving members. Contrasting with *NewOrderStory* (1993), *Joy Division* shows Sumner, Hook and Morris remembering Curtis with stark emotion. Wilson is interviewed, and over a dozen others who had interacted with the band. However, the cult value of Curtis's life story continues to be evident. In the most arresting implication of audiences being taken somehow closer to Curtis's aura, Gee's film includes extracts from a tape of the singer, weeks before his suicide, being hypnotized to recall a past life. While the film effectively opposes Factory's presentation of Joy Division as a decidedly elusive entity, some emphasis on mystique thus persists.

Gee's film locates Joy Division within contexts of post-war England and, especially, 1970s Manchester. In terms of popular music history, the overall narrative is more insular, beginning (like Winterbottom's film) with The Sex Pistols' first Manchester gig, attended by Sumner and Hook. Joy Division emerged in a post-punk era when new musicians and journalists were striving to establish distance from earlier mainstreams. Dominated by this generational sensibility, Gee's interviews risk keeping Joy Division in a post-punk historiographical rut, partly because Hannett's role, though acclaimed, is not significantly detailed. For example, The Beatles may not have influenced Curtis, Hook, Sumner or Morris, but the Liverpool foursome influenced Hannett, and therefore Joy Division.[49] This is most audible in their 1979 recordings, including reversed guitar overdubs ('Autosuggestion'); 'found' ambient details (breaking glass in 'I remember nothing'); and even aerosols as percussion ('She's lost control'), as on Paul McCartney's self-produced *McCartney* album (1970).

Factory's history has become characterized by cult value less through spatial than temporal separation; as already noted, an elite few, who personally observed parts of this history, have dominated its historiography. Although Gee, like Winterbottom, was a relative outsider, *Joy Division* reinforces the centrality of honorary Factory scribes. Savage is credited as the documentary's writer; Morley is interviewed in depth. Another prominent interviewee is writer and graphic artist Jon Wozencroft, who began writing about Joy Division in 1984 (contributing, with Morley, to *An Ideal for living*, an illustrated miniature biography of the band).[50] Savage, Morley and Wozencroft also wrote sleevenotes for London Records' Joy Division boxed-set *Heart and soul* (1997) and would pen further notes for London's 2007 expanded re-releases of Joy Division's 1979–81 albums. All three writers evocatively combine information and impression in their responses to Joy Division. However, their prominence in the band's historiography (albeit well-earned after their roles as early, creative popularisers) has become inseparable from Joy Division's post-Factory marketing. Meanwhile, the repackaging continued. Deviating from the titular subtleties of *Still* (1981), *Substance* (1988) and *Permanent* (1995), a 2008 compilation from London was *The best of Joy Division.*

Critiquing the emerging role of film in mass culture, Benjamin quotes Georges Duhamel's 1930 observation: 'I can no longer think what I want to think. My thoughts have been replaced by moving images'.[51] In Factory's own history, film played a relatively slight role, despite the IKON partnership. Yet the twenty-first century film and documentary narratives, both in content and proliferation, have an interpellative effect, *telling* the Factory story in ways that reverse (while also exploiting) the label's originally minimal aesthetics and their room for interpretation. However, another effect was to create exhibition value for interpretations of actual events, often challenging the mythology hitherto curated by Factory's dominant voices.

Factory historiography post-2007

In developments that would seem to honour (though perhaps unwittingly) the late Wilson's aptitude for post-Situationist PR surrounding *24 hour party people,* the post-2002 mythologizing also helped to generate an audience, and indeed authors, for Factory-related narratives attempting boldly, and at times iconoclastically, factual accounts. While these continue to be led largely by insiders, the focus has broadened significantly, thanks significantly to the emergence of several seemingly more impartial authors.

A welcome offshoot of Joy Division's heightened profile has been increased recognition of Martin Hannett. Playwright and (briefly) Durutti Column vocalist, Colin Sharp, authored an eccentric biography of Hannett (2007). A close friend in the 1970s, Sharp recalls their conversations to detail the producer's musical interests, but recounts Hannett's post-Factory life through impressionistic vignettes, noticeably similar to Winterbottom's narrative. Hannett is also the subject of one of the first Factory-related narratives initiated from a younger perspective. Olivia Ford's 2012 audio documentary on Hannett, produced as part of her Journalism degree at the University of Leeds, features interviews with several Factory figures.[52] Refreshingly, Ford's respectful yet discerning questions prompt measured discussions of Hannett the producer, rather than reinforcing the troubled autocrat caricatures of earlier representations. Musician Chris Hewitt's documentary film *He wasn't just the fifth member of Joy Division* and book *Martin Hannett – Pleasures of the Unknown* appeared in 2014. They are both rooted in a rich body of interview material..

An aesthetic casualty of the digital download age is the sleeve as a visual and textural aspect of the album. Thus, a timely testimony to the work of Saville and many other, lesser-known Factory designers is Matthew

Robertson's *Factory Records: The complete graphic album* (2007), bearing Wilson's foreword, plus Robertson's often highly-informative commentaries on each sleeve. Designs for other Factory projects, including the Haçienda, are also represented. However, the lavish book exploits the cult value of original Factory records only insofar as it keeps this intriguingly intact, reproducing just front-sleeve designs.

In a different redevelopment of the graphic emphasis, Rob Gretton's 1978–80 notebooks were reproduced as the 2008 book *1 Top-class manager*. Beyond Jon Savage's foreword, the book consists primarily of Gretton's handwritten lists. While conveying his meticulous planning for Joy Division's career week-by-week, the content is often impenetrable for outsiders, to the degree that the book almost recalls Factory's early, enigmatic designs. Overseen by the late manager's partner Leslie Gilbert in collaboration with Manchester District Music Archive, Gretton's reproduced notebooks are invaluable to researchers in providing extensive chronologies of Joy Division's gigs, plus numerous aborted negotiations. More broadly, they indicate much regarding the methods, commitment and cost involved in managing a Manchester-based band in the post-punk period. Prose is scarce in this book, though a striking January 1979 statement – seemingly for a meeting with Joy Division, following a conversation with Paul Morley that evidently impacted on Gretton – declares the future Factory co-director's priority to be to 'approach everything from a different viewpoint – not having everything dictated by money' (original emphasis).[53]

Gretton's notebooks, and, to a lesser extent, Robertson's graphic album, appear in the fuller view of Factory historiography as new emphases from the label's inner-circle on the factual and tangible, somewhat apart from the mythologizing in whose wake they emerged. A related development was the first biography of Wilson, David Nolan's *You're entitled to an opinion ... The high times and many lives of Tony Wilson, Factory Records and the Haçienda* (2009). While providing an affectionate portrait, Nolan is emphatically sceptical towards Wilson's own narratives regarding Factory. Nolan had interviewed Wilson for his independently-researched but eventually semi-authorized biography of New Order's Bernard Sumner *Confusion* (2007), a title reflecting in part the careful, indeed, dignified privacy favoured by this musician.[54]

In terms of physical presence and both intellectual and emotional directness, Peter Hook remains a most compellingly human representative of Factory Records, an enterprise whose latter-day mediation might otherwise have been somewhat pompous. The frequency and manner of Hook's public appearances create the impression of a genial individual, proud of his achievements while seldom seeming to lose self-awareness and never appearing to neglect opportunities to acknowledge the contributions of others. Hook's 2009 memoir *The Haçienda* notably counters Wilson's praxis rhetoric through its subtitle, *How not to run a club*.

Here, Hook combines energetic raconteurship with lists of the club's annual schedules, as well as extracts from the Hacienda's increasingly ominous account books. Hook's 2012 memoir *Unknown pleasures: Inside Joy Division* seeks in part to redeem the band's image from its solemn iconography by detailing their laddish camaraderie. Hook's book about New Order (from whom he bitterly split in 2007) is currently in preparation.[55]

James Nice's 546-page *Shadowplayers: The rise and fall of Factory Records* (2010) is a year-by-year narrative of Factory from 1978–92. In 1983, Nice established his own independent label, LTM, who adopted former Factory artists Crispy Ambulance and Section 25. Nice also worked for Factory's Belgian imprint, Factory Benelux. Nice now runs a revived imprint of Factory Benelux, and in 2012, began reissuing expanded editions of albums by original Factory artists including Crispy Ambulance and The Durutti Column. While this background could make Nice's loyalties appear ambiguous, as a former Factory employee on an unremarkable wage, his published viewpoints on the original label, while tirelessly enthusiastic, are far from idealistic. As well as utilizing music magazine archives, Nice's 2010 tome provides dozens of exclusive interviews with individuals including Wilson and (unusually) Erasmus, but most revealingly, with lesser-known Factory employees and artists. This, plus Nice's readiness to question official Factory mythologies, endows *Shadowplayers* with timely qualities of history from below. Selections from Nice's interviews formed the DVD *Shadowplayers: Factory Records 1978–81* (2006), which Nice intended would counter various 'crass myths' perpetuated by Winterbottom's film.[56]

Lindsay Reade, Wilson's wife from 1977–83, closely witnessed Factory's origins and early years. Reade also briefly worked as supervisor of Factory's overseas licensing. She retained intimate friendship with Wilson until his death. Reade's memoir *Mr Manchester and the Factory girl: The story of Tony and Lindsay Wilson* (2010) is invaluable for researchers of Manchester music beyond Factory, while her accounts of the label itself, including its eventful afterlife, are indispensable for their level of detail, often drawing on Reade's diaries, as well as interviews with Factory associates. Reade highlights numerous occasions on which Factory, even in its earliest months, fell short of its radical ideals, an example being Wilson's effective 'selling' of Orchestral Manoeuvres in the Dark in spring 1979 to Dindisc, a Virgin Records imprint.[57]

Although Factory has received little academic study in its own right, several related critiques are valuable. Liz Naylor, who became acquainted with Factory while writing for fanzine *City fun*, explores in her 2007 postgraduate research how Manchester's decaying landscape influenced the city's post-punk music.[58] Since 2007, Joy Division have been the subject of three scholarly articles, all concerning film. Constantine Verevis' 2009 documentary study critiques Gee's film in relation to Situationist notions

of place.[59] In a pioneering 2009 article, Mitzi Waltz and Martin James discuss film representations of Curtis's illness, indicating the singer's potential importance for Cultural Disability Studies.[60] Noel McLaughlin compares cinematic depictions of Joy Division and U2 in an excellent 2011 article, which also indicates how these two bands' careers might bear further comparisons.[61] Meanwhile, Richard Witts' 2010 appraisal of North Manchester band The Fall discusses how Factory's post-1992 mythology has distracted problematically from the cultural legacies of other Manchester post-punk artists.[62]

The Durutti Column's Vini Reilly in 2013.

Photo, Elspeth Moore

Conclusion

Factory was fundamental to the construction of Joy Division's mythology, and vice versa. Yet the career which most fully attests to Factory's ethos is arguably that of The Durutti Column, the first act approached by Erasmus and Wilson. Posthumous attention to Joy Division easily obscure show, in Factory's earliest years, it was (and with significant reason) guitarist Vini Reilly who was represented, even promoted by Factory, as a perilously mortal musician. Max Bell's February 1980 *NME* profile of Reilly stressed the guitarist's serious health troubles, including depression.[63] Yet The Durutti Column, still fronted by Reilly, continue as a dynamic, if in every sense unpredictable, group of experimentalists over thirty albums later. Their infrequent, mostly Manchester-based live performances, present spectacular demonstrations of aura in the living moment, peerlessly fusing past, present and found music as Reilly, with charismatically robust drummer-manager Bruce Mitchell, combine samples from songs and films with original compositions, often works in progress. Their gigs often include Reilly's tribute to his friend Ian Curtis, 'The missing boy' (1981), and dedications abound to Wilson and others.

Factory issued nine Durutti Column albums from 1980–90. Despite none of these registering on mainstream UK charts, mutual support between band and label continued. In 1985, Reilly commented that Factory gave him the creative freedom to do 'what I want when and where I choose.'[64] Wilson adopted The Durutti Column as his main signing for Factory Too, the 1994–98 Manchester label he ran as a subdivision of London/Polygram. He ceased managing Reilly in 1998, but in 2005, Wilson's final, short-lived label F4 Records issued the band's EP 'Heaven sent (It was called digital. It was heaven sent)', one of the first download-only releases. The Durutti Column's *Sex and death* (1994) had been issued, on Wilson's suggestion, as a CD-ROM. Their Factory release *Domo arigato* (1986) was Britain's first CD-only album. Factory's very first band, and the act with closest connections to Wilson, would continually be associated with risk-taking steps forward in the history of mechanically-reproduced music.

Despite being under-represented in the three films by Winterbottom, Corbijn and Gee, Reilly would prove the Factory survivor to most creatively eulogize Wilson. Premiered at the 2009 Manchester International Festival, The Durutti Column's *A Paean to Wilson* (released 2010) celebrates Reilly's late mentor through lengthy instrumentals (for decades, Wilson ineffectually discouraged the guitarist's singing). Perhaps appropriately, Reilly's nominal tribute to Wilson is also replete with allusions to other Factory pioneers, including samples of Hannett laughing, and the instrumental 'Alan', honouring Erasmus.

This article has sought to demonstrate possible further approaches to Factory Records by offering new perspectives on key texts within and surrounding the label's history. In particular, I hope to have indicated, by adapting a selection of Benjamin's terms, how aspects of critical theory can broaden the conceptual frameworks for discussing Factory in cultural historical terms. Benjamin observed that the film industry sought to compensate for the elusiveness of aura by creating film stars as celebrities; he called this 'the spell of personality', and in other words, 'the phony spell of a commodity'.[65] This might explain some processes at work in Factory's twenty-first-century cultural presence, and might be equally, if differently, pertinent to the label's original albums. Benjamin is concerned with mass-production in specific relation to mass culture; but the pattern does not differ significantly from the commodification of the writer's personality since the age of the printing press. It remains instructive to consider Factory Records itself in terms of a spell of personalities. Yet the commodities discussed above as texts promoted ideas and attitudes, as well as industries. One such underlying notion throughout Factory's eventful history is that it can pay, in a variety of ways, to prioritize creativity over calculable monetary gain. For this reason, as well as those I have sought to demonstrate above, the legacies of Factory Records might prove heartening to people working and studying in Arts and Humanities departments.

Madchester and the representations of the North–South divide in the 1980s and 1990s

Georgina
Gregory

The term 'Madchester' is often invoked to describe a localized music scene emerging in Manchester between the late 1980s and the early 1990s, where artists recording for independent labels eventually became the subject of intense media interest. Groups associated with the phenomenon including The Stone Roses, Happy Mondays, 808 State and Inspiral Carpets, created a distinctive musical style synthesizing elements of indie rock, pop, dance with flourishes of 1960s psychedelia.[1] Like many other musical subcultures, the style was accompanied by an equally recognisable visual identity and fashion sensibility, referred to in the media as the 'baggy' look. The fashionable image saw the revival of 1960s flared jeans, loose long-sleeved T-shirts decorated in a mish-mash of swirling, psychedelic colour. The resultant identity created by artists and designers connected to the scene contrasted sharply with the contemporary image of the city as a grey, rain-soaked and culturally impoverished provincial outpost.

In this paper, I will show how, rather than celebrating Manchester's unique creativity, the Madchester label was used by the media to reinforce class stereotypes, the hegemony of the south and notions of the north as 'other'. During a period of extreme social and economic division, the depiction of Manchester as home to the workshy, hedonists and drug abusers set Mancunians apart from the media depiction of 'Yuppie' culture and its headquarters in the southern-centred finance sector. Furthermore, I will argue that the reception of Madchester was somewhat conflicted. While it resonated with certain individuals and groups, notably people from outside the city, for those involved in the scene, Madchester was an unwanted label. Northern youths' apparent refusal to conform to the zeitgeist of aspirational conservatism will be placed within the context of more longstanding historical divisions between the south and the north of England. Since stereotypes of the region as an uncivilized, lower class and hostile hotbed of rebellion informed popular opinion, I will consider how these cultural tropes fuelled the media reception of Madchester and whether the artists themselves deliberately played up the popular image of northern identity.

The foundations of the North-South divide

A divide between the north and the south of England is a well documented historical schism which according to historian Helen Jewell is, 'as old as the hills'.[2] The division is at the heart of the image of the north as the less civilized region, where locals are renowned for their pride, independence and non-conformity. According to McArthur, the Romans' separation of *Britannia superior* in the south from *Britannia inferior* was one of the earliest recorded examples of the split.[3] As the conquering armies moved northward, their perception of the inhabitants via the descriptor *Britannia Barbara,* served to amplify the idea that distance from the southern epicentre was a measure of cultural degradation. This view of the north established a social agenda which has been maintained in various guises ever since and, in many respects, the attitude of the national press to music and musicians emanating from the Manchester region mirrors that of the Romans.

Although it is not within the scope of this article to explore mythological misrepresentation of the south, Dave Russell's work on northern identity draws attention to the dangers of oversimplifying the stereotyping of regional identities and it is fair to say that the process is a reciprocal one.[4] As he points out, the south is also subject to pervasive stereotypes, many of which are equally unhelpful and unrepresentative. Furthermore, at any one time conflicting representations of the regions which surface within the discourses of culture can lead to contradictory stereotypes. Some of the hackneyed clichés of the north invoke quite positive connotations, imbuing the region with imagined qualities of ruggedness, virility and authenticity. Clearly, the well-worn tropes do not in themselves create hierarchies of social class. Inequalities are established by the ways in which stereotypes are mobilized by competing groups in society and certain representations of the north serve the purposes of those who wish to diminish the cultural contribution and the people of the region.

If we return to the mythical separation of a civilized south from an uncultured north, this particular perception was further magnified during the industrial revolution as northerners emerged as a visible force due to the evolution of a fast-growing and distinctively urban, working-class. Katie Wales explains how the north-south divide was strengthened by industrialisation and the arrival of a new type of workforce, different from the agricultural labourer or cottage based craftsman.[5] According to Donald Read, whereas in preindustrial communities, social cohesiveness was maintained through traditional hierarchies of subservience, the new working class showed fewer obeisances to their economic 'superiors'.[6] Hence, although stereotypes of northern identity may incorporate notions of rugged rural life, hardy folk and picturesque, albeit craggy landscapes, the concept of the rebellious working-class northerner is typically located within industrial cities. In particular, the city of

Manchester has a reputation for anti-authoritarianism political leanings via its associations with protest groups such as Chartism, the Anti-Corn Law League and the women's suffrage movement.

Paradoxically, considering its assignation to an inferior social and geographical position, the city of Manchester has often exhibited something of a superiority complex. More millionaires may have resided in the south of England during its nineteenth-century zenith but Martin Pugh says that northern manufacturing centres such as Manchester experienced such self-confidence during the Industrial Revolution, that they began to see London as somewhat backward.[7] By 1850 the city was the eighth largest in Europe and like other provincial outposts Manchester displayed great pride, even arrogance, concerning its role as a regional capital.[8] Evidence of this self-assured attitude was clearly articulated in the magnificence of municipal buildings such as the neo-Gothic town hall, completed in 1877. Its soaring bell tower and elaborate statuary signify the sense of pride, swagger and ambition. While the streets of Manchester may not have been paved with gold this certainly did not deter the inhabitants from feeling a deep loyalty to the city and its distinctive culture.

Economic decline and the geopolitics of difference

Although Victorian Manchester's identity as an independent and prosperous regional centre was indisputable, by the early years of the twentieth century its fortunes were reversed when various factors led to a protracted waning of economic stature. Although the end of the First World War fuelled a continued market for the products of heavy industry, during the inter-war period the staple industries of the north shouldered the brunt of successive economic slumps. As Jones argues, 'In every year from 1925, London, the South East, the South West and the Midlands experienced unemployment rates below the national average'.[9] Although subsequent governments have attempted to redress regional disparities through policies designed to bring prosperity to the regions, the north-west is regularly marginalized within national political campaigns and its inhabitants continue to experience higher levels of poverty, ill health and unemployment.[10]

Within the geopolitics of difference the region's physical environment is seen as inferior to the south. Wales says the view of the north as unattractive stems from enduring stereotypes, most of which, 'derive from the industrial revolution and the huge expansion of industry and growth of the Midland and northern towns'.[11] In 1807 the poet Robert Southey claimed it would be hard to find a place, 'more destitute than Manchester' a vision embellished by George Orwell (1937) in his account of the north where he advises those travelling 'northward' to expect an aesthetic deterioration once they go beyond Birmingham where they will, 'begin to encounter the real ugliness of industrialism- an ugliness so frightful and so arresting that you are obliged, as it were, to come to terms with it'.[12]

Media depiction of northerners

Those living within the confines of these dismal vistas are often seen as equally abject in discourses where their characters and speech are contrasted less favourably with the refined demeanour and voices of cultivated southerners. Northerners are more likely to be portrayed as uncouth or unsophisticated and while these negative descriptors apply to both men and women, it is northern men who bear the brunt of the lengthy repertoire of shortcomings. In films, television and literature they are frequently represented as misogynistic, coarse, rebellious, workshy, or clumsy. For example, although we are never told where he was born, Emily Bronte's brutal protagonist Heathcliff creates a template for a procession of damaged northern male characters that resurface across a range of media. The angry protagonists of late 1950s and early 1960s social realist novels and films such as Alan Sillitoe's rebel Arthur Seaton in *Saturday Night and Sunday Morning*, are followed by other equally flawed individuals. From Ken Loach's roguish and volatile family man Bob Jones in the film *Raining Stones*, to Jim Royle the lazy, sexist head of TV soap's *The Royle Family* and Jackie Elliot, the gruff, domineering unemployed miner who tries to prevent his son from becoming a dancer in *Billy Elliot*. Regardless of any redeeming qualities they share, the men of the north are routinely portrayed as physically strong and emotionally unstable.

Compounding these character defects, the northern accent is presented as inferior, a perception Wales traces to Roman Britain. By the sixteenth century, literary scholar George Puttenham advises poets, 'neither to take the termes of Northern men such as they use in dayly talke . . . nor in effect any speech beyond the river of Trent', suggesting instead, to 'take the vsuall speech of the court and that of London'. Regional accents and dialect continue to attract unwanted negative connotations.[13] In Chambers and Trudgill's words, low status language is, 'generally associated with the peasantry, the working class, or other groups lacking in prestige, and within the hierarchy of preferred speech, standardized southern accents have become hegemonic'.[14] Regional accents may now be more accepted but southern accents are still accorded more prestige. Hence, those who speak 'properly' are seen as more intelligent and of a higher social class than northerners regardless of their true socio-economic position, a prejudice which lingers into the present day.

Northern Identity and Pop Music

Although stereotypes of northernness are embedded across a range of broadcast media, whether such imagined differences can be detected in music emanating from the region is a question which invites interest. According to Tim Wall, scholarly work on the link between regional identity and popular music is growing as various studies attempt to uncover precisely how music texts represent the cultural groups which produce them.[15] Music's combination of images, sounds and performances can undoubtedly draw on a deep reservoir of symbolic public language but whether these cultural texts are symptomatic of a fixed, underlying identity or if identity is always subject to renegotiation, is a continuing theme in cultural and media studies.[16] Nevertheless, a body of work by Gilroy, Marks and Negus supports the concept of an identifiable relationship between music, national identity and notions of ethnicity,[17] while other writers have uncovered a relationship between both musical and regional discourses.[18] Furthermore, as Osgerby notes, provincial youth cultures operate below the radar of national scrutiny, as 'micro-heritages' within the confines of their own region and for this reason they are largely ignored by the media.[19] In the 'swinging Sixties' for example, media interest focussed almost entirely on events happening in London and although the regional music scenes, especially 'Merseybeat', regularly surface, it was expected that the artists involved will eventually sever their local ties to take up residence in the South. More recently the roots of Two Tone and Heavy Metal, musical subcultures of the 1970s, can be traced to the particular conditions of urban life in the Midlands.[20] Historical templates such as these, illustrate that music texts do indeed communicate meanings emanating from their location.

In the case of Manchester, the city's position as a separate creative centre is fully exploited in its popular music and in the post-war period, Mancunians have been particularly productive in establishing local fashions, subcultures and music scenes. The city had its own beat groups in the 1960s with artists such as Freddie and the Dreamers, Herman's Hermits and The Hollies providing an alternative to the Merseybeat sound. During the same decade, a particular style of soul music played in Manchester's iconic dance clubs also established a distinctive identity around the city, with clubs like The Twisted Wheel establishing a regional subculture style. Later, during the darker years of economic decline, the self-sufficient attitude of punk artists of the 1970s led to the emergence of a string of independent record labels and at this time, Manchester developed its own localized musical culture separate from the metropolis. Emphasising the sense of difference, themes of 'otherness' are frequently invoked by local musicians who play on the existing repertoire of northern stereotypes. In the lugubrious strains of Morrissey's social realism, the gloomy intensity of New Order, and the cryptic misanthropy of The Fall, a distinctively imagined landscape portrays the character of Mancunian life, from its grey skies and wet pavements, to the self-effacing humour attributed to the city's laconic inhabitants. In refusing to conceal their flat, nasal accent and thus amplifying the sense of regional identity, their collective endeavours embody Shepherd and Wicke's contention that music's aural and linguistic elements evoke a symbolic structuring in awareness, enabling people to reproduce themselves materially.[21] Another important factor in Manchester's success in hosting alternative music scenes is its historical involvement in the textile industries, an important factor during the Madchester years, when local design companies created an identifiably northern fashion style. The strong visual identity of the scene was driven to a great extent in the 1980s and early 1990s by small and flexible Manchester companies based in Manchester capable of responding the nuances and trends established locally.

The political context of Madchester

If we look now at the political backdrop to Madchester, it was established against a scenario of deepening recession where Conservative politics were a dominant force in shaping and directing the fissure between the northern and southern regions. In a study of the impact of UK regional policy making, Harrison and Hart point out how the 1980s saw Britain becoming increasingly polarized in terms of both political allegiance and prosperity.[22] Changes in the global economy were particularly uneven during the 1980s when deindustrialization had a disastrous impact on jobs in UK manufacturing. However, the financial services sector grew considerably, leading to a widening of the traditional division of the north from the south.

After the public sector strikes which dominated the 1970s, Margaret Thatcher won the general election of 1979 promising to bring about a new economic order but the early 1980s were initially blighted by further economic recession. That slump was experienced keenly in Manchester, where the collapse of the old manufacturing industries and associated unemployment contrasted sharply with the surge of prosperity experienced in some parts of the south. Local unemployment statistics illustrate the gravity of the problem.

> In 1986, over 59% of adult males living in Hulme were unemployed; in Miles Platting the figure was 46%; Cheetham Hill and Moss Side both had an unemployment rate of 44%. The main group (both sexes) of unemployed were young people under the age of 21. Hulme's youth employment was recorded at 68%, and Cheetham Hill suffered 59%.[23]

In her recollections of the effects of unemployment in the 1980s, a former Deputy Leader of the City Council describes neighbours collecting money for the funeral of a local youth whose inability to find work led him to take his own life. Other memories include, 'canvassing one street in Gorton South on the Suttons Estate [where] every single man was out of work. A lot of those men never worked again and started the dreadful spiral of benefit dependency through one or more generation.'[24] While pockets of wealth undoubtedly existed in the more exclusive suburbs of Manchester, for unemployed Mancunians the grim realities of life without work contrasted sharply with the media image of the 'Yuppie' lifestyle. Furthermore, in an increasingly overheated micro-economy southerners had access to more jobs and higher levels of disposable income than their northern counterparts. Although the unemployed were advised by the employment secretary Norman Tebbit, to 'get on their bikes' in search of work, any efforts to relocate were thwarted by soaring house prices in the south. Not surprisingly, allegiance to Thatcherism was weak or non-existent in the northern cities and as Taylor points out, the prime minister further alienated potential northern voters by referring to those living in the region as 'moaning Minnies'.[25]

Madchester Style

Illustrating the capacity of creativity to thrive in challenging circumstances the music scene in Manchester flourished during the 1980s and, despite the economic difficulties, various artists were simultaneously working on the creative projects eventually subsumed under the Madchester umbrella. While there were differences in approach, the overall constitution of the music scene had little in common with New Romanticism and New Wave electronic pop which dominated the UK charts during the 1980s. These genres resonated more with the conservative ethos of materialism and individualism for, as Borthwick and Moy contend, unlike other more politically motivated examples of popular music:

> ... synthpop chose not to deal explicitly with the continuing social issues of high unemployment, the decline of traditional industries and a burgeoning revival in right-wing politics, and instead chose flamboyant, overt commercialism and escapism as its central tenets.[26]

Instead, the stylish, well-groomed, metrosexuality of pop groups like Duran Duran and Spandau Ballet and the cool and mannered electronic music of The Human League and Eurythmics articulated messages of detachment and emotional constraint. By contrast, the libidinous, drug-inflected dance rhythms and joyful directness of The Happy Mondays and Inspiral Carpets offered a refreshing antidote to the posturing artifice of 1980s synthpop and New Romanticism.

In a similar manner, Madchester fashions provided an alternative to the upwardly mobile Yuppie identity of the 1980s that was epitomized in the executive clothing of chain store 'Next'. Where 'Next' celebrated sophistication and the work ethic through its elevation of the suit and smart business wear, Manchester's independent design companies turned instead to the sphere of escapism and leisure, with the revival of flared jeans, trainers and baggy tops more redolent of the Woodstock era. The bright florescent colours of the local fashions also contrasted with the sober greys, browns and blacks favoured by young executives working in the southern-based financial sector. Long hair was also preferred by Mancunians, providing diametric opposition to the neatly coiffeured look favoured by the feminized 'New Man' identified by both Mort and Nixon in advertising and magazines of the 1980s.[27]

In many respects, the Manchester based clothing company Joe Bloggs conforms to the internal homology of the Madchester scene with its emphasis on hedonism as opposed to corporate values. Also the design ethos relates to the city's independent, entrepreneurial past. Therefore, rather than hailing the New Man or the company man, Joe Bloggs spoke to the average man in the street, inviting ordinary people to identify with an inexpensive clothing range of casual separates and accessories. Owner Shami Ahmed's approach was typical of the new generation of businesses run in Manchester by youthful entrepreneurs with an ability to keep one step ahead of high-street chain stores. A feature in the March 1990 edition of *The Face*, attributes the success of another clothing company, Funki Junki, to the ability of the 17 year old manager Jason Keller and his workforce of under-18s who regularly trawled clubs and raves in search of new ideas. The speed with which these small northern companies could respond to subtle changes in street and club fashions was fundamental to their success and Manchester's ability to lead as a fashion capital during the Madchester years. Where established southern-based fashion companies could only offer annual collections, the new Manchester designers turned out monthly collections based on the most up-to-date street style.

If we look next at some of the individual elements of the Madchester style there is a homology in the music and fashions where each aspect articulates the character of Mancunian culture during the period in question. For example, as with fashion, the oxymoronic name 'Happy Mondays' connotes the possibility of eliding the constraints of the corporate world. Where in 1979 London based punk band, The Boomtown Rats recording, 'I Don't Like Mondays' tapped into the consciousness of a reluctant but compliant workforce, unemployed Mancunians were at least liberated from the dreaded 'Monday morning feeling'.[28] The Inspiral Carpets may have taken their name from a local shop but the descriptor also conjures up escapism while alluding to the drug-induced mind expansion of the Manchester music scene. In choosing their name The Stone Roses, ensured that the harsh grittiness of northern masculinity was carefully protected from the soft feminising image generated by the flower of romance. The names of other groups create other reference

Happy Mondays, Manshester Ship Canal, 1987. An iconic image of the Happy Mondays captured by leading rock photographer Ian Tilton.

points to the mood and spirit of the scene. Northside express regional pride to outsiders and more esoterically, to those who know the city well, to their roots in the poorer, more abject, northern side of Manchester, where levels of unemployment and social deprivation are far higher than on the south side. Similarly, the group, The Charlatans, used a name that could be read as playing on the stereotypes of workshy, criminality associated with the working classes living in northern cities.

Madchester and the Media

It has been argued that Madchester was the first British music scene to happen without the permission of the music press.[29] What the eventual coverage does show is how well-worn tropes already embedded in the national psyche were mobilized by the media and sometimes the artists themselves to dramatize and overstate difference. According to Middles, until The Stone Roses and Happy Mondays appeared together in the weekly television programme *Top of the Pops* in 1989, the music press failed to recognize the importance of Madchester. Moreover, he reports how a representative of The Stone Roses had bemoaned the fact that 'no London papers will listen to us'.[30]

Soon the situation reversed and Madchester eventually dominated the prestigious front pages of the influential *NME*. However, having been blindsided, the media responded in ways which attempted to shore up the hegemony of southern-based music journalism. The name 'Madchester', was itself a descriptor used by journalists from outside the city with a nationwide readership in mind, providing an insight into the subsequent stereotyping process. As Kitzinger explains, because the press cannot cover all music scenes and genres, 'rhetorical shorthand', is used to make sense of any new development, offering easy reference points for readers.[31] By foregrounding insanity, the word connotes a combination of danger, lack of wisdom and disorder. However, while the 'Madchester' label was seized on by the media, Shaun Ryder of the Happy Mondays claimed the descriptor was never embraced by Mancunians as self-representative.

> It was our video directors, the Bailey Brothers, who came up with the term 'Madchester', but we said, 'Great, yeah, go with it', because Manchester was mad at the time. But no one used the term in Manchester, unless they were a prick.[32]

The media was also quick to emphasize any elements of 'roughness' and in doing so they strengthened long-established southern fears of the north as an uncivilized place. In the words of Miranda Sawyer, a Wilmslow-born journalist living in London:

> People in London . . . seemed scared of the place, talked about it as though it was really rough, like an English New York ghetto. When I told them that they would love the Haçienda, that it was brilliant, a fantastic club with amazing music and enough space for anyone and everyone to express themselves, they looked at me as though I were mad.[33]

In an era when relatively few Londoners appear to have ventured north, her report fuelled the dark fantasies which abounded. The Madchester label also implied a degree of homogeneity as though bands operated together representing the city. Dave Haslam, a DJ and veteran of the era, claims otherwise.

> People mistake the whole Manchester music history and the tradition that we have –the whole story, the whole mythology – for some kind of local pride . . . I interviewed Joy Division, The Smiths, Stone Roses, all those iconic bands and none of them wanted to be 'local' bands. They were all inspired by widely different things.[34]

His observations are endorsed by Shaun Ryder of The Happy Mondays who, in a contemporary interview, claims that the band, '... wanna keep moving. The world's too small. It doesn't end at Manchester' and 'I don't see us as part of a Manchester scene as such'.[35] Furthermore although lumped together, the groups referred to as Madchester bands came from quite disparate locations. For example, the founder members of The Happy Mondays were from Little Hulton, a village within the borough of Salford, almost ten miles away from the city centre. Inspiral Carpets, hailed from Oldham, a quite separate town, seven miles north of Manchester and The Charlatans were formed in Northwich, a town close to the heart of rural Cheshire. As southern-based reporters were often unaware of these subtle distinctions, they go unnoticed and, whilst the members of the groups were northerners, their origins and social affiliations were much more varied than the media led readers to believe.

Contriving class credentials

It is also interesting to note how the working-class credentials of the scene were regularly overstated to secure the traditional class distinctions of the north-south divide. Both John Squire and Ian Brown of Stone Roses went to Altrincham Grammar School for Boys, and lived as children in the quiet suburb of Timperley in Cheshire. Clint Boon of Inspiral Carpets was educated at the prestigious independent Roman Catholic day school St Bedes and the band's frontman Tom Hingley was the son of an Oxford don. However such middle-class qualities were carefully played down in the process of pigeonholing and instead, contemporaries were presented with a determinedly lowbrow and stereotypical portrayal of Mancunian masculinity. Needless to say, this conformed to readers expectations of 'typical' northern manhood and the media coverage embodies Nathan Wiseman-Trowse's argument that regardless of the true class position, because of the city's strong historical links with socialism and its fame as a manufacturing centre, 'The very notion of a band from Manchester suggests an urban working class position'.[36]

The self-representation of those involved in Madchester does little to counter these views. For instance, despite the fact that their work is being exhibited in a London gallery, in a contemporary *NME* article dedicated to the work of Central Station Design, the graphic artists responsible for the unique visual identity of local bands are portrayed as inarticulate, uneducated and workshy.[37] Keen to emphasize his plebeian lack of qualifications, designer Matt Carroll reportedly says, 'I only got an "E" for me art' and 'My art teacher was like all those old fellas come into the room to mark me work they weren't into it at all. They failed me and I didn't give a shit'. Speaking of his attitude to his studies, Carroll goes on to live up to the coarse, lazy, anti-establishment leanings of the textbook northerner:

> All we really learnt how to do there was drink. Going to the Tech was a way of avoiding the type of people we knew were waiting for people like us, 'cos once you're in that routine of a shitty nine to five, its more and more difficult to get out of it.[38]

The historical propensity for non-conformity is foregrounded within much media reportage where any signs of recklessness or hedonism are used to overshadow deeper discussion of creative effort. On occasion the artists themselves collude by paying homage to the stereotype of the rebellious northerner. A Stone Roses interview in national music magazine, *Sounds*, is quick to move from analysing reasons for the band's lack of popularity beyond Manchester, to recount the Roses' story about felonious past of fellow bandmates, The Happy Mondays:

> One story I heard was about the time that they bought a gun from a gunshop sale, took it back to school and sat on the school playing field all afternoon playing Russian Roulette with it. And when I was a scooter boy they used to kick my scooter over when I parked it outside ...[39]

The discourses of dialect

The speech of Mancunians is an important class marker and there are numerous examples of journalism capitalising on the differences in southern and regional ways of talking. An article in *The Face* begins innocuously enough by introducing The Happy Mondays as potentially world-leading artists. However, journalist Nick Kent soon moves on to a discussion of dancer Bez's drug-addled shenanigans – taking care to draw attention to the nuances of the band's northern accent. Readers are offered lead vocalist Shaun Ryder's inarticulate account of Bez's antics where he informs readers how: 'Last night his bed caught fire 'cause of smoking that [cannabis]. There were flames comin' up from 'is pillow. He didn't know 'owt about it tho'. He were too fookin' comatose'.[40]

In his laboured attempts to reproduce the northern pronunciation of the vowel 'u', and, since these efforts are unnecessary, we must assume that Kent has deliberately invoked what Wales refers to as 'one of the most culturally salient markers of a linguistic "North-South divide"'.[41] Whether or not this was a conscious decision, taken alongside the fact that the speech of southerners is not transcribed in a similar fashion within the publication, it diminishes the potential for more serious readings of the article. Furthermore, because the northern accent already has associations of inferiority, the artists are portrayed unfavourably in relation to their southern counterparts.

A related example of linguistic stratification, presents Kent's transcription into 'Mancunian' of Ryder's unintelligible response to a question about his drug use: 'Uh ... well ... uh ... illumination pal. Yeah! Illumination, definitely. Well illumination, like, half the time anyway. Cos t'other half we just like to get fookin' roarin' shit-faced, y'knowharramsayiin'?'.[42] This deliberately contrived translation raises issues of dominance and control: because the southern accent is over-represented throughout the media, regional accents are marginalized. To northerners, whose voices are so often depicted as comic, southern speech has come to represent authority and the political power of the south-east.[43] Possibly, this motivated local artists like Ryder to assert their northerness via provocative displays of florid Mancunian.

Rather than trying to conform to dominant linguistic codes as many northerners feel they must in order to gain social acceptance, their stance represents a spirited display of the local pride traditionally exhibited by northerners. By owning the negative stereotypes and metonyms, the local musicians take on the mantle of other artists and writers who have refused to abandon markers of regional identity.

Fashioning difference

Café Society. An advert for Affleck's Palace from City Life, October 1988.

Abigail Ward, Aidan Cartwrite and Manchester District Music Archive

The patronising media put downs are not confined to the sphere of music but spill out into discussions about the fashion sensibilities of Madchester; the coverage invokes a caricature of the style, with a limited set of signifiers comprising flared jeans, pudding basin haircuts, beanie hats and loose fitting tops defining the look of Manchester youth. Under the overall umbrella of 'baggy' these elements of style conform to what is depicted as a faintly ridiculous local fashion. In *The Face*, a report on a Stone Roses concert begins by informing readers that Manchester's Piccadilly Bus Station is filled with '13 year olds with wide bottomed jeans and Stone Roses T shirts'.[44] The description diminishes the significance of the occasion, by implying that Madchester music lovers are children rather than sophisticated adults. Meanwhile, evidence of a more grown-up fan following is ignored as are subtler manifestations of the local fashion styles. As Manchester-based brand consultant, Gary Aspden, explains:

MANCHESTER, Afflecks Palace,
Afflecks Arcade
CHESTER, 40 Bridge Street Row
LIVERPOOL, Bold St.

For me, there are two Madchesters. The first is the media cartoon version with students wearing Joe Bloggs and those long-sleeve Ts, listening to 'baggy' bands and shopping in Affleck's Palace.[45] I find this version simplistic and irritating. The real version was something far more switched on. The 10 years prior to acid house in Manchester had seen various fashions that had been huge among working-class northern youth but had never been picked up on by the mainstream media. And much of that style was reflected in what people were wearing in Manchester in 88/89.[46]

Fortunately, these subtle and not so subtle efforts to diminish the significance of regional style did not go uncontested and in the battle between the regions, the tradition of northern pride sometimes surfaces in media coverage. For instance, journalist Rob Sandall, discussing the entrepreneurial spirit of the city in 1990, describes printed T-shirts bearing the less than humble message: 'On The Sixth Day God Created Manchester'. In the same feature Manchester shop owner Leo Stanley makes a caustic observation regarding the reversal of the usual order of leadership in matters of style claiming that:

> Five or six year ago people here used to go down south to shop just so that could come back with a bag with the name of a big London store on it. Now I get Londoners coming up here to buy their flares and Manchester T-shirts.[47]

In conclusion, the sounds and images of the subculture and their nostalgic references to the psychedelia and associated drug culture of the 1960s, were symptomatic of an escapist solution to the economic and social problems affecting Manchester during the late 1980s and early 1990s. On the one hand the music drew unselfconsciously on the quirkiness of local culture and the city's strong history of both dance and rock music without regard to national tastes. If, as Umberto Eco claims, we 'speak through [our] clothes', Mancunians gave an equally forceful message of indifference to southern style and values.[48] It seems that once the music scene became visible to the national media, the efforts of artists and entrepreneurs in and around Manchester were met with a level of hostility surfacing in patronising, stereotypical media coverage. The media circus brings to mind Durkheim's delineation of modern society as complex and driven by, intricate divisions of labour and conflicting and competing social groups.[49] Increasingly this competition has been played out within the visual arena of personal style and the sonic dimension of popular music where sounds, clothing and accessories provides opportunities to escape from the pressures of everyday life. The Madchester scene, offering what Steve Redhead refers to as 'Hedonism in hard times', did not provide a political solution to those in search of an answer.[50] Instead through escapism, it offered a temporary respite from the suffering and, at the same time, the music and fashions helped to give Manchester a recognisable new identity which transcended the city's image as a social and cultural backwater. The numerous references to the irreverent behaviour of the artists and the contrived efforts to represent the local dialect illustrate the extent to which the music press was determined to secure the hegemony of the culture of London and the South East in a particularly troubled political period.

The Manchester Lesbian and Gay Chorus: Manchester, the Gay Village, and local music-making practices

Esperanza
Miyake

I moved to Manchester in the summer of 2003, just as I was beginning to undertake fieldwork for my PhD research. The underlying concern of my project had been to investigate the relationship between music and sexuality. My aim was to move away from the tendency in feminist understandings of music,[1] queer musicology,[2] popular music studies[3] and subcultural studies[4] to conceptualize music and sexuality mainly through two interrelated ways: a) gendered performances and/or gendered readings of music where there is a conflation between the terms 'gender' and 'sexuality'; b) the emphasis of *sex*-uality, where the relationship between music and sexuality involves an erotic or eroticized exchange. I wanted to explore music and sexuality in an *everyday* life context, particularly outside of an eroticized field.

Manchester was really the best place I could be: both a 'musical city' of the North rivalling Liverpool and also, the 'Queer Capital of the North,' complete with an area now known as the Gay Village. The most obvious place to start my exploration was Canal Street, the main artery running through the Village, pumping with activity as gay bars, clubs and pubs open both day and night. Initially, I conducted interviews with lesbian and gay DJs, alongside revellers out on Canal Street for the night. I wanted to understand what music meant for them in their lives. Apart from the practical problems I faced – interviewees thinking my project was a 'pick-up' strategy, high noise levels, drunkenness and so on – I also found it very hard to escape the eroticization of music (and of myself within this field) within this social context, which is precisely what I was trying to avoid: I wanted to explore the music-sexuality relationship beyond questions of gender and the erotic.

Rather serendipitously, I discovered and consequently joined the Manchester Lesbian and Gay Chorus (MLGC) in February 2004, initially as a leisure activity. What had attracted me was MLGC's homepage, which advertised the following: 'We meet to rehearse, socialize, to give concerts and to perform at events promoted by other LGBT community groups and affiliated organisations'. I immediately realized that the

MLGC could be a potential field for my PhD research. Because the choir is also regarded as a social space allowing for socializing and getting to know people through conversation, I had no problems in approaching people with my project. Whilst the question of sex might be one aspect of the MLGC's social interactions, the prime reason for the members' presence was to make music with other members of the lesbian, gay, bisexual, and transsexual (LGBT) community. Even the physical setting of rehearsals and performances ensure that music is what brings people together, not sex. Whilst the bar is open during rehearsals, it is used for refreshment rather than socialisation purposes and in fact, members are discouraged from talking during rehearsals. Despite being part of the Village as a designated LGBT area, the MLGC is positioned away from the main ground of eroticized queer spaces: thus an ideal location for my research.

In becoming part of the MLGC's organized choral sound, I also became an ethnographic chorister, conducting participant observation (or singing) within the auditory and ethnographic field. Here, participant observer and chorister are one through the voice, where both positions are dependent on being part of the existing organized choral framework. I also conducted qualitative interviews with 14 members (9 women, 5 men) between the ages of 25–65, along with the musical director (MD). The ethnographic material gathered for the project presented different social contexts in which we might understand the relationship between music and sexuality: from group discussions on music, individual reflections on their relationship to music and the choir itself, different kinds of musical events they choose to participate in, incidents that arise during rehearsals or performances. By analyzing their everyday life musical activities both as a group and as individual members, I drew out what kind of factors – which might include issues surrounding gender and the erotic but also move beyond these concerns – bring the concepts of music and sexuality together.

I will initially provide a brief background of the MLGC as a way of contextualizing the ensuing discussion on the relationship between the MLGC, the Village, and Manchester. By drawing on fieldwork material gathered between 2003 and 2005 with the chorus, I will: then firstly, examine the relationship between the local music scene in Manchester and the emergence of a more open gay subculture in the Village between late 1980s throughout the 1990s; and, secondly, explore Manchester's own urban transformation starting in the early 1990s, and how this consequently opened up new socio-cultural and political opportunities for the local LGBT community. Here, I want to focus on how localized lesbian and gay music-making practices define and/or or challenge the changing position of queers living in the city in the twenty-first century within this context. Overall, this article thus addresses issues relating to local music-making and LGBT subculture in order to understand one aspect of the music-sexuality relationship beyond questions of gender and the erotic.

Introducing the participants: Manchester Lesbian and Gay Chorus

In early 2000, a very small group of Manchester-based singers from the LGBT community met informally at the St Peter's Chaplaincy building in the University of Manchester. At this point, there was no formalized structure in place and meetings were irregular. However, according to founding member, Chongwei, by early 2001, the group decided to become a constituted organisation with a mission 'to provide a safe environment for the LGBT community to participate in music'. Membership was open to anyone who identified with this mission statement, and after a series of discussions, the name 'Manchester Lesbian & Gay Chorus' was formally adopted. In the summer of 2001, the MLGC attended and performed a small repertoire at the first ever Sing Out event in Norwich at the University of East Anglia. Sing Out is an association of LGBT choirs from across the UK. The fact that such an association emerged in the early 2000s demonstrates the growing *cultural* – as opposed to the political – visibility of the LGBT community in the UK, perhaps as a result of queer activism and its politics of visibility starting in the 1990s.[5] I shall discuss these ideas in further depth later, but this event and association needs highlighting here as it marked a turning point for the MLGC. Having attended this event, the MLGC realized there was no LGBT voice that represented the city of Manchester within this queer musical network.

Chongwei felt that 'divisions arose within the group at this point', where some members were unwilling to prepare for or take part in the event: some argued that those unwilling to prepare or participate were uncommitted, both as musicians and as members of the LGBT making 'a stand'; others argued that due to external pressures and/or not having come out and wanting to retain anonymity, they should not feel pressured to participate in activities beyond casual and private rehearsals.[6] The eight members who *did* attend (seven women and one man) decided to carry on and successfully re-launched the Chorus in September 2001, securing a room free of charge at the Hollywood Showbar in the Village and hiring a professional MD. About 30 new members joined in the autumn in response to a publicity campaign involving flyers, a BBC Radio Manchester interview and other promotional activities in the Village. However, just as the group's repertoire and membership were growing, the MD left with disastrous consequences: membership dwindled and by May 2002, the second version of the Chorus collapsed.

Fortunately, prior to the collapse, the group had submitted a successful bid for funding from Awards for All, a National Lottery funding scheme.

The Manchester
Lesbian and
Gay Chorus in
performance.

Esperanza Miyake

With this financial backing, Chongwei re-launched Chorus once again, with a new MD, and a free room at the Taurus Bar, also in the Gay Village. Between September 2002 and July 2003, the Chorus developed a full performance repertoire with a steady membership of 20 singers. Using his network of contacts, Chongwei (by then the Chorus's chair) secured two important performances as part of the Europride 2003 celebrations in Manchester: a performance at the Manchester Museum and a more pivotal performance, singing with the London Gay Men's Chorus (LGMC) in their in *Tying the Knot* show at the Library Theatre.[7] Inspired by these events, in September 2003, three 'New Members' Evenings' were held in the Taurus Bar which led to 45 new members joining the Chorus. The sudden growth in numbers created a logistical problem as the room in Taurus was quite small, and so after negotiations, the Chorus moved to a bigger venue: upstairs in Manto, a bar-club in the Village.[8] By then, the Chorus had a new MD, with around 110 members. It was at this point, that I joined. During my time with the choir, it moved yet again to Hollywood Showbar – still within the Gay Village – to accommodate for the further expansion in group size. The Chorus is now an expected part of Manchester Pride celebrations – extending into Europride in Trafalgar Square, London – and has moved on to win third and second place at the International World Outgames Chorus Competition in 2006 (Montreal) and 2009 (Copenhagen) respectively. The MLGC now organizes its own independent events and performances, and has sung at local, national and international events. These include a joint concert in Berlin with a German choir at which it recorded its first CD in 2008; a West End stage debut at Trafalgar Studios the same year, and a performance as guests at the Paris Pride in June 2010. 2011 marked the MLGC's 10th Anniversary, and in the words of the MLGC website, 'instead of going abroad, we chose to celebrate this landmark by bringing our music back home to Manchester'. The MLGC thus concentrated on local performances, some of which include: the LGBT Families annual picnic; the Co-operative Family Fun Day in Morecambe; a concert entitled, 'Beyond the Rainbow' in the Royal Northern College of Music; and finally, the MLGC took part in the Royal Exchange Theatre's new production of *Beautiful Thing*.

This brief history of the MLGC demonstrates that its success depended not just on the existence of LGBT members wanting to sing together, but also on the existing buildings, musical and LGBT social networks and cultural practices of Manchester (as shall become apparent in the course of my discussion), and the Gay Village as both a geographical and social space to accommodate their activities in; as their mission statement states, a 'safe environment for the LGBT community to participate in music'. The fact that the MLGC began only to thrive after its move from being outside of the Village to being *inside* it, became stable enough to perform *outside* it (not only the rest of Manchester, but also outside the region and the country), to then come back *inside* the Village as a celebrated part of it, suggests the development of the MLGC as a musical and LGBT group seems to run concurrently with Manchester and the Village's own socio-cultural development. Therefore, I want to now focus more closely on the relationship between the Village and Manchester, particularly as they relate to local music and music-making practices.

'Gaychester': the gay subcultural scene

One of the concerns of queer historian George Chauncey is to challenge popular conceptions of the lesbian and gay community as only 'coming out' post-Stonewall, a pivotal and visible incident in LGBT politics and activism which occurred in New York in 1969, when the LGBT community engaged in a series of demonstrations and riots against police raids against it.[9] Following Chauncey's argument, it is important to note that there was a thriving LGBT community before the formal demarcation of the 'Gay Village' in Manchester in the mid-1990s. For example, the pubs on Canal Street once catered to the dock-workers and sailors who were working or stopping by at the canal during the Industrial Revolution in the late nineteenth-century. The still existing New Union Pub hosted a lesbian three-piece band and was frequented by men in drag during that time. Throughout the pre-Stonewall twentieth-century, the area continued to host a hidden LGBT subculture, albeit subject to many a police raids, particularly between the 1950s and 1960s.[10] Such snippets of history reveal the close relationship between the process of industrialization and urbanization, and the emergence of a hidden homosexual subculture.

But as mentioned earlier, Manchester today paints a very different picture. Most visiting the city will find that Canal Street is now a very open and public area – particularly famous for its nightlife – where

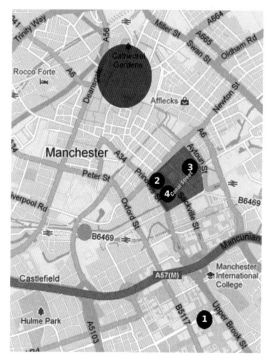

Key

The orignal site of the Hacienda, now converted into luxury flats: 'Hacienda Apartments'.

1996: I.R.A Bomb hits Corporation Street. Consequently, an Urban Regeneration Scheme is set up for the renovation of Manchester's City Centre.

1990 - present: The Gay Village

MLGC Trail

1 2000: St Peter's Chaplaincy, University of Manchester. A small group of LGBT singers get together informally. First public performance at the World AIDS Day Vigil around the Beacon of Hope in Sackville Gardens, an annual event the Chorus has supported since.

2 2001: Chorus draws up a Constitution and mission statement, formally christening itself as: 'Manchester Lesbian and Gay Chorus'. Re-launch in September and move to Hollywood Showbar, with a professional Musical Director and approximately 30 new members.

3 2002: In May, the Musical Director suddenly left, almost ending the Chorus. However, with a successful National Lottery funding bid and another new Musical Director, the Chorus re-launches again and moves to Taurus Bar.
2003: The Chorus prospers and performs at two pivotal events: Europride; and Manchester Museum with London Gay Men's Chorus. Inspired, they began 'New Members Evenings' attracting more members from the LGBT community.

4 2003: As a result of all the promotion earlier on in the year, the Chorus suddenly outgrew Taurus Bar. In September, the Chorus re-located to a bigger venue upstairs Manto Bar. I joined the Chorus at this point as part of my fieldwork research.
2005: The Chorus continues to perform annually at Manchester Pride on mainstage and the closing A.I.D.S. Vigil ceremonies; Green Room; Royal Northern College of Music; and private civil partnerships/birthday events.

2 2006: The Chorus are now successful and stable, growing continuously in numbers. This prompted a re-location back to Hollywood Showbar. The Chorus also participated in their first international event, a LGBT chorus competition at Montreal's World Out!Games, winning 3rd Place.
2007: As an award-winning Chorus, the MLGC started to perform bigger venues, including organising their own show at the Royal Northern College of Music.
2008: The Chorus go to Berlin to participate in a joint concert with German choir, Cantare. The Chorus also record their first CD, 'Beautiful Rain', and give an eponymous concert at the RNCM. The MLGC make their West End stage debut at Trafalgar Studios as part of the Eloquent Protest project for Remembrance Sunday.
2009: In May, the Chorus go to London for 'Various Voices', an European LGBT choirs festival. In the summer, the MLGC go to Copenhagen for the second World Out!Games, coming 2nd place this time, and appearing on Danish radio. The Chorus then participate in Paris Pride.
2011: The Chorus celebrate their 10 year Anniversary by 'staying home'; performing a joint event with the London Gay Men's Chorus in London; in September the Chorus give their most ambitious concert to date in the RNCM's large concert theatre; they perform at the Royal Exchange Theatre's new production of 'Beautiful Thing'.

it is not uncommon to find drag queens and LGBT couples, groups of domestic tourists, and even heterosexual crowds celebrating their stag- and hen-nights in gay bars. Somehow, there was a transition between Canal Street being a geographical closet hiding a homosexual subculture, and its extension into what is now the 'Gay Village' as a whole sector of the city.[11] I want to argue in the following that local music and music-making activities played a crucial role in bringing this localized hidden culture 'out' and further into the public.

Factory Records was a Manchester-based independent record label started in 1978 by Tony Wilson, a presenter for Granada Television, and Alan Erasmus, an unemployed actor and band manager. Together they managed The Durutti Column, Cabaret Voltaire, and most famously Joy Division (later New Order), Happy Mondays, and A Certain Ratio: bands which created a certain 'Manchester sound', part of a new local rave scene. In 1981, Wilson and New Order decided to fund and found a nightclub and took a lease on an abandoned yacht showroom (which became part of the club's overall distinct post-industrial décor) and named it the Hacienda. During the late 1980s, local bands – like Joy Division, The Fall, Happy Mondays, and Stone Roses – mixed Manchester's post-industrial miserablism (The Smiths being a notable example), the existing dance culture surrounding Northern Soul, and the new Ecstasy culture connected to the House scene from the US and Amsterdam, to create the movement known as 'Madchester'.

MLGC trail
Trail produced by the Manchester Lesbian and Gay Chorus in 2011.

Manchester Lesbian and Gay Chorus

Local musician and writer CP Lee states, 'Manchester's music scene was content to proceed along on its own way until, in 1988, something happened to it that had never happened before it caught the attention of the world's media'. Local music-making activities escalated into what is now commonly referred to as 'Summer of Love' in 1988, a defining moment for Manchester where the city was detected by the national and international cultural radar.[12] However, despite thisr international and commercial recognition, by the mid-1990s, the Hacienda lost money due to problems arising from drugs and gun-related crime.[13] Manchester was even dubbed by sections of the media as 'Gunchester'. In an attempt to revive the Hacienda's financial loss, the organizers opened a gay night called, *Flesh* in 1991 and thus a new era, 'Gaychester', began. If the initial 'Summer of Love' in Manchester meant a musical 'something happened to Manchester', then *Flesh* had a bearing on a similar 'something' for the LGBT community.[14]

Flesh created a new gay consciousness in Manchester, a mode of being 'out' which was defined specifically through music and the body's relationship to it, where embodying dance music was to embody an out queer identity. There is a body of work which addresses the close relationship between male gay subculture and dance/disco scene, interlinking the idea of gay pleasure, homosexual identity, and dance music as a strong gay subculture.[15] Queer sociologist Jeffrey Weeks, for example, discusses how in the UK, the arrival of mega-discos during the mid-1970s in effect created a gay subculture in Britain. Weeks argues that these mega-discos symbolized a 'new hedonism, where sexual pleasure was placed at the heart of the new gay identity', and consequently, the gay community experienced an 'increasingly overt sexualization of the gay male subculture'.[16] In Manchester, *Flesh* was indeed a catalyst for shaping a localized, new, and more open gay identity tied to dance, clubbing and the subcultural music scene. For example, in an image posted on a website now unfortunately unavailable, the phrase 'queer as fuck' is literally inscribed on a dancer's body, where the homosexual body and visibility are inseparable from club music and its subcultural scene. *Flesh* thus opened up the means for queers (particularly gay men) to be 'out' within a public space, albeit within a confined area. The very words, 'Queer as Fuck' reveal the manner in which indeed, 'for queers *eroticism is the basis of community*' (emphasis in original).[17] To consume music was to thus consume gay subculture defined by erotic sociality.

In studying the 'Liverpool Sound', Sarah Cohen argues that 'locality can be seen as a political strategy within a global, plural system ... within this strategy, music exercises territorializing power, framing public and private spaces and domains'.[18] Within this context, *Flesh* as a local music scene opened up a new spatial possibility for gay men, vital to the eventual demarcation of the Gay Village as a separate area in the city, a geographical closet. Furthermore, the localization of a gay subculture through music

was politically significant during the AIDS crisis.[19]
For example, the Village formed an important point
of contact for those involved in its activism: at every
AIDS Vigil, this point is made clear by those who
were there at the height of the crisis, or through
second-hand accounts. In this manner, existing urban
and local music-making practices played an important
part in the production and consumption of Gaychester
as a localized gay subculture, signalling a moment when Manchester's
LGBT community became more 'culturally intelligible' and also marked
the start of the Village area's transformation.[20]

'Gaychester, 1994', part of the art work on the Hacienda apartments, built after the club was demolished in 2002.

Esperanza Miyake

MLGC member, Charlotte, remembers this process as being closely
linked with the opening of Manto.

> Probably early 1990s, which was sort of the start of the Village. It was
> kind of Manto's really, it started the Village, the Gay Village. The move
> from pubs where you couldn't see through the windows and all the bars
> were empty, and you know it was a lesbian and gay bar. But I think we all
> fantasize about the Village and I never was sure whether it ever was that
> cosy. I never go there, I eat out in Chorlton [...] Well I guess they want to
> make money out of it. But I suppose it's better than (pause) like when I first
> moved to Manchester there were lots of isolated bars you know, and I think
> it's probably better than that. You don't get beaten up, you know.

The club's own website, unsurprisingly takes a similar view:

> Manto originally opened in 1990 when the Gay Village wasn't really a
> village, 'AIDS' was how many people saw us, and what passed for a gay
> bar was firmly rooted in the 1970s. In its 10 year history, Manto became
> synonymous with changing attitudes, throwing parties, just for the hell of
> it, like the Gay Village has never seen: big wheels and circuses, legendary
> all-nighters, cutting-edge music and design, beautiful people, warehouse
> parties, a record label and Top 20 singles.

Manto is the first bar to have opened on Canal Street with clear windows
and to bring homosexual bar life out onto the streets for the eye to see:
as Charlotte states, this was the 'start of the Village, the Gay Village'. The
city planners regarded 'Gaychcester's' subcultural capital as translating
into economic capital.[21] Further reinforcing the start of the Village's
transformation, in 1991, the city-planners formally named the area
around Canal Street as the 'The Gay Village' – its name borrowed from
New York's Greenwich Village – as a separate planning area. In both
Charlotte's account and Manto's self-description, life before Manto and
the start of the Village are presented under a rather negative light and the
mega-disco culture explored earlier is referred to as being *passé*. Between
the city's and the Village's own efforts to encourage and maintain the
gay subcultural scene – the active conversion of subcultural capital
into economic capital – the entire Village went through a process of

commercialization, altering both the physical and social landscape of the Village. For example, policing increased around Canal Street, bars began to use clear windows so people could see both from inside and outside of the venue, and the opening of more gay bars meant that over all, there was an increase of gay migration into Manchester.[22]

As Dereka Rushbrook argues in her work exploring queer tourism, 'while CD collections, restaurant choices, and clothing may mark our cosmopolitan consumption of other races and cultures, the consumption of gayness is much more difficult to demonstrate without marking gayness ... the artefacts of queerness depends on interaction [...] where the deliberate consumption of queerness almost necessarily takes place *in* place'.[23] The commodification of the Village is probably most evident during events like Pride. Whilst fund-raising and awareness-raising based on entertainment – having fun whilst causing disruption and noise – have been long-established queer street tactics, Pride events are often lucrative business occasions for Village bars/clubs. Bar owners raise their drinks prices and even charge an entrance fee, while Pride ticket prices are raised each year: Pride has become a predominately a white, middle-class, gay male affair and is criticized for its exclusivity by those who are marginalized from 'this globalized McPink economy, those who are trapped in poverty, unable to buy into the global gay lifestyle'.[24]

Running parallel to the commercialization of the Village was the 'queerification' of Manchester, the increasing presence of gay references, images and activities within mainstream culture and spaces. This process was exemplified by festival events like *QueerUpNorth*[25] which occur openly and around the city to celebrate LGBT culture, or Granada TV's soap-opera *Coronation Street* which broadcast the programme's first (in) famous 'gay kiss' in 2003: such events demonstrate how localized LGBT culture has 'queered' not just the local but also national mainstream culture. In addition, whilst not Manchester-made (as opposed to *Coronation Street*), Channel 4's series *Queer as Folk* in 1999 which used Canal Street as its backdrop probably epitomizes the extent to which Manchester has become queerified. In almost every scene with Canal Street in the background, the sound of techno and pop dominate the series and subtitles even state, 'Booming Techno Music'. The previously stigmatized gay club- and sub- culture suddenly became a 'cool' and even 'quirky' part of mainstream culture. Musically and culturally, what was once a local gay subculture is now very much a part of Manchester and a dominant culture.

However, Charlotte's account reveals there is also a deliberate consumption of queerness *outside* of the Village. Charlotte even thinks 'we all fantasize about the Village', and as an advertisement, Manto's self-description is perhaps an example of such an idealized version of the Village, presented as a haven for queers: 'big wheels and circuses, legendary all-nighters, cutting-edge music and design, beautiful people, warehouse parties'. The contrast and difference between the two accounts suggest that indeed there is a tension between the fantasy or imaginary Village as it is presented and the local queers.[26] There is even a website called 'The*Real*Manchester.com' (many of the *MLGC* members use this site) where people's pictures, profiles, announcements, and blogs from the Village are posted, again, as if there is another more authentic version of Village life.

Both Charlotte's remarks and the existence of TheRealManchester. com website suggest how the transformation of the Canal Street area into The Gay Village has had an effect on the local queer community. There is now an alternative queer social life (for example, Chorlton) to what was once the alternative place in Manchester for queers, like *Flesh*. In this light, we must interrogate terms like 'alternative' or 'subcultural' in relation to queers: does coming out in the Village mean the same thing it did back during the *Flesh* days? How are queers defining themselves within this context, and furthermore, how is music configured within this process?

Coming out in 2000s: entertaining the gay scene, and singing for the queer community

On Saturday 15 June 1996, a 1500kg IRA bomb exploded in Manchester's city centre, injuring more than 200 people and requiring the reconstruction of 50,000 square metres of retail space and 25,000 square metres of office space. After the event, central government set aside £1million of European Union finance, and a further £20 million from the European Union regional aid budget (from 1997 to 1999) for the redevelopment of the damaged sector. The Village as an area was included in the city-developer's Regeneration Scheme and similarly, the local queer community was incorporated as part of Manchester's overall active cultural drive to present itself as a cultural capital: tourist maps, events listings, guidebooks, or the BBC local news page listed the Village and local queer activities in its own separate category as one of the city's several cultural 'experiences'.[27]

Since the IRA bomb, there has been steady increase of consumerist culture and commerce in the Village with businesses like *CloneZone* and the Village Business Association network being set up in the area.[28] In addition, there have also been significant changes to gay civil rights in the UK since the initial transformation of the Village: most notably the repeal of Section 28, the introduction of Employment Equality Regulations both in 2003 and the Sexual Offence Act, Gender Recognition Act, and the legalization of civil partnership for same sex couples, all in 2004. Such commercial and social changes mean there is a shift in the positionality of queers within the city, and the manner in which the local LGBT community demarcates its cultural and spatial identity.

Much work has been conducted concerning the effects of globalisation and the emergence of a more homogenous queer identity since the 1990s, where discussions cover issues surrounding commercialism, visibility, the pink economy, and mobility.[29] Whilst this body of work provides an in depth understanding of the movement from local to global, very little attention has been given to the effects of the global on the local. Queer scholar Jasbir Puar focuses on the relationship between the construction of homosexual identities and tourism, within which are configured ideas on marketing, advertising, and 'how in the face of the nation's marketing as a gay-friendly destination, local homo/sexual cultures are affected by queer tourism; how (global) tourism affects (local) sexualities; and how (local) sexualities are perceived by (global) tourism'.[30] In the context of this study, the question I wish to pose now is: how are such transformations affecting local gay and lesbian music-making practices? How is music configured and configuring the 'local homo/sexual culture'?

> I've been in Manchester twenty years so you know, I've got a good group of friends but when I came out, there were a lot of things that weren't commercial. ... then there was a time where there didn't seem to be much that wasn't part of the commercial scene and I think if I'd been coming out at that point, or moved to Manchester, that would have been really hard. And then the choir's there [...] Cause I mean as well as being fantastic singing and all that, I just think there's *another part of it which is about the community and that it's quite hard getting to know people on the scene, if you're going on the commercial 'scene'* (Eleanor, a MLGC member. Italics mine).

Eleanor's juxtaposition between her coming out amongst friends whom 'I had something in common with', like the Young Lesbian Single Mothers' Group (YLSMG), and her belief that it 'would have been really hard' to come out in the commercial scene demonstrates the marked separation between community – to mean a body of people whom you have 'something in common with' (Eleanor) – and the commercial scene which is regarded as devoid of a sense of shared meaning. Many of my interviewees set up such an oppositional and comparative relationship between themselves (and the choir) as an alternative and community-based place, and in contrast, what they perceive as being the rest of the Village's bar/club-based commercialism, or 'going on the commercial "scene"' as Eleanor articulated it. Tinny, another choir member, and other interviewees told me how they were 'purposefully looking for stuff that was going on in Manchester because I wanted to find something to do that didn't involve going clubbing or pubs'. As I experienced myself at the start of my fieldwork with the MLGC, the choir is thus regarded as a place which is specifically non-scene – not specifically eroticized – a place where people 'feel more part of the community' (David). A social space where they are there 'to meet other people as well within the lesbian and gay community' (Kristen) and here, 'community' is always referred to it in terms of forming 'real friendships' and meeting people 'without sex in mind' (Jed). The divide between community-as-commonality and scene-as-commodity is geographically manifest too. Charlotte, for example, states how she 'never goes there (Village), I eat out in Chorlton' where she feels that she is part of the community more. How then does the choir *musically* experience this divide?

> David: I suppose when we were wearing the T-shirts, that identifies us as the choir but the policeman said some nice things about us ... he said that our voices were representing the community and we were singing out, and we were being heard and all that ... I mean it was a bit corny but it was a nice thing to say I thought.

> Author: So why did you like that one particularly?

> David: It just seems like ... because we were doing something that was connected to the lesbian and gay community ...

> Author: Did you feel like that during Pride?

> David: I did at the Vigil, I didn't feel that on the main stage ... I thought that was more 'entertainment' (laughs) people had come to just watch drunkenly and didn't really care about what we were singing and so I didn't enjoy that as much. But the Vigil definitely felt more ...

David is referring to an event which was organized by the Manchester City Council and it was to raise awareness about homophobia. The Manchester Metropolitan Police were present as part of awareness raising and as a campaign for increasing safety for queers out on the streets. What David liked about this event which he relates to the Vigil was how it was something about the 'lesbian and gay community' and most importantly, feeling though as though the choir was 'representing the community'. The events which members list as being meaningful are usually those concerned directly with political and civil issues surrounding queer lives: AIDS Vigil, memorial service, private performances for a charity and home set up for those who are HIV positive, called *BodyPositive*, civil partnership and christening ceremonies. In contrast, the events where the members felt they had not gained as much satisfaction from performing were those which they considered as being for entertainment. These are events like Pride mainstage or concerts unrelated to the queer community – such a request from an anti-nuclear weapons group, which the MLGC declined on the grounds that it would not benefit the local LGBT community – where members feel 'out of place and dunno, a bit weird' (Tinny) or because people 'didn't really care about what we were singing' (David). Therefore, running concurrently with the community-as-commonality and scene-as-commodity is the divide between music-as-meaningful (often to mean political) and music-as-entertainment.

I want to now expand upon these two strands in greater depth before I discuss the significance behind the choir's attempts to bring them together. Broadly speaking, most of the choir's performances fall into two kinds of occasions: events where singing is for the sake of entertainment and serious events where the choir takes on a more supportive role, with singing a contemplative background to more prominent activities of the event. I want to examine these two kinds of occasions because they correspond directly to the two main aspects of contemporary queer culture as discussed so far: 'going on the commercial scene' (Eleanor); and the 'grass-roots politics of queers' (Charlotte).

(i) Music for the community: Soundtrack to the politics of Manchester

> Without question, Manchester Lesbian and Gay Chorus is about fun, community and inclusiveness. We may compete again in the future, but the joy of singing with such a great community and supporting local, charity and LGBT events is far, far more important to us than competition. (Jed, interview with BBC Manchester, Aug 2006)

> I think that the overall sound is fucking great, and the community feel is great, and it does feel like a real community thing and I never actually felt that doing a lesbian and gay thing before ... it's like ... cause it doesn't feel competitive, and everyone's just got ... everyone's got the right to be there, and I think that's really cool. (Tinny, interviewed by the author)

Jed is discussing the choir's participation in an international competition for queer choirs which took place in Montreal as part of the Outgames in 2006. Jed emphasizes the local 'community and inclusiveness', in contrast to the more globalized and international LGBT community denoted by the choir's participation in Montreal (registration for the event was over £100). Similarly, Tinny enthuses about the 'community feel' of the choir in contrast to other more competitive spaces outside. Within the context of these two discussions, both seem to prefer the choir directing its musical energies towards generating a 'community feeling' rather than towards gaining fame or engaging in competition within a wider LGBT community. What *is* the sound of the community, and how why do the choir wish to produce this sound?

One of the main, local LGBT charity events the MLGC supports year after year is the Manchester AIDS Vigils in Sackville Park. The Vigil represents a moment where Manchester, queer politics, and music come together: as Charlotte states, the choir provides 'the soundtrack to queer politics in Manchester'. During each Vigil, the choir always sings next to the Beacon of Hope and the statue of Alan Turing. Singing beside these two landmarks is significant and symbolic as they stand as a mark of queer solidarity, in relation to both AIDS and the stigmatisation of homosexuality: the Beacon is a pillar-shaped sculpture by Warren Chapman and Jess Boyn-Daniel (erected in 2000) and the UK's only permanent memorial dedicated to all those lost and still fighting against AIDS; and Alan Turing was an English mathematician and 'father of computer science' who committed suicide in 1954, unable to cope with the persecution of his homosexuality. These two monuments make the park an area of reflection in contrast to and removed from the main area of the Village (Canal Street) with its noisy bars. In other words, the event is always spatially and culturally separated from the more commercial and club cultural aspect of the Village and the queer community. The Vigil for Pride 2005 was covered by Manchester BBC and Manchester Radio and broadcast across the nation so in this sense it was a high-profile event. The prominent British soul singer and active campaigner against AIDS and homophobic lyrics in urban music, Beverley Knight, performed on the night and in contrast to her as an established and, in the words of organizer, Michelle, a 'famous face', the choir as a large group of anonymous faces were to represent the local LGBT community. During Pride Vigil 2006, this metaphor was actively enacted where the organizers wanted that year's theme to have a 'focus on community' and thus placed the choir as the main performing act to emphasize this point.

The choir performed 'Step by step', a song by Pete Seeger who put music to words from a nineteenth century American mining union rulebook. The song has a militant feel because of its lyrics ('step by step the longest march, can be won, can be won ... and by Union what we will, can be accomplished still ...') and marching tempo: all aimed to reflect the idea of the community acting together to fight against AIDS, or as organizer Michelle stated, to be 'angry at the horrible bug'. The choice and singing of 'Step by step' was significant. A choir member named Martin made the effort to research the origins of the song and, upon discovering them, posted this information to everyone. Some members even commented upon Manchester's LGBT community's strong links with the National Union of Mineworkers' ever since their support for one another during the Miner's Strike (1984–5) in Manchester. In this light, singing 'Step by step' was not only meaningful to the members of the MLGC as it connected them to local LGBT history, but sung in juxtaposition to Beverley Knight's 'A change is gonna come' became emblematic of local community activism more generally.[31] Hence such occasions mark a moment when the choir's music practices are localized through music of local reference, and in turn, how the choir's music-making practices become part of the local community and its socio-political practices.

(ii) Music for entertainment: 'people had come to just watch drunkenly'
If making music is more meaningful when it is, in David's words, 'something that was connected to the lesbian and gay community', the question is, why then does the choir keep agreeing to perform at events like Pride mainstage every year, where they are presented as

'entertainment', part of a more commercialized enterprise? One answer is that in being part of mainstage events, the choir gets 'free' publicity. Europride 2003 did bring a fresh batch of members which boosted the numbers in the choir from less than ten members to thirty: the founding members, like Eleanor, Charlotte, and Chongwei all use the term 'turning point' in reference to what Europride achieved for the choir by way of publicity. By 2005, the MLGC's reputation had grown and suddenly the choir were an awaited 'quirky' (Kristen) addition to the rest of the sexy clubby acts. Even David who had hated the Pride mainstage events until that point, when I asked him again, stated he really enjoyed mainstage that year and was 'on a high'.

Much discussion always goes into what should be incorporated into the repertoire but one of issue that the committee, the MD, and the members all agreed upon was that the repertoire should 'suit each occasion'.[32] The choir committee carefully chose 'Downtown' and 'I'm beginning to see the light' – both popular 'gay anthems' – because they suspected these songs would be a 'sure hit' (Jed and Geoff) with the Pride crowd: and they were right, in the words of the MD, 'the audience didn't know whether to watch or to sing along with us, it was great' (Jeff).[33] Since then, the committee have strategically chosen songs they believe would be 'sure hits' for entertaining a queer crowd: 'It would be good to sing songs that everybody, including the audience knew, to maintain our popularity'.[34] Such a statement reveals the choir's willingness to popularize itself, and *popular* in this case is defined by the committee as something familiar enough for audiences to sing along to. Why is this important?

> Author: You know there's all this talk about changing the repertoire. Would you change anything? I mean for example, did you put in requests?
>
> Kristen: Yeah I did, the song that was in the Coke ad (laughs)? We've sung it once or twice in the choir but I'd quite like to go back to it. I like songs that you know, they're popular, and that they've got quite a good beat and feel to them really.

Kristen is referring to the song, 'I wish I knew how it would feel to be free' written by jazz pianist Billy Taylor, and recorded originally by Nina Simone. Since then, it has been covered by Solomon Burke, Ray Charles, remixed, sampled, and has been used in countless of films. As a song it is, as Kristen states, 'popular': her reference to 'the Coke ad' being an indication of its ubiquity. Interestingly enough, this song was mentioned by other interviewees like Denise or Jude who arrived to it through Nina Simone, but whatever route they came to the song, the underlying feeling is that they feel positive when they listen or sing the song: 'good beat and feel' (Kristen), 'it's so inspiring!' (Denise). Thus there is another reason why singing songs for entertainment is significant for queers today: the pleasure of popularity. Kristen states, 'they're popular, and that they've got quite a good beat and feel to them'. Such a statement suggests how there is pleasure in singing these songs and what's more, in singing them for the sake of singing them with the audience.

In discussing the idea of value judgements made in popular music, popular music theorist Simon Frith argues that judging music – whether it is 'good' or 'bad' – moves beyond the issue of taste, and is about how 'we establish our place in various music worlds and use music as a source of identity'.[35] Therefore in choosing 'Downtown', for example, the MLGC was being judged ('they were judging us' Tinny states referring to Pride 2005) not just musically but as queers: it is about seeking queer social validation and acceptance through an articulation of knowledge of queer culture, and in the process creating a sense of togetherness. For as Jeff's statement regarding 'Downtown' implies, familiar songs can diminish the clear divide between audience and performer and singing together creates a sense of shared togetherness ('everybody, including the audience'): 'I felt *closer to the community* that way' (emphasis mine) states David, in reference to how the audience sang along with the choir for 'Downtown'. In this sense, *popular* to mean familiar ('songs that everyone, including the audience knew, to maintain our popularity') is an important social process by which queers feel a sense of belonging despite the apparent homogeneity and commercialism of events like Pride.

Local brands of queer choirs: You'll never walk alone

The MLGC took part in a national festival in Leeds College of Music called 'Out Tonight!' as part of the *Rainbow Weekend*, 2004. The festival brought together queer choirs from around Britain who all performed their repertoires individually, but as a grand finale, all the choirs came on stage to sing a song together which had been learnt throughout the day; 'You'll never walk alone' from the musical *Carousel* (Rodgers and Hammerstein, 1945) and arranged for the *Pink Singers* (London's mixed LGBT chorus) by W. Stickles. 'You'll Never Walk Alone' is a piece which appears in the musical *Carousel* at two points: the first time, it is sung at a rather poignant death scene, where one of the protagonists (Julie) is comforted by those around her because her lover (Billy), who had turned to crime, has just killed himself and gone to heaven. The reprise occurs when Billy – having been sent back down to earth by angels to redeem himself – tells his daughter, Louise, to be strong. Upon hearing his words, both Julie and Louise join in together in song with Billy. The manner in which the piece was sung at Leeds mirrored the reprise: an accompanied soloist began as one voice in the room, and gradually, other vocal parts joined in one after another to escalate towards a Bolero-esque climactic moment which filled the room with queer singing voices. This marked a turning point for the choir for several reasons.

The occasion is referred to by the interviewees as being one of the most memorable. Ironically, 'You'll never walk alone' was a hit released in 1963 by Liverpool band Gerry and the Pacemakers and which has become the Liverpool Football Club's anthem: the phrase is also used as a general motto by the club and its fans. However, despite the long-standing rivalry between Manchester and Liverpool – of which football and music are two cultural manifestations – not one of my interviewees alluded to Liverpool in relation to this particular song. Instead, all of them seem to place importance on the meaning of lyrics within that specific social context: singing with other LGBT choirs. One theme which arises from all the members' accounts is the shock of realizing the sheer number of queer choristers in one room: 'And then singing *with* everybody, it's like singing ... you know like 'Never Walk Alone' ... I mean it's just incredible with that *many*' (June); 'And then when we sang together at the end (quietly, whispering) ... it was phenomenal! (Katya). As if mirroring the song's effect in the musical, the choir's microcosmic existence in the Village as choristers was suddenly placed within a larger macrocosmic community – specifically a queer choral community – itself a part of the larger, queer community in UK: indeed, using June's words as an analogy, 'music's been a thing that has been a one-person affair, a very individual thing ... it was the first time that I actually felt part of it more.' Singing this particular song marked an almost symbolic initiation of the choir into the 'rest of the community' (Chongwei), a process of coming out as a group in public through music. In other words, for the choir, this moment marked a time when musical community was directly related to the queer community and thus being part of it was a necessary, or at least, symbolic rite of passage.

In a discussion concerning the process of coming out, Ken Plummer states that coming out is a 'process by which individuals pass of the moratorium ... and are "reborn" into organized aspects of the homosexual community, a process during which they come to identify themselves as "homosexuals"'.[36] The LGBT community had originally been defined through the differences in culture, social relationships and practices, politics and so on. This is why the idea of the closet was so significant in the construction of homosexual identities in the city. Paradoxically, in attempting to become culturally intelligible by coming out of this closet, these differences have become displaced through processes of commercialisation, tourism and queer mobility, and legislative changes as has been discussed. In this manner, coming out in contemporary British queer culture is about going back in, so to speak, finding the queer community again. This is not to say that the community cannot exist outside of the closet; on the contrary, it is about finding Tinny's 'community feeling' outside of the closet by recreating a sense of communal belonging. The event in Leeds demonstrates how music-making as a social process is a meaningful way to come out again into the queer community from a localized position.

Chongwei: [...] I think a performance is something for the group to work towards otherwise we'd be singing songs and getting them to a good standard, but we'd be only singing for ourselves. I don't think that's what I want the group to be like, it is for us to share the music

Author: With the rest of the world!

Chongwei: With rest of the world, and the rest of the community.

So the two things that could stamp our identity are: location, which is about community; and our sexual orientation, which is the community. And I think if we can just do that, if we can do that by next year, by next Mardi Gras, I think people are going to be, 'Oh. My. God.' (John)

Chongwei corrects my excited outburst, and relocates or at least refocuses my direction ('the rest of the world!') to face the local audience ('rest of the community'); furthermore, the manner in which he indicates the importance of breaking the interiority of the choir ('but we'd be only singing for ourselves') to be part of the exterior but local queer community reveals a simultaneous desire for a localized cultural incorporation and recognition through the 'sharing the music'. Whilst singing together is important, it only gains political and cultural momentum when is part of a recognized wider queer community. Similarly John, who was giving me ideas on how the choir could change its repertoire, brings together 'community' with 'location', which are then juxtaposed against the more international and global event of Mardi Gras (Pride). Furthermore, John's wanting to shock the Mardi Gras audience for example, suggests a desire for the choir to be somehow different from the other acts whilst simultaneously wanting to be considered, if not admired, as part of them. It is precisely this dual force which drives the choir and propels it forward, between wanting to form an uniquely localized lesbian and gay identity through music against the homogeneity of the Village *whilst also* seeking a more globalized cultural incorporation – even acceptance – into a larger queer culture, represented by events like Mardi Gras.

I want to conclude this article by reflecting on something the compère at the Leeds event said when she welcomed everyone: 'it's wonderful to see all our local brand of queer choirs brought together'. I think 'local brand' describes the conditions of queers in the city today: wanting to be part of a localized sense of communality and belonging, whilst also recognising the need for and seeking acknowledgement from a more global and competitive community. Whether it is for entertainment or as a political instrument, music enables local queer musicians to adopt a position of partiality. Queer theorist Arlene Stein refers to artists like Canadian singer k.d. lang who 'embrace lesbian identifications while achieving mainstream success, simultaneously acknowledging both lesbian marginality and membership in the dominant culture'.[37] Stein's overall argument being that queers 'comprise a "partial culture", that is we share some basic interests that separate us from the rest of society, but we also wish to belong to the mainstream society'.[38] What I want to suggest here is that whilst queers still comprise a partial culture, it is one which is defined less by being partial along the mainstream/subcultural axis. Instead, the partiality is one that is now defined by questions of local/global identifications. This point seems even more relevant now: for example, as noted earlier, the MLGC wished to bring their music 'back home to Manchester'. Within this context, coming out in contemporary queer culture is about creating a sense of queer belonging outside of what has increasingly become a diffused closet. Music spatializes the closet once again by creating pockets of queer belonging despite or because of the increasing fragmentation of the queer community. Being part of this sound through the social process of music-making can thus form part of a process of coming back out of (or going back into) the closet.

Digging (out) the beat: sources and resources for the study of popular music in the Manchester region

Dave
Russell

The *Manchester Region History Review* traditionally complements its themed editions with essays that explore museums of related interest and examine the research potential offered by particular archival/library collections. Popular music, however, does not altogether easily lend itself to such treatment. Although it has frequently featured in specific museum and gallery exhibitions, there is no single regional institution devoted to the subject. Similarly, archival material is relatively thin for the obvious reason that so much popular music-making leaves little in the way of formal records; minutes of the last meeting have never exactly been 'rock 'n' roll'. What follows, therefore, is a general survey of available resources, rather than a detailed consideration of a specific institution or set of material. Although largely focused on the period from 1950 and on popular music as 'pop' and 'rock', it strays a little beyond this terrain both in terms of chronology and content in order to provide a reminder of the wider fields that beckon.

Primary sources: archives and libraries

Archival collections are certainly far from absent, although they usually relate to the period before the 1960s.[1] *Manchester Central Library's Special Collections* holds a large collection of broadside ballads most of which were printed about the time of the Napoleonic Wars or between 1850 and 1875. The largest body comprises the Pearson Collection, and relates to the output of Thomas Pearson, a printer active in the city's Oldham Street area in the 1860s and 1870s. The Harris Library in Preston holds the Harkness Collection, a corpus of several hundred broadsides, mostly of the first half of the nineteenth century, including many produced by local printer, John Harkness.[2] Formally organized amateur institutions such as brass bands, and choral and amateur operatic societies, feature quite largely. Small collections of band material such as minute books, membership lists, concert programmes, press cuttings and photographs are held in a number of record offices – the minute books of Heap Bridge

Band from 1895 to 1914 are held in Bury Archives, a substantial collection relating to Denton Band in Tameside's Local Studies and Archives Centre – while Manchester's Chetham's Library holds a collection of site-specific Victorian banding material in its Belle Vue archive.[3]

Collections relating to professional popular musicians and recent commercial ventures are much rarer, although two deserve special mention. Jack Hylton (1892–1965) was born in Bolton and led one of Britain's most highly successful dance bands in the 1920s and 1930s before becoming a leading impresario. Lancaster University holds his personal archive which includes band parts, press cuttings, programmes, photos, scripts, adverts and recordings.[4] It is likely that many performers, of equal or lesser fame, have gathered collections of this type and it is to be hoped that families and friends will feel able to let at least some of these, often financially valuable items, found space within the public realm. In 1998, Rob Gretton, a director and major figure within Factory Communications Limited, deposited a large personal archive relating both to the company and to his role as Manager of Joy Division and New Order at the Museum of Science and Industry in Manchester's Castlefield. It includes financial records, especially relating to the Hacienda night club, business correspondence and a rich array of posters, videos and original artwork for record sleeves.[5] Finally, although much of the material relates to the Hallé orchestral concerts, The Greater Manchester County record office holds a collection of concert programmes (GB127.M619/4) from the city's Free Trade Hall for the period 1951–1974 which include items relating a considerable number of leading national and international jazz, folk and rock acts (for full listing see http://www.concertprogrammes. org.uk/html/search/verb/GetRecord/4004).[6]

If the record office is likely to be an infrequent stop on the popular music historians' journey, the library will always be a common one for it invariably holds a source long the backbone of much historical scholarship. For the local and regional historian of almost any subject in the post-1800 period, the newspaper has always been absolutely central and music is no exception. While the dozens of daily and weekly titles that served the region could never record every element of popular musical activity, much of its formal existence is neatly captured in its dense columns of classified advertising, that most revealing index of shifting tastes. Concerts, venues, times and prices are faithfully recorded, allowing for the kind of close, numerical measurement of different musical genres and types of activity that should underpin much historical research. Alongside this raw data, many papers included music criticism, comment and news. In the six days from 22 to 27 March 1965, for example, the *Manchester Evening News* carried a review of a concert by Thelonius Monk at the Free Trade Hall by 'Jack Florin' (actually journalist, Alan Stevens), a feature in the weekly 'Roderick Random' column on Middleton pop group, The Measles, and news stories on local stars Freddie and the Dreamers and Herman's Hermits. Several other weekly features such as the Tuesday 'Showpage', the Wednesday 'Entertainment Parade' and the Friday 'Jazz roundabout' (again with Jack Florin) also frequently covered local musical life; even when the focus was national, these columns provide an interesting insight into contemporary musical debate and socialization. Listings magazines such as *What's on in Manchester*, published from 1971 and held in Manchester Central Reference Library can provide a useful subsidiary source to the local press, not least because the illustrations and graphics used in adverts are a useful guide to the image that venues sought to foster.

For many music followers, of course, the local press would have been seen as having little value beyond the dissemination of basic information, and, sometimes, not even that. From the 1970s, the alternative press generally and fanzines specifically, grew up as a way of allowing fans to discuss and explore particular musical sub-cultures and to challenge dominant views in ways that were entirely impossible within the mainstream media. Many towns produced some form of non-commercial 'other paper' or 'free press' in the later 1970s and 1980s in which music had at least some presence. The fortnightly *New Manchester Review* (1975–1980) and *City Life* (1984–2005) are good examples – although the latter title eventually evolved into a lifestyle magazine – and, once again, are available in the city's Central Reference Library.[7] Both carried detailed listings, record, concert and venue reviews as well as some detailed articles, often well-illustrated. Bob Dickinson's contribution to this volume demonstrates extremely effectively both the role and style of the fanzines that captured and shaped Manchester's musical scene from the punk and post-punk era onward. Often printed in extremely small quantities and, unsurprisingly, not usually purchased for libraries, they are often found in the hands of individual collectors and fans rather than in public repositories. However, as will be discussed below, the Manchester District Music Archive has been digitising a complete set of *City Fun* (founded 1978), perhaps the best known local title, and clearly a similar strategy provides the way forward for this type of publication more generally.

The popular music industry has also long nurtured a strong trade press, which, although invariably published in London, offers much regional coverage, particularly of the larger centres. For historians of nineteenth-century music hall, the theatrical newspaper *The Era* is available within the '19th Century British Library Newspapers Online' facility which is now subscribed to by virtually all university and larger public libraries. The paper continued until 1938 although post-1900 runs do not appear to be held in any local institutions and is not yet available electronically. *The Stage* (1880 and continuing) provides a valuable source for studying 'mainstream' popular music, especially as encountered on the variety stage, in cabaret and working men's clubs and summer seasons. Beyond recent editions, it does not appear to be held in any of the region's libraries, but its entire archive is available electronically to the public via subscription. Better known to fans of pop, rock and jazz are such weekly titles as *Melody Maker* (1926–1999), *New Musical Express* (1952 and continuing) and *Sounds* (1970–1991). Some, albeit incomplete archived collections, do exist in the region. Manchester Central Library holds microfiche copies of *Melody Maker* from 1986–1997 and microfilm of *New Musical Express* from the late 1950s to 1971 and from 1991, while Salford University has some copies of *Melody Maker* from 1988 and *New Musical Express* from 2001. These and many other key titles can be accessed via the electronic site, http://www.rocksbackpages.com, although I have not yet found any examples of regional libraries subscribing to it.

Autobiography is invariably one of the most prominent and popular genres within public libraries and it can obviously offer much to historians. Certainly, most are skilfully constructed so as to offer a particular view of an individual and are frequently more useful as studies of how stars wish to be represented rather than of 'reality'. Cultural historians seeking to explore the construction of particular narratives and versions of history will hardly find this a problem, while those with slightly more empirical ambitions will invariably find invaluable material and leads to pursue. Manchester is not notably well blessed in this regard, although, again as will become apparent later, websites will play an increasingly central role here, especially in regard to those from outside the star category. Recent titles that have received relatively favourable receptions include *Mr Manchester and the factory girl. The story of Tony and Lindsay Wilson* (2010), by Lindsay Reade, first wife of Factory founder, Tony Wilson, and which marries autobiography with biography; Joy Division bassist Peter Hook's *The Hacienda: how not to run a club* (2009) and *Unknown pleasures: inside Joy Division* (2012).

Talking about music can sometimes feel almost as important to its devotes as the music itself. Most books about Manchester music are heavily coloured by personal analysis, reminiscence and opinion although formal oral histories are not notably common. Arthur Taylor's *Labour and Love* (1983), focusing on twentieth-century brass bands, is an early and valuable example that, while national in scope, has much to offer local band historians. In the field of rock and later popular musical forms, John Robb, *The north will rise again. Manchester music city, 1976–96* (2009) presents much valuable material drawn from interviews with many of the city's leading musicians, journalists and entrepreneurs. While many local studies collections now hold oral history material, the major repository for the region has long been the North West Sound Archive, housed in Clitheroe Castle.[8] The collection does contain a number of 'traditional' oral history interviews (interviewee responding to historian's questions) that include material relating to various aspects of music and it also has a valuable archive of music-centred radio programmes that would prove useful to students of folk, country and brass bands. The interviewing of the region's musicians, especially those who were never in the national spotlight, remains a priority for the historical community.

A brief breath of fresh air

At first sight, it is difficult to see popular music's architectural heritage as serving any great value to historical projects, not least because a remarkable number of the region's key venues have been demolished or altered beyond recognition. Even those that remain offer little of the tangible, useable evidence offered by many other elements of the built environment. Nevertheless, as Bob Dickinson's article in this volume demonstrates with great clarity, even as empty spaces, boarded up sites or in their new guises as office blocks, apartments or supermarkets, venues past play an enormously important role in stimulating the historical imagination. As I began researching the history of local cabaret clubs, I was increasingly drawn into a series of lunch-time walks during which I gazed knowingly at the unlikeliest of sites, attracting *en route* the kind of head-shakingly sympathetic stares that tend to greet the behaviour of the unthreatening eccentric. At one level, this desire to see where something once was can seem as merely a form of anorakistic obsession, but it is to be encouraged. It can lead to a far closer understanding of the role and practicalities of location – proximity to transport routes and so forth – but, more importantly, for so many of us it seems to be an essential aid to the recall or conjuring up of particular sounds, cultures and moments. Therefore interpretative maps and guidebooks are an invaluable aid. The 'Salford music map', produced in conjunction with the Salford Museum and Art Gallery's 'Quiffs, riffs and tiffs' exhibition (2008) is a useful reference point, but by some way the most comprehensive work yet is by Phill Gatenby and Craig Gill, *The Manchester musical history tour* (2011). Although lacking maps, the book is a well illustrated and well informed guide to the major popular musical sites of Manchester and its suburbs by two well respected local musical figures. The work grew out of the authors' involvement with Manchester Music Tours, a company which offers a variety of themed guided walks around the city.[9]

Webbed feet

While Manchester's climate is the source of much unfair and lazy comedy, there is no doubt that on occasions, a virtual tour might be preferable to a physical one and the web contains many opportunities for dry (although only meteorologically speaking) encounters with the past. The web has become so central to so many lives so quickly that it is easy to forget what a recent phenomenon it is and the extent of the changes it has wrought. Two points strike especially clearly in regard to specialist music sites. The first is the extent to which many now serve as a major source of personal testimony and reminiscence as often geographically scattered members of musical communities and taste publics gather virtually to recall (or re-invent) past times. In this, they complement rather than challenge traditional oral history as a source. Individuals posting on line can obviously be approached and asked to provide further information or even become formal face-to-face interviewees, but, in their virtual guise, they can only stand as uninterrogated autobiographical voices. Within those limits, however, those voices can be extremely valuable. Just as oral history has always been strongly advocated as a method of exploring 'history from below', a way of accessing the life stories and memories of those largely excluded from the historical record, the best web sites can sustain similar claims. It is here that the recollections of rank and file musicians, front-of-house staff and, crucially, audience members can be found in abundance. At the same time, websites are increasingly taking on the appearance, wittingly or otherwise, of virtual museums, galleries and archives. Popular music has proved slightly troubling territory for museums in that, while aspects of it have been featured in various themed exhibitions, it has not proved possible to provide a national museum or interpretative centre for it. The short and unhappy life of the Sheffield-based National Centre for Popular Music (1999–2000) has hardly proved an encouragement for such an endeavour.[10] The web, however, has become a manageable place within which to present visual material and ephemera.

In order to provide an insight into what will undoubtedly become an ever more critical element of the music historian's environment, two key local sites were approached and asked for comments on their history, aims and perceived achievements.[11] Beyond a little editing in the interests of space, their responses are printed below, largely *verbatim*. As both their respective commentaries and their sites demonstrate, they have very different philosophies and approaches, but, in their distinctive ways, provide key resources which often cannot be easily accessed elsewhere. Both invite readers of this journal to utilize and, if appropriate, to contribute to their sites. We begin with the Manchester District Music Archive, and a statement produced by Joe Beech.[12]

> Manchester District Music Archive was founded by Matthew Norman and Alison Surtees in 2003 in a bid to celebrate Greater Manchester music, protect its heritage and promote awareness of the city's cultural importance. Since its inception, the group has grown to over 2,000 members. Their contributions have created an invaluable online resource collecting the stories behind a globally renowned music scene. The archive emerged out of a campaign for a museum dedicated to Manchester's rich and diverse music history. "We believed there should be a proper space dedicated to storing Manchester music [so] we, as an organization, campaigned for a

couple of years to get a physical music museum in Manchester", explains MDMArchive Project Manager Abigail Ward.

Frustrated with a lack of progress towards this end, Abigail Ward and web designer Ashley Kennerley set up the website to create a user-led, virtual resource. It has developed hugely over the past seven years, despite sparse funding. Submissions come from all over the city, from artists and industry personnel to fans and cultural historians, discussing their experiences and sharing their tapes, tickets, flyers and photos. Today, the archive contains memorabilia from over 4,000 bands, venues and DJs hailing from Manchester, dating as far back as 1912. An impressive range of artefacts includes an original '84 New Order master tape and 460 artefacts from the Hacienda. Yet the project also aims to recognize unsung heroes from areas such as Moss Side and Hulme, whose reggae and blues traditions are often overshadowed by the more renowned Factory Records bands, celebrated in recent popular films such as 24 Hour Party People and Control. There is also space for folk and other musical traditions that pre-date sound recording, complemented by a detailed chronology of Manchester's musical history from 1422 to present day. Embedded videos show a wide range of material and a recital of ballads emphasizes the historical link between music and events like Peterloo.

Despite the lack of a permanent physical museum, MDMArchive also hold various events, including exhibitions, seminars, film screenings and club nights. Their Manchester Punk Exhibition at Urbis boasted rare memorabilia and footage from Joy Division and the Buzzcocks, while film and music night "The Blues and Gospel Train" attracted fans from around the world. In 2010, they hosted an ambitious event celebrating the history of Manchester's gay music culture at The Deaf Institute. The night was so successful that the group launched an online exhibition on the subject, called "Queer Noise". This virtual museum, showcasing the history of LGBT music in Manchester, was curated by Abigail Ward and writer Jon Savage. Ward says, "Queer Noise is a digital museum experience ... hundreds of artefacts relating to LGBT clubbing and gay live music, all grouped together in a really exciting, cutting-edge, interactive display". There are further physical and digital exhibitions in the pipeline: "We're almost ready to launch our next online exhibition, which is a complete archive of Manchester's post-punk fanzine City Fun. We are dedicated to unsung eras, so we wouldn't want to touch on 'Manchester and Factory' anymore because there's no need for us to do that". The archive is broadening its scope to paint a detailed picture of the Manchester music scene, from unsigned artists and buskers to thought to be lost rarities from underground movements. With an enthusiastic swathe of contributors, it is likely to keep expanding.

Manchesterbeat, in its turn, is an individually self-funded site dedicated to the music of the 1960s.[13] Its founder and webmaster is Paul Mlynarz, originally a north-west musician who has lived in Australia since 1986 and who thus, in his phrase, runs 'the site at a slight distance'.

'The origin of the Manchesterbeat is, I suppose, based in my early aspirations "to be in a group". That would be the life for me – the girls, the money, the girls, the music and … the girls! I did it, although we didn't make much money and nobody ever told me about the loss of sleep and those cold winter nights in the Bedford on the way home from Carlisle, facing the even frostier looks of my section head at the CWS, when I arrived just a little late the next morning. But who cared? I was in my teens and life was great – even when playing in those many groups that never quite got on the road or did so, only to fold a short time later. Shift forward many years – a move to Wrexham, a year in Merseyside then "down south" where I worked with a ska band and fronted a comedy band. Then a bigger move to Papua New Guinea and finally Australia. But the old groups and old friends were still part of me – never forgotten, despite the distance and time.

They do say that "necessity is the mother of invention", so when I decided I needed to get into this "web thing", learn HTML and other mysterious acronyms, what better basis for learning than to set up a site for one of the few things I really knew about. Groups. Not the famous ones; not interested. I liked the ones I loved seeing each week at the local youth centres and clubs. The Dyleks at St Crispins, the Starlights at St Kents and the Focal Points and Mobile Unit at The Pop Inn. There were initially probably 6 or 7 pages but a start. Incredibly someone saw it and added some information, told their friends and they told their friends and off we grew. Twelve, thirteen, perhaps even fourteen years later and we now have probably over 700 pages – too many to count and who cares anyway. There's hardly a day goes by without changes – its way of life for me now.

Oddly, I do have policies put in place. Firstly, the site is about the 60s and generally for groups that were from, or played in the Greater Manchester area in the 60s. But I do realise that the 60s groups did not all break up at midnight on NYE '69, so we are quite lenient with dates. Rule two is that I include everything that people send – if it interests just one person (usually the writer) then in it goes! I break this rule occasionally, when people send in "I think my sister knew a guy in a group that might have played in Halifax". Rule three should perhaps have been rule one, because it is so important. The "scene" wasn't just about groups. There was a very wide range of venues, DJs, agents, managers and, of course, punters. Plus we all ate in 60s places (remember Wimpy bars?), dressed in 60s clothes and bought 60s gear from 60s music shops (what, a hundred quid for that PA?). All of these elements feature on the site.

Rule four is that while I sometimes use the term "I" for the site it should be "we"; the contributors are the site. I recognize that and, apart from a few minor irritations, our readers/contributors are incredible and the site is a real co-operative! Finally, Rule five is that "thou shalt not steal". I never knowingly include "stuff" from other sites. It happens, of course, as contributors may not be fully aware of what they are doing and don't tell me the origin.

What of our achievements? This is certainly the first site to be based on un-famous groups in the north-west, and possibly the only one to offer such a wide field of information, having being going for so many years. We have also produced five books based on material from the site (I see them as souvenirs of the era). For our readers/contributors, we have found long lost friends, assisted with re-unions, discovered lost photos, helped university students with theses, assisted with finding lost blood fathers (its usually the roadie), smoothed over squabbles that have lasted over 40 plus years and introduced children/grandchildren to (some) of the exploits of dad/granddad. We are still fresh and relevant, I feel, with the occasional bit of cheekiness. Manchesterbeat continues to grow, widening its audience and broadening its subject matter. The beat goes on ...'

Secondary sources

The Manchester city-region's popular music scenes have generated a substantial body of writing over the last thirty years in particular from journalists, industry-insiders and, increasingly, academic scholars. While it is clearly not possible to provide anything resembling a definitive listing or discussion of this secondary material here, it is useful to identify some of the most significant texts.

Although a single-volume history covering an extensive time-period does not exist, Dave Haslam, *Manchester, England* (1999) provides a strong starting point for individuals seeking a long view. While the core of the book concerns the period from the 1970s, Haslam, amongst other things a Haçienda DJ and a significant figure within the city's popular culture, begins his narrative in the nineteenth century and gives some weight to the urban musical genres that preceded that decade. In general, popular music from much before the 1970s has not yet received the level of attention it deserves, although some pioneering work has mapped out territory that demands further exploration. Roger Elbourne, *Music and tradition in early industrial Lancashire, 1780–1840* (1980) explores the musical life of the county's textile communities as they were shaped by the experiences of industrialization and urbanization. The performance and composition of sacred music formed a key element of the resultant music-making and the activities of one particularly noted group within this tradition, the Rossendale-based 'Larks of Dean', have been studied by Sally Drage in her, 'The Larks of Dean: amateur musicians in northern England', in Rachel Cowgill and Peter Holman, eds, *Music in the British provinces, 1690–1914* (2007). Robert Poole, *Popular leisure and music hall in 19th-century Bolton* (1982), does much to demonstrate the important role that the Lancashire industrial region played in the establishment of music hall, while Chris Waters, 'Manchester morality and London capital: the battle over the Palace of Varieties', in Peter Bailey ed., *Music hall: the business of pleasure* (1986), discusses the evolution from music hall to variety via a study of attempts to establish a profitable large-scale variety theatre in Manchester in the 1890s. David Hindle, *From a gin palace to a King's Palace* (2007), traces that same evolution in a case study of Preston.

Frank Pritchard, *Dance band days around Manchester* (1988), one of the many valuable titles published by the late Neil Richardson, provides an insight into inter-war dance hall and dance band life. Leading local bandleader, Phil Moss, takes the story into the post-war period in two further Richardson titles, *Manchester's music makers* (1994) and *Manchester's dancing years* (1996). Two of the region's greatest ever popular musical stars, Rochdale's Gracie Fields and Wigan's George Formby, are the subjects of thoughtful biographies by David Bret, namely *The real Gracie Fields* (1995) and *George Formby, troubled genius* (1999). Stan Hibbert, once a trumpeter with the BBC Northern Dance Orchestra, presents an interesting memoir-cum-history of the band in 'The Northern Dance Orchestra: a brief history', *Manchester Sounds*, 2 (2001).

CP Lee, *Shake, rattle and rain. Popular music making in Manchester, 1955 to 1995* (2002), provides a wide-ranging survey from folk and skiffle onward that serves as a rewarding introduction to the rock era; the book makes extensive use of oral testimony. Although much of his work took place away from his Salford roots by the 1950s, the life of Ewan MacColl has a central role for any student of folk music, and Ben Harker, *Class act. The cultural and political life of Ewan MacColl* (2007) stands as one of the best biographies of a local musical life.[14] Alan Lawson, *It happened in ~~Liverpool~~ Manchester: the true story of Manchester's music, 1958–1965* (1998) offers an enthusiastic and informative survey of the city's remarkably rich beat culture, while Keith Rylett and Phil Scott, *CENtral 1179. The story of Manchester's Twisted Wheel Club* (2001) provides a history of the iconic 1960s blues and soul venue, as well as providing a full listing of acts that performed there. Bill Sykes, *Sit down! Listen to this! The Roger Eagle story* (2012) uses interview material with a variety of musicians and others to consider the life of the DJ and club promoter who began his career at the club in 1962.

The Twisted Wheel was one of the most important foundation sites for the Northern Soul dance scene that emerged from the late 1960s. This has generated several good popular works, including David Nowell, *Too dam soulful. The story of northern soul* (2001), but also a body of academic accounts exploring its role in working-class life in urban communities: while considering far more than simply the Manchester region, they feature it extensively. These include Katie Milestone, 'Love factory: the sites, practices and media relationships of northern soul', in Steve Redhead with Derek Wynne and Justin O'Connor, eds, *The clubcultures reader* (1997); Joanne Hollows, and Katie Milestone 'Welcome to dreamsville: a history and geography of northern soul', in Andrew Leyshon, David

Matless and George Revill, eds, *The place of music* (1998), and Barrie Doyle, 'More than a dance hall, more a way of life: northern soul, masculinity and working-class culture in 1970s Britain', in Axel Schildt and Detlef Siegfried, eds, *Between Marx and Coca-Cola. Youth cultures in Changing European societies, 1960–1980* (2006).

Studies of Punk have only infrequently considered the northern provincial experience, but Paul Cobley, '"Leave the capital". On being a punk in Wigan', in Roger Sabin. ed., *Punk rock. So what?* (1999) remains a valuable corrective to London-centric approaches. Comfortably the largest body of Manchester music writing concerns the period from the foundation of Factory in 1978 to the waning of 'Madchester' and Factory's bankruptcy in 1992. James Nice, *Shadowplayers. The rise and fall of Factory Records* (2010), comprises a meticulously researched, year-by-year account of the label and its associated business empire, while, David Nolan, *Tony Wilson. You're entitled to an opinion* (2010), provides a portrait of that empire's most high profile figure through the use of extensive interview material. Joy Division/New Order have undoubtedly attracted the largest degree of critical attention of the Factory bands. Deborah Curtis, *Touching from a distance. Ian Curtis and Joy Division* (1995), an autobiographical/biographical account of Joy Division's vocalist by his wife, was an important early title, while ex-*Sounds* journalist, Mick Middles, has contributed importantly here, notably with *From Joy Division to New Order* (1996) and *Torn apart: the life of Ian Curtis* (2006), co-written with Lindsay Reade. Stockport-born music writer Paul Morley's *Joy Division. Piece by piece* (2008) is a compendium of his many reviews, sleeve notes, articles and criticism about the band. David Nolan, *Bernard Sumner* (2007), offers a biography of the guitarist and keyboard player from his Joy Division days onward.[15] Late 1980s 'Madchester' has produced several biographies of individuals or groups including John Robb, *The Stone Roses and the resurrection of British pop* (1997), Mick Middles, *Shaun Ryder. Happy Mondays, Black Grape and other traumas* (1997) and *The Stone Roses. Breaking in to heaven* (2000). Simon Spence, *The Stone Roses. War and Peace* (2012) was published in the year that one of the era's most significant bands unexpectedly re-formed and brought a quarter of million people into Manchester's Heaton Park for three June concerts.

The Smiths (1982–1987) and the subsequent careers of singer/lyricist, Morrissey, and guitarist/song-writer, Johnny Marr, have also been the subject of a substantial literature; indeed, Morrissey is probably Manchester's most written about musical figure. Johnny Rogan, *Morrissey and Marr. The severed alliance* (1992) and Tony Fletcher, *A light that never goes out. The enduring saga of The Smiths* (2012) are highly detailed and well researched narrative accounts, which have been followed by, amongst others, Simon Goddard, *The Smiths: Songs that Saved Your Life* (2004) which tells the story of, and behind, all of their output, and his *Mozipedia: The Encyclopedia of Morrissey and The Smiths* (2009), explores Morrissey's wider aesthetic and intellectual universe. Gavin Hopps provides a detailed and scholarly literary analysis of Morrissey's lyrics in *Morrissey. The pageant of his bleeding heart* (2009), while Sean Campbell and Colin Coulter eds, *Why pamper life's complexities? Essays on The Smiths* (2011) comprises fourteen essays that seek to place the band's work into a variety of social, cultural and political contexts. Richard Carman, *Johnny Marr, The Smiths and the art of gun-slinging* (2006) focuses on a highly influential guitarist.

Michael Goddard and Ben Halligan, eds, *Mark E. Smith and the Fall. Art, music and politics* (2010), provides a set of writings on a band that the editors believe to have been unjustly neglected because of its failure to fit neatly into the key narratives that tend to frame and structure the city's musical history. Mick Middles, who has played a consistently important role in responding in print to new developments, has written on two other Manchester region bands that have achieved national and international eminence, *Oasis: round their way* (1996) and *Reluctant heroes. The story of Elbow* (2010). This brief listing could clearly be much extended as many worthy titles have been excluded and, of course, many more will undoubtedly appear. The words, like the beat, thankfully go on.

Notes

Editorial *Dave Russell*

1. Dave Haslam, *Manchester, England* (London, 1999), p. 106.
2. A useful introduction to some recent thinking is provided by the 'virtual symposium' held by advisory editors to the journal *Popular Music* and reprinted in Allan F. Moore, *Critical essays in popular musicology* (Aldershot, 2007), pp. 35–48. Some writers now reject the term as being too imprecise, particularly in our own age when boundaries between musical forms have become so porous.
3. Haslam, *Manchester, England*, p. xxviii.
4. Quoted in Haslam, *Manchester, England*, p. 110; quoted in James Nice, *Shadowplayers. The rise and fall of Factory Records* (London, 2010), p. 7.
5. See essays by Richard Witt and Katie Hannon in Michael Goddard and Benjamin Halligan (eds), *Mark E. Smith and the Fall: art, music and politics* (Farnham, 2010).

Going with the mainstream: Manchester cabaret clubs and popular music in the 1960s
Dave Russell

1. *Manchester Evening News*, 6 Feb. 1964. Henceforward, cited as *MEN*. Biographical information cannot be provided on the many performers noted in this article. Guidance to musicians can often be found in Colin Larkin (ed.), *The encyclopedia of popular music*, 10 vols (Oxford, 4th edn, 2006), and Louis Barfe, *Turned out nice again* (London, 2008) and Tony Hannan, *On Behalf of the Committee. A history of northern comedy* (Leeds, 2009), provide useful guides to some other fields of entertainment.
2. 'Casino Society' was broadcast on 3 March 1966; *Guardian*, 9 July 1966; *The Stage and Television Today*, 19 Oct. 1972. Henceforward, cited as *Stage*.
3. Although see, Mark Jarvis, *Conservative governments, morality and social change in affluent Britain, 1957–1964* (Manchester, 2005) and Frank Mort, *Capital Affairs. London and the making of the permissive society* (New Haven, 2010). Louise A. Jackson, '"The coffee club menace". Policing youth, leisure and sexuality in post-war Manchester', *Cultural and Social History*, 5 (2008), pp. 289–308.
4. Dave Russell, 'Glimpsing *la dolce vita*: cultural change and modernity in the 1960s English cabaret club', *Journal of Social History*, 47 (2013) pp. 297–318.
5. For perceptive comments in the wider historical literature, Dominic Sandbrook, *Never had it so good. A history of Britain from Suez to the Beatles* (London, 2005), pp. 430–434 and *White heat. A history of Britain in the swinging sixties* (London, 2007), pp. 411–413.
6. Dave Harker, 'Still crazy after all these years: what was popular music in the 1960s?', in Bart Moore-Gilbert and John Seed (eds), *Cultural revolution? The challenge of the arts in the 1960s* (London, 1992), pp. 241–3, 251; Derek B. Scott (ed.), *The Ashgate research companion to popular musicology* (Farnham, 2009), p. 4.
7. Michael Brocken, *Other voices: hidden histories of Liverpool's popular music scenes, 1930–1970* (Farnham, 2010), p. 24.
8. *Guardian*, 9 July 1966, on Manchester striptease.
9. Often butts for humour, the best were of a very high standard. Derek Hilton, for example, who led a trio at Mister Smiths from 1963, was a highly regarded and well-trained musician and arranger who

eventually became Director of Music at Granada TV in the 1970s. Obituary, *Daily Telegraph*, 1 Aug. 2005.

10. Bill Harry, *'Whatever happened to ...?* (London, 1999), p. 8; Penny Valentine and Vicki Wickham, *Dancing with demons* (London, 2000), p. 128; Hannan, *On Behalf*, p. 274.

11. *The Stage Year Book*, 1968, p. 363; *Wythenshawe Express*, 10 Oct. 1968; *Stage*, 3 Aug. 1972. Blighty's opened in December 1971.

12. *MEN*, 7 Oct. 1968; *Stockport Express*, 5 Dec. 1968.

13. This is based on club advertisements in *MEN*, February to March 1970.

14. *MEN*, 7 Oct. 1967.

15. *MEN*, 4 Oct. 1967; *Stage*, 7 Dec. 1961.

16. *Stage*, 16 Oct. 1966, 26 June 1969, 14 Oct. 1971. When the Stockport Empress, later the Poco-a-Poco, opened in 1962, its owner described it as 'a casino for workers'. *MEN*, 13 Feb. 1962.

17. On opening in 1954, the Cromford set its subscription at 3 guineas. Club Index, Greater Manchester Record Office, M117/176, Register G. 225. Henceforth 'Club Index'.

18. See comments by James Towler, *Stage*, 10 Feb. 1966.

19. *Stockport Express*, 5 Dec. 1968.

20. *MEN*, 19 Oct. 1963. The club used both this form and the 'Mister Smiths' used in this article.

21. Evidence from Martin Mitchell, an ex-police sergeant with extensive experience of monitoring the city's clubs.

22. David Kynaston, *Family Britain, 1951–57* (London, 2009), p. 178.

23. Department of Economic Affairs, *The North West. A regional study* (London, 1965), Table 34, p. 167.

24. 'Drinking clubs and the law', *Manchester Guardian*, 29 Dec.1958.

25. Alan Kidd, *Manchester. A History* (Manchester, 2006, 4th edn), p. 226. Tameside figures extracted from David Owen, *A history of the theatres and cinemas of Tameside* (Radcliffe, 1985).

26. *Manchester Guardian*, 30 Dec. 1958 for

shrewd observations on the relationship between TV and the emerging club scene.

27. Peter Hepple in *Stage*, 31 Jan. 1980.

28. *Manchester Guardian*, 29 Dec. 1958.

29. All dates are those at which the clubs formally registered. See Club Index, M117/80, A-J.

30. *Stage*, 19 Nov., 3 Dec., 10 Dec., 30 July 1959. A number of pubs, notably the Fusiliers, Salford, and the Yew Tree, Wythenshawe, also began hosting live shows in the 1950s.

31. *MEN*, 5 Oct. 1959.

32. *MEN*, 5 Oct. 1959; *Stage*, 2 April 1959, 19 Nov. 1959.

33. John Taylor, *From Self-help to glamour. The working man's club, 1860–1972* (Oxford, 1972), pp. 72–89; Ruth Cherrington, *Not just beer and bingo! A social history of working men's clubs* (Bloomington, Indiana, 2012), pp. 62–86.

34. On M.E.C.A.A., *Stage*, 31 Dec. 1959, 26 March 1964. For publications, *Stage*, 21 Feb. 1958, 19 Nov. 1958.

35. *MEN*, 29 June 1961.

36. Jarvis, *Conservative governments*, pp. 1–11.

37. Parliamentary Debates, Commons, 1959–60, vol. 613, 1039–40.

38. Report of the Gaming Board for Great Britain, Parliamentary Papers, 1970, vol. vi, p. 563.

39. Parliamentary Debates, Commons, 1960, vol. 631, 41–2.

40. I am again extremely grateful to Martin Mitchell for expert guidance on this and the wider issues of licensing.

41. George L. Bernstein, *The myth of decline. The rise of Britain since 1945* (London, 2004), p. 308.

42. *Guardian*, 9 July 1966.

43. David M. Smith, *Industrial Britain: The north west* (Newton Abbott, 1969), p. 38.

44. John K. Walton, *Lancashire. A social history, 1558–1939* (Manchester, 1987), pp. 283–324.

45. *Guardian*, 14 June 1962.

46. There are some biographical details in *Stage*, 26 Nov. 1959.

47. *Stage*, 20 Feb. 1964, 12 Oct. 1967.

48. Brocken, *Other voices*, p. 185; *Guardian*, 14 June 1962.

49. Graham Turner, *The north country* (London, 1967), p. 236, reported locals explaining Sheffield's lack of clubs as reflective of a culture that objected to 'flaunting' money.

50. Club Index, M117/179, J. 9; Jonathan Margolis, *Bernard Manning* (London, 1996).

51. These figures have been constructed from advertisements in *MEN* and listings in *Stage*.

52. Brocken, *Other voices*, p. 181. Organs were undoubtedly common but, once again, popular memory masks complexity. For organs in clubs, *Club and Institute Journal*, 1 Jan. 1968.

53. In recent years, the term 'middlebrow' has increasingly been denuded of its negative connotations and used as a valuable tool for opening up neglected cultural practices, especially within literature. The same process is required in music. See http://www.middlebrow-network.com/.

54. *Stage*, 28 March 1963; Manchesterbeat.com posting by 'Collette', 28 March 2010.

55. Performance diary constructed from *MEN*. Although individual sets were rarely recorded in detail in the trade press or other sources, sufficient evidence is available to allow some reconstruction of performance histories.

56. *Stage*, 26 March 1963.

57. *Stage*, 20 May, 16 Sept. 1965.

58. *MEN*, 2 March, 16 March 1970.

59. *Stage*, 17 June 1965; *MEN*, 4 March 1965.

60. Alan Lawson, *It happened in Manchester* (Unsworth, Bury, 1990), pp. 25–6; *MEN*, 10 June 1966.

61. http://www.manchesterbeat.com/, testimony of Dave Anderton [posted 17 June 2012, accessed 8 October 2012].

62. http://www.discogs.com/Chris-Rayburn-Chris-Rayburn/release/3757303 [accessed 8 October 2012].

63. Roger Elbourne, *Music and tradition in early industrial Lancashire, 1780–1840* (Trowbridge, 1980).

64. *Musical Times*, Nov. 1911; John D. Vose, *The Lancashire Caruso* (Blackpool, 1982).

65. *MEN*, 6 Feb. 1964; *Stage*, 2 Jan. 1964 for Hughes.

66. *MEN*, 16 March 1970; Turner, *North Country*, pp. 251–2; *Stage*, 9 March 1967.

67. *MEN*, 27 Aug. 1966; *Stage*, 30 April 1964, 29 April 1965.

68. Melinda Bilyeu, Hector Cooke and Andrew Môn Hughes, *The Bee Gees. Tales of the brothers Gibb* (London, 2001), pp. 343–4.

69. *Stage*, 23 Jan. 1964, 23 November 1967.

70. For Rockin' Berries, Alan Clayson, *Beat Merchants* (London, 1995), pp. 121, 141–4, 283; Harris, *Stage*, 26 March 1964 and in Manchester Region, *MEN*, 4 Feb. 1964 (Cromford Club, Manchester), 5 Feb. 1964 (Wishing Well, Swinton).

71. Gerry Smith, *Noisy island. A short history of Irish pop music* (Cork, 2005), pp. 11–16.

72. http://www.margo-burns.co.uk/The_Beginning/the_beginning.html [site created 2002, accessed 17 October 2012]. *MEN*, 26 Feb. 1966.

73. Mahora Peters with James George, *Showband. Mahora and the Maori Volcanics* (Karori, New Zealand, 2005).

74. *Stage*, 28 March 1968; *MEN*, 6 May 1966, 26 Sept. 1966, for Castaways at Manchester's Piccadilly Club.

75. *Stage*, 19 Oct. 1967.

76. Bert Weedon at the Burnley Cabaret and Brierfield New 77 Clubs, *Stage*, 20 Feb. 1964; Morgan James Duo at Piccadilly Club, *MEN*, 2 April 1966, 20 May 1966 and Palladium Club, *MEN*, 7 June 1966; Gina Brannelli, *Stage*, 15 March 1973 and http://www.ginabrannelli.co.uk/ [site updated 16 July 2012, accessed 10 August 2012].

77. *Stage*, 5 Oct. 1967, 21 March 1968, on the breathalyser. Report of the Gaming Board for Great Britain, 1969, *Parliamentary Papers*, 1969–70, vol. 6, 676.

78. *MEN*, 10 Nov. 1970. The club closed in late 1970 when it emerged that its premises were to be demolished for redevelopment in the next year; Cromford Court now lies buried under the Arndale Centre.

79. Jackson, '"The coffee club menace"', pp. 289–308.

80. City of Manchester Watch Committee, Chief Constable's Report for 1967, p. 2.
81. Information from Martin Mitchell, a member of this unit in 1968.
82. *MEN*, 7 Oct., 5 Dec. 1967, 16 Jan. 1968.
83. For example, *Stage*, June 20, 1968, 24 Dec. 1969.
84. *Stage*, 16 Dec. 1982, 8 Dec. 1982.
85. Dave Haslam, *Manchester, England* (London, 1999), pp. xxii, 146.

Shebeens and black music culture in Moss Side, Manchester, in the 1950s and 1960s   *Dennis Bourne and Melanie Tebbutt*

1. F. Wertheimer, 'Recording 1960s Manchester's buzzing Caribbean scene', *The Guardian*, 31 May, 2011. The Commonword project resulted in a publication, Martin De Mello (ed.), *Moss Side stories* (Manchester, 2012). We have also used the original 2011interview transcripts, currently held by Commonword Publishing and we are grateful to Yvonne McCalla for access to these. See, also, *Moss Side stories: the hidden history of Moss Side and Hulme club culture*, online exhibition: http://www.mdmarchive.co.uk/mosssidestories/ [accessed September 2013].
2. OED Online. September 2012. Oxford University Press. http://oed.com/view/Entry/177737?redirectedFrom=shebeen, [accessed 22 October 2012]. As will be seen, the word is also sometimes rendered as 'shabeen'.
3. Jo Stanley, 'Mangoes to Moss Side: Caribbean migration to Manchester in the 1950s and 1960s', *Manchester Region History Review*, 16 (2002–3), pp. 40–50.
4. Thanks to Bill Williams for advice on these matters. The name was given to a network of poor streets stretching southwards from New Park Road (which ran between the dockside Trafford Road and Oldfield Road) to Monmouth Street. Number 69 Monmouth Street was a boarding house well-known to seamen, run between 1907 and 1923 by a Mrs. Emma Taylor.
5. Manchester City Planning Department, *Ethnic minority groups in Manchester* (Manchester, 1984), cited in Stanley, 'Mangoes to Moss Side', p. 43.
6. Colin Holmes, *John Bull's island: immigration & British society, 1871–1971* (Basingstoke, 1988), p. 167; E.J.B. Rose, *Colour and citizenship: a report on British race relations* (London, 1969), p. 65. Ian Spencer also provides a more detailed breakdown of the numbers enlisted from the Caribbean, arguing that approximately 10,270 were recruited from Jamaica, and 800 from Trinidad and other smaller islands, mainly for the RAF. Ian R.G. Spencer, *British immigration policy since 1939: the making of multi-racial Britain* (London, 1997), pp. 17–18.
7. Spencer, *British immigration*, p. 18.
8. Ibid. Spencer states that the *SS Almanzora*, which left Jamaica in late 1947, carried 94 former members of the RAF. Two-thirds of the passengers on the Empire *Windrush*, which arrived in June 1948, were ex-servicemen who had been to Britain during the war.
9. P. Panayi, *The impact of immigration: a documentary history of the effects and experiences of immigrants in Britain since 1945* (Manchester, 1999), p. 63.
10. Bill Williams, "46. The post-war years: the West Indians', unpublished paper.
11. Stanley, 'Mangoes to Moss Side', pp. 40–1.
12. Paul Mosley and Barbara Ingham, *Fighting discrimination: W. Arthur Lewis and the dual economy of Manchester in the 1950s* (Brooks World Poverty Institute, Working Paper 179, 2012), p. 7
13. Alan Kidd, *Manchester* (Edinburgh, 2002), pp. 219. Karen Evans, *et al.*, *A tale of two cities: global change, local feeling and everyday life in the North of England. A study in Manchester and Sheffield* (London, 2003), p. 209.
14. Bill Williams, 'Post-war years'.
15. *Report on the health of the City of Manchester for 1954 by the Medical Officer*

of Health p. 23, cited in Bill Williams, 'Post-war years'.

16. Mosley and Ingham, *Fighting discrimination*, p. 6.

17. Ibid.

18. CP Lee, 'Popular music in Manchester: 1950–1995' (unpublished PhD thesis, Manchester Metropolitan University: Manchester Institute of Popular Culture, 1996), p. 29

19. Neil. A. Wynn, 'Race, war and black GI's and West Indians in Britain', *Immigrants and Minorities*, 24 (2006) p. 327.

20. Ibid.

21. For detailed information about the general history, see Aldon P. Ferguson, *Eighth Air Force Base Air Depot "Burtonwood"* (Berkshire, 1986).

22. Peter Fryer, *Staying power: the history of black people on Britain* (London, 1984), p. 347.

23. Dorothy Jasper, in De Mello, *Moss Side stories*, p. 172.

24. Lee, 'Popular Music', p. 29

25. Ibid, p. 33.

26. Holmes, *John Bull's island*, pp. 202–204.

27. Wynn, 'Race, War and Black GI's', p. 332.

28. Ibid.

29. Dorothy Jasper, in De Mello, *Moss Side Stories*, p. 175.

30. Ibid.

31. *Roots oral history: rude awakening* (UK Roots Oral History project, 1992), pp. 42–43.

32. Minutes of General Annual Licencing Meeting, Thursday 4th February, Greater Manchester Record office, M117/4/1/2/4.

33. L. Bradley, *Bass culture: when reggae was king* (London, 2001) p. 117. The Blue Spot was the top-shelf radiogram, a large, freestanding polished-wood unit imported from Germany. It was made by Blaupunkt, which translates to 'Blue point'.

34. Dorothy Jasper, interview transcript, 2011.

35. Dorothy Jasper, in De Mello, *Moss Side stories*, pp. 170–1.

36. Kenneth Williams, in De Mello, *Moss Side stories*, pp. 147–8.

37. Sydney Lewis, interview transcript, 2011.

38. Ibid.

39. Ibid.

40. Dorothy Jasper, interview transcript, 2011

41. Sydney Lewis, interview transcript, 2011.

42. Bradley, *Bass culture*, p. 115

43. Sydney Lewis, interview transcript, 2011.

44. Kenneth Williams, in De Mello, *Moss Side stories*, p. 148.

45. Dorothy Jasper, in De Mello, *Moss Side stories*, pp. 173–4.

46. Bradley, *Bass culture*, p. 115.

47. Lee, 'Popular music', p. 35.

48. Interview with Yvonne McCalla, Commonword, reproduced on the website of Manchester District Music Archive, http://79.170.40.161/mdmarchive.co.uk/archive/showartefact.php?aid=8397&uid=8&pageid=5 [accessed April 2012].

49. Soul Persian, in De Mello, *Moss Side stories*, pp. 177–8.

50. Bradley, *Bass culture*, p. 117.

51. Interview, *Roots oral history: rude awakening*, pp. ??

52. Soul Persian, in De Mello, *Moss Side stories*, p. 177.

53. D. Haslam, *Manchester, England* (London, 1999), p. 222.

54. Lee, 'Popular music', p. 34. See, also, Adrian Horn, *Jukebox Britain; Americanisation and youth culture 1945–60* (Manchester: Manchester, 2009).

55. Tosh Ryan, quoted in Lee, *Popular music*, p. 25.

56. S. Cohen, *Decline, renewal and the city in popular music culture: beyond the Beatles* (Farnham, 2007), p. 31.

57. Dorothy Jasper, in De Mello, *Moss Side stories*, p. 169.

58. Bradley, *Bass culture*, part 1: 'Boogie in my bones'.

59. Victor Brox, quoted in Lee, 'Popular music', p. 35. Fela Ransome Kuti (1938–1997, who changed his name to Fela Anikulapo Kuti in the late 1960s), was a Nigerian multi-instrumental musician, composer, pioneer of Afrobeat music and leader of the band Fela Ransome Kuti and Africa '70. In 1958 Kuti moved to London with the intention of studying medicine but decided to study music instead at the

Trinity College of Music. Much of his politics and lifestyle are controversial, but he influenced artists ranging from Jimmy Cliff to Talking Heads' David Byrne. Aldwyn Roberts [1922–2000], a calypso composer and performer born in Arima, Trinidad and Tobago, is best known as Lord Kitchener, a sobriquet derived from the British soldier of the First World War. He started his career as a calypsonian and was sometimes called just 'Kitchener' or 'Kitchie', by those who knew him well.

60. Bradley, *Bass culture*, p. 17.
61. Dorothy Jasper, in De Mello, *Moss Side stories*, p. 169.
62. Kenneth Williams, in De Mello, *Moss Side stories*, p. 146.
63. Dorothy Jasper, in De Mello, *Moss Side stories*, p. 169.
64. Dorothy Skinner, in De Mello, *Moss Side stories*, p. 141. Tab Hunter, an American actor, singer and author, starred in over forty Hollywood movies including the 1955 World War drama *Battle Cry*. Apart from the 'Red Sails in the Sunset', Hunter had other hit singles including the 1957 release '*Young Love*', which reached number 1 on the U.S. Billboard Hot 100 chart.
65. Record Shops, The Beat goes on … Manchester, http://www.manchesterbeat.com/shops/shops_record.php [accessed 21 March 2012].
66. Lee, 'Popular music', p. 35
67. Ibid, p. 29
68. Ibid, p. 35.
69. See, in particular, Dave Haslam, *Manchester*, Chapter 9, 'Hard Times and Bass lines: The Moss Side Story', which provides a whistle stop tour of the area and the influence it had on Manchester music and cultural life. Unfortunately, it feels as if this issue is rather tacked on, and the chapter fails to address the full significance of the black community and its impact on wider mainstream music culture.
70. Haslam, *Manchester*, p. 222.

Bob Dylan, Folk Music and Manchester   *CP Lee*

1. First published in 1998. A second and revised edition was published by Helter Skelter Publishing in 2004.
2. Georgina Boyes, *The imagined village* (Manchester, 1993).
3. Sharp has been, to say the least, a controversial scholar amongst students of the first revival. Michael Heaney's essay in the *Oxford dictionary of national biography* (Oxford, 2004), vol. 50, provides a thoughtful assessment, although was probably in press before the publication of C.J. Bearman, 'Cecil Sharp in Somerset: Some Reflections on the Work of David Harker', *Folklore* 113 (2002): 11 -34), a powerfully argued critique of Sharp's detractors.
4. The originator of this memorable line was probably the Scottish composer and writer Guy Warrack.
5. For more information on Jordan see liner notes on his album *Fred Jordan – Songs of A Shropshire farm worker* (Topic 12T150, first released, 1966)
6. Dave Harker, *Fakesong. The manufacturing of British 'folksong' 1700 to the present day* (Milton Keynes, 1985), pp. 231–53.
7. Michael Brocken, *The British folk revival, 1944–2002* (Aldershot, 2002), p. 37.
8. Colin Harper, *Dazzling stranger* (London, 2000), p. 26.
9. Ben Harker, *Class act. The cultural and political life of Ewan MacColl* (London, 2007).
10. Peter Cox, *Set into song – Ewan MacColl, Charles Parker, Peggy Seeger and the radio ballads* (London, 2008).
11. Brocken, *Folk revival*, p. 37.
12. Brocken, *Folk revival*, pp. 37–8.
13. 'Man of the people', BBC Radio 4 *Archive Hour*, broadcast 18 Nov. 2006. See http://mudcat.org/thread.cfm?threadid=96422#1885541.
14. *North West Labour History*, 26 (2001), p. 36.
15. Harper, *Dazzling stranger*, p. 11; Robin Denselow, *When the music's over* (London, 1989), p. 29.

16. Reprinted at http://www.edlis.org/twice/threads/open_letter_to_bob_dylan.html.
17. Ewan MacColl, 'Folk music: The singer and the audience', *Folk Music Magazine*, 1 (Nov. 1963), pp. 2, 3, 17.
18. CP Lee, *Like the night (revisited). Bob Dylan and the road to the Manchester Free Trade Hall* (London, 2004 edn), pp. 118–33.
19. Donovan was a Scottish singer-songwriter whose early hits such as 'Catch the wind'

(1965) led to his being labelled very much a Dylan imitator. His music did evolve beyond this.
20. Lee, *Like the night*, p. 159.
21. Lee, *Like the night*, pp. 169–78. Andy Kershaw and CP Lee's, 2000 *Ghost of electricity* was broadcast by BBC Radio 1 in 2000.
22. Brocken, *Folk Revival*, pp. 55–61, 146–216.

Audiences in punk and post-punk Manchester *Bob Dickinson*

1. Naomi Klein, *The shock doctrine* (London, 2007).
2. Jon Savage, *England's dreaming* (London, 1991), p. 298.
3. Dave Haslam, *Manchester England: the story of the pop cult city* (London, 1999), p. 117.
4. Kevin Cummins, *Manchester: Looking for the light through the pouring rain* (London, 2009), pp. 48–49.
5. Ibid, pp. 64–65.
6. Ibid, pp. 68–69.
7. Ibid, pp. 70–71.
8. *Shy Talk*, 2 (April 1977), p. 2.
9. Bob Dickinson, *Imprinting the sticks: the alternative press beyond London* (London, 1997), p. 145.
10. Linder Sterling and Jon Savage, *Secret public*, Manchester, New Hormones ORG 2.
11. Dickinson, *Imprinting the sticks*, p. 146.
12. Ibid, p. 147.
13. A full account of Rock Against Racism appears in David Widgery, *Beating time* (London, 1986).
14. Simon Reynolds, *Rip it up and start again: post punk 1978–84* (London, 2005), p. xxv.
15. *City Fun*, 2 (Nov. 1978), p. 8.
16. *New Manchester Review*, 92 (2–15 Nov. 1979), p. 15.
17. *City Fun*, 1 (Oct. 1978), p. 9.

18. Alan Wise, interviewed by Bob Dickinson, 19 Oct. 2012.
19. Jon Savage, *England's dreaming* (London, 1991), p. 406.
20. Reynolds, *Rip it up*, p. 442. Bill Sykes, *Sit down! Listen to this! The Roger Eagle story* (Manchester, 2012).
21. Elias Canetti, *Crowds and Power* (London, 1973), pp. 16–17.
22. ATV, 'The Image Has Cracked', Deptford Fun City, 1978, DLP01, Side 1, track 1.
23. *City Fun*, 'Downtown' column, 2 (Oct. 1981), p. 8. Edwards' recollection of the incident, in which he states, '... the crowd had started to invade the stage to try to pull me into the crowd to beat me up. It was getting very dangerous, on the verge of a riot', is included in the liner notes to the Gods Gift CD *Pathology*: Manchester 1979–84, Hyped2Death/Messthetics 218, 2009.
24. *City Fun*, 2 (July 1981).
25. Reynolds, *Rip it up*, p. 270.
26. Richard Schechner, *Performance theory* (London, 2003).
27. Josephine Machon, *(Syn)aesthetics: redefining visceral experience* (London, 2011), p. 24.
28. The distancing effect, also known as the alienation effect or estrangement effect are translations from Brecht's original German term, *verfremdungs effekt*.

'Closer from a distance': The auras of Factory Records in music, place, film, and historiography   *James McGrath*

1. Tosh Ryan, *Black Monday: The last days of FAC 251, the Factory Records office* (2012), Oz/IT/Dandelion DVD.
2. James Nice, *Shadowplayers: The rise and fall of Factory Records* (London, 2011), p. 36.
3. See Nice, *Shadowplayers*, chapters 1–3.
4. Mick Middles, 'Joy Division', 1978, http://www.rocksbackpages.com/article.html?ArticleID=10649.
5. New Order, *Play at home* (RPM/Channel 4, 1984). Christopher Gray (ed.), *Leaving the 20th Century: Incomplete work of the Situationist International* (London, 1998).
6. Howard Slater, *Factory Records scrapbook*, 1998, http://home.wxs.nl/~frankbri/slaterfac.html.
7. Walter Benjamin, *Illuminations* (London, 1999), p. 214–5.
8. Benjamin, *Illuminations*, p. 214.
9. Jon Savage, 'Joy Division: Unknown pleasures', *Melody Maker*, July 1979, www.rocksbackpages.com/article.html?ArticleID=1444. Max Bell, 'Joy Division: Unknown pleasures', *New Musical Express*, July 1979, www.rocksbackpages.com/article.html?ArticleID=17211.Therein, *NME*.
10. See Chris Rodley, *Factory: Manchester from Joy Division to Happy Mondays*, 21 September 2007, BBC4.
11. For the full catalogue list, see David Nolan, *You're entitled to an opinion: The high times and many lives of Tony Wilson, Factory Records and the Haçienda* (London, 2009), pp. 245–74.
12. Max Bell, 'It's Martin Hannett! A legend in his own town!! Didsbury', *NME*, 19 Jul 1980, pp. 6–7.
13. Matthew Robertson, *Factory Records: The complete graphic album* (London, 2007), p. 9.
14. See Guy Debord, *Beneath the paving stones … Situationists and the beach, May '68* (London, 2001).
15. Robertson, 2007, p. 29.
16. The Fall, 'Cash 'n' carry', *A part of America. Therein*. Rough Trade, 1982.
17. 'IKON/FCL', *NME*, 21 Aug. 1982, p. 27.
18. Joy Division, *Here are the young men*, IKON/FCL, 1982. See http://www.youtube.com/watch?v=NtkaaAT3JcA.
19. Benjamin, *Illuminations*, p. 217.
20. Nice, *Shadowplayers*, p. 238.
21. Mick Middles, *Factory: The story of the record label* (London, 2009), p. 170, pp. 383–4
22. Tony Wilson, *24 hour party people* (London, 2002), p. 119. Compare with Gray, *Leaving the 20th Century*, pp. 15–18.
23. Audible at http://www.youtube.com/watch?v=A-T2a0OE9cA.
24. Amrik Rai, 'Fac51: The Haçienda', *NME*, 29 May 1982, pp. 50–51.
25. See Peter Hook, *The Haçienda: How not to run a club* (London, 2009).
26. 'The Haçienda Club and Dry 201: A sponsorship opportunity' (9 Mar 1995). Factory Communications Ltd Archive, Manchester Museum of Science and Industry, 1999, 16, Box 32.
27. See former Haçienda DJ Greg Wilson's comments to journalist Jon Robb. http://www.gregwilson.co.uk/2012/05/the-hacienda-30-years-on/.
28. 'Stark raving Madchester', *Newsweek*, 22 Jul 1990. http://magazine-directory.com/Newsweek.htm.
29. 'Pillars of the establishment', *NME*, 4 Aug. 1990, p. 24–5.
30. Nolan, *Entitled to an opinion*, p. 158.
31. Gray, *Leaving the 20thCentury*, p. 16.
32. Benjamin, *Illuminations*, p. 218–9.
33. Available as a DVD extra on Anton Corbijn, *Control* (Momentum, 2008).
34. Saul Austerlitz, *Money for nothing* (London, 2007), p. 74.
35. 'Joy Division to be canonised – official', *NME*, 22 Mar 1980, p. 15.
36. *NME*, 22 Mar 1980, p. 15.
37. *Wired: Joy Division*, Channel 4, 1 July 1988.
38. Ibid.
39. Nice, *Shadowplayers*, p. 1.

40. CP Lee, *Shake, rattle and rain: Popular music making in Manchester, 1955–1995* (Ottery St. Mary 2002), pp. 154–5.

41. See Nolan, *Entitled to an opinion*, pp. 163–66.

42. Wilson, *24 hour*, p. 150–51.

43. Nolan, *Entitled*, p. 91; Nice, Shadowplayers, p. 210.

44. http://www.lexisnexis.com/uk/nexis/.

45. See http://www.musicweek.com/news/read/large-crowd-for-bbc-ian-curtis-tribute/033957.

46. A transcript of the press conference is available via Cerysmaticfactory, a highly-recommended Factory website http://www.cerysmaticfactory.info/ian_curtis_movie_press_conference_050117.html.

47. On Half-Man, Half-Biscuit, *Achtung Bono*, Probe Plus, 2005.

48. David Ward, 'Soundtrack of a generation plays out final farewell to Mr Manchester', *The Guardian*, 21 Aug. 2007 http://www.guardian.co.uk/media/2007/aug/21/musicnews.music.

49. Colin Sharp, *Who killed Martin Hannett?* (London, 2007), p. 97). See also Savage's 1988 interview with Hannett, the fullest transcript of which appears in the notes of the Hannett-production compilation CD *And here is the young man* (Debutante, 1998).

50. Mark Watson (ed)., *An ideal for living: An history of Joy Division* (London, 1984).

51. Benjamin, *Illuminations*, p. 231.

52. Olivia Ford, *Martin Hannett documentary* (2012) https://soundcloud.com/oliviasinterviews/martin-hannett-documentary.

53. See Rob Gretton, *1 Top class manager* (Manchester, 2008), p. 52.

54. David Nolan, *Bernard Sumner: Confusion – Joy Division, Electronic and New Order versus the world* (London, 2007).

55. Bernard Sumner's eloquent autobiography, *Chapter and verse –New Order, Joy Division and Me*, was published by Transworld Publishers in 2014.

56. Nice, *Shadowplayers*, p. 495.

57. Lindsay Reade, *Mr Manchester and the factory girl: The story of Tony and Lindsay Wilson* (London, 2010), pp. 126–7.

58. See Liz Naylor, 'Must the Haçienda be built?' in Ros Crone (ed.) *New perspectives in British cultural history* (Newcastle, 2007), pp. 255–65.

59. Constantine Verevis, 'Disorder: Joy Division', *Studies in Documentary Film*, 2 (2009), pp. 234–46.

60. Mitzi Waltz and Martin James, 'The (re) marketing of disability in pop: Ian Curtis and Joy Division', *Popular Music*, 28 (2009), pp. 367–80.

61. Noel McLaughlin, 'Rattling out of control: A comparison of U2 and Joy Division on film', *Film, fashion & consumption*, 1 (2011), pp. 101–20.

62. Richard Witts, 'Building up a band: Music for a second city' in Michael Goddard and Benjamin Halligan (eds), *Mark E. Smith and the Fall: Art, music and politics* (Farnham, 2010), pp. 19–32.

63. Max Bell, 'The emaciated line between art and ambience', *NME*, 2 Feb. 1980, p. 8.

64. Middles, *Factory*, p. 283–4.

65. Benjamin, *Illuminations*, p. 224.

Madchester and the representations of the North-South divide in the 1980s and 1990s   *Georgina Gregory*

1. Not all music under the 'Madchester' umbrella conformed to this template. There were other artists such as MC Tunes whose work featured rap and hip hop influences.

2. Helen Jewell, *The North-South divide: The origins of northern consciousness in England* (Manchester, 1994), p. 28.

3. Tom McArthur 'The superior, inferior and barbarous Britains', *English Today*, April 1985, p. 24.

4. Dave Russell, *Looking North: northern England and the national imagination* (Manchester, 2004), p. 3.

5. Katie Wales, 'North and South: an English linguistic divide?' *English Today*, 16 (2000), pp. 4–15.

6. Donald Read, *Peterloo: the massacre and its background* (Manchester, 1958), p. 6.

7. Frank Musgrove, *The north of England: A history from Roman times to the present* (Oxford, 1990), p. 262; Martin Pugh, *We danced all night: a social History of Britain between the wars* (London, 2009), p. 418.

8. Tertius Chandler and Gerald Fox, *3000 years of urban growth* (New York and London, 1974), p. 322.

9. M. Jones, 'The economic history of the regional problem in Britain, 1920–38', *Journal of Historical Geography*, 10 (1984), p. 388.

10. See NHS report: http://www.nhs. uk/news/2012/11November/Pages/ North-South-divide-in-heart-disease-deaths.aspx.

11. Wales, 'North and South', p. 5.

12. George Orwell, *The road to Wigan Pier* (London, 1937), p. 26.

13. Katie Wales, *Northern English: A social and cultural history* (Cambridge, 2006), quoted in Joan Beal, *English in modern times* (London, 2004), p. 118.

14. J.K. Chambers and Peter Trudgill, *Dialectology* (London, 1980), p. 3.

15. Tim Wall, *Studying Popular Music Culture* (London, 2003).

16. Alan Durant, 'Representing Culture,' *British Studies Now* (London, 1984), pp. 3–5.

17. Paul Gilroy, *There ain't no black in the Union Jack: the cultural politics of race and nation* (London, 2002); Anthony Marks, 'Young, gifted and black: Afro-American and Afro-Caribbean music in Britain 1963–88', in Paul Oliver (ed.) *Black music in Britain: essays on the Afro-Asian contribution to popular music* (Buckingham, 1990); Keith Negus, *Popular music in theory: an introduction* (Oxford, 1996).

18. Ruth Finnegan, *The hidden musicians: music-making in an English town* (Cambridge, 1989); Sara Cohen, *Rock culture in Liverpool: popular music in the making* (Oxford, 1991); Keith Halfacree and Rob Kitchin, '"Madchester rave on": placing the fragments of popular music', *Area* 28 (1996), pp. 47–55.

19. Bill Osgerby, *Youth in Britain* (London, 1998), p. 170.

20. Michael Ray (ed.), *Popular music through the decades: disco, punk, new wave, heavy metal and more* (New York, 2013), p. 42 and p. 163.

21. John Shepherd and Peter Wicke, *Music and cultural theory*, Cambridge, 1997), p. 199.

22. Richard Harrison and Mark Hart) *Spatial policy in a divided nation (regions, cities and public policy)* (London, 1993), p. 44.

23. 'Manchester in modern times: the Second World War & after', http:// www.manchester2002-uk.com/history/ modern/20thcent-2.html.

24. Val Stevens, 'Youth Unemployment – Now and the 1980s' (posted 12 January, 2012) http://manches-teryounglabour.co.uk/2012/01/ youth-unemployment-now-and-the-1980s/.

25. Ron Martin, 'The political economy of Britain's North-South Divide', *Transactions of the Institute of British Geographers*, 13 (1988), p. 390; Michael Wild 'On your bike', 2007, http://news.bbc.co.uk/1/hi/ programmes/politics_show/6660723.stm> [accessed 5 November 2012]; Peter Taylor, 'The meaning of the North: England's "foreign country" within?', *Political Geography*, 12 (1993), p. 143.

26. Stuart Borthwick and Ron Moy, *Popular music genres* (Edinburgh, 2004), p. 124.

27. Frank Mort, *Cultures of consumption: masculinities and social space in late twentieth century* (London, 1996); Sean Nixon, *Hard looks: masculinities, specta-torship and contemporary consumption* (Basingstoke, 1996).

28. 'I Don't Like Mondays' was a song recorded by Irish group, The Boomtown Rats, in 1979. It draws on the Western aversion to the start of the working week.

29. Ted Kessler (ed.), *Madchester: original reviews, interviews & photos from the archives of NME* (London, 2003), p. 8.

30. Mick Middles, *Breaking into heaven: the rise and fall of the Stone Roses* (London, 2000), p. 91.

31. Jenny Kitzinger, 'Media templates: patterns of association and the (re)construction of meaning over time', *Media, Culture & Society*, 22 (2000), pp. 61–84.

32. Luke Bainbridge, 'Madchester remembered: "There was amazing creative energy at the time"', *The Observer*, 21 April 2012 http://www.guardian.co.uk/music/2012/apr/21/madchester-manchester-interviews-hook-ryder [accessed 20 October 2012].

33. Miranda Sawyer, 'How Madchester put the E into enterprise zone', *The Observer*, 21 April 2012, http://www.guardian.co.uk/music/2012/apr/21/madchester-manchester-stone-roses [accessed 20 October 2012].

34. Anne Louse Kershaw, 'Mr Dave Haslam discusses "Madchester"', *Manchester's Finest*, 23 August 2012, http://www.manchestersfinest.com/category/articles/ [accessed 20 October 2012].

35. Nick Kent, 'The Stone Roses and The Happy Mondays', *The Face*, January 1990, www.rocksbackpages.com/article.html?Article1D=11057 [accessed 12 November 2012].

36. Nathan Wiseman-Trowse, *Performing class in British popular music* (Basingstoke, 2006), p. 162.

37. Central Station Design was the design company which created artwork for The Happy Mondays, Northside and James. See: 'Hello playmates', *NME*, article No 17, November 1990, http://cerysmaticfactory.info/central_station_design.html.

38. Mandi James, 'Central Station Design: south central reign', *New Musical Express*, 17 November 1990. Carroll was Shaun Ryder's cousin and created the group's graphic identity and many of the signifiers associated with Madchester.

39. John Robb, 'The Stone Roses: trunk call – romancing the stone', *Sounds*, 27 January 1988, www.rocksbackpages.com/article.html?Article1D=18695 [accessed 10 November 2012].

40. Kent, 'The Stone Roses'.

41. Katie Wales, *Northern English: a social and cultural history* (Cambridge, 2006), p. 20.

42. Kent, 'The Stone Roses'.

43. Michael White, 'Prescott's survival hopes recede as MPs speak out', *The Guardian*, 30 May 2006, http://politics.guardian.co.uk/labour/story/0,,1785526,00.html [accessed 20 May 2010].

44. *The Face*, July 1990.

45. Affleck's Palace is a shopping emporium situated in the Northern Quarter of Manchester. It houses a collection of independent shops, stalls and boutiques selling fashion, music and accessories.

46. Bainbridge, 'Madchester remembered'.

47. Robert Sandall, 'A music scene to stir the soul', *The Sunday Times*, 11 February 1990.

48. Dick Hebdige, *Subculture: the meaning of style* (London, 1979).

49. Emile Durkheim, *The division of labour in society* (New York, 1984).

50. Steve Redhead, *Rave off: politics and deviancy in contemporary youth culture* (Aldershot, 1993), p. 4.

The Manchester Lesbian and Gay Chorus: Manchester, the Gay Village, and local music-making practices   *Esperanza Miyake*

1. After Susan McClary's seminal *Feminine endings* (Minneapolis, 1991), feminist anthologies on music and gender and/or sexuality followed: Leslie C. Dunn and Nancy A. Jones (eds), *Embodied voices: representing female vocality in western culture* (Cambridge, 1994); Susan C. Cook and Judy S. Tsou (eds), *Cecilia reclaimed: feminist perspectives on gender and music* (Chicago, 1994); Susan J. Leonardi and Rebecca A. Pope (eds), *The diva's mouth: body, voice, prima donna politics* (New Brunswick, N.J., 1996); Elaine Barkin and Lydia Hammessley (eds), *Audible traces: gender, identity and music* (Zurich, 1999).

2. Following feminist music scholarship, queer musicology emerged as a field consisting largely of musicologists who extended the lines of feminist enquiry into music to include issues of sexuality,

sexual identity, and queer politics alongside gender. For example, Ruth Solie (ed.), *Musicology and difference, gender and sexuality in music scholarship* (Berkeley, 1993); Phillip Brett, Elizabeth Wood, Gary Thomas (eds), *Queering the pitch: the new gay and lesbian musicology* (New York, 1994).

3. Peter Webb, 'Interrogating the production of sound and place: the Bristol phenomenon, from Lunatic Fringe to Worldwide Massive', in Sheila Whiteley, Andy Bennett, and Stan Hawkins (eds), *Music, space and place* (Aldershot, 2004); Simon Frith, *Performing rites: evaluating popular music* (Oxford, 1998); Sheila Whiteley, *Women and popular music: sexuality, identity, and subjectivity* (New York, 2000), and ed., *Sexing the groove: popular music and gender* (London, 1997); Thomas Swiss, John Sloop, and Andrew Herman (eds), *Mapping the beat: popular music and contemporary theory* (Oxford, 1998); Will Straw, 'Seizing up the record collections: gender and connoisseurship in rock music culture', in S. Whiteley (ed.), *Sexing the groove*, pp. 3–16, and 'Communities and scenes in popular music', published in 1991 and reprinted in Ken Gelder and Sarah Thornton (eds), *Subcultures reader* (London, 1997), pp. 494–505.

4. Angela McRobbie, *In the culture society: art, fashion, and popular music* (New York, 1999); Ben Malbon, *Clubbing: dancing, ecstasy and vitality* (London, 1999); M. Bayton, 'Women and the electric guitar', in Sheila Whiteley (ed.), *Sexing the groove*, pp. 37–49.

5. During the 1990s, the philosophy and politics behind queer activism (such as that associated the New York-based Queer Nation) used 'a performative politics that associated identity less with interiority than with the public spectacle of consumer culture'. Rosemary Hennessy, *Profit and pleasure: sexual identities in late capitalism* (New York, 2000), p. 127.

6. The term, 'coming out' refers to the process where a member of the LGBT community reveals their sexual identity, whether it is to family members, friends, or at work. Because of the prosecution against and stigma surrounding homosexuality, 'coming out' is often considered as a political and personal process relating to being 'proud' and not ashamed of one's sexual identity.

7. Pride' is a British term for 'Mardi Gras' (San Francisco, New York, Sydney all hold famous Mardi Gras events are festivals that celebrate gay pride). Depending on the size of the city and how active the LGBT community are, Pride/Mardi Gras events can be anything from a single parade to a week-long event. Manchester's Pride events are one of the biggest and longest with the UK.

8. I shall discuss Manto in further depth later, but its importance to the LGBT community in Manchester should be noted here as it was the first openly visible 'gay bar' to have established itself in the Village in 1990.

9. George Chauncey, *Gay New York: gender, urban culture, and the making of the gay male world, 1890–1940* (New York, 1994).

10. Source: John Atkin, contact for the *Manchester Lesbian and Gay History Trail*, a local walking tour for the LGBT community about local LGBT history.

11. Michael. P. Brown, *Closet space* (London, 2000) and Dennis Altman, *Global sex* (Chicago, 2001), explore spatial demarcations of queer communities in relation to political activism, and their global replication. In Manchester, this model has been adopted both in name and culture: 'The Gay Village' being a direct reference to New York's gay area. See also a collection of essays on spatiality and sexuality in David Bell and Gill Valentine (eds), *Mapping desire: geographies of sexualities* (London, 1995).

12. CP Lee, *Shake, rattle and rain: popular music making in Manchester 1950–1995* (Ottery St. Mary, 2002), p. 2.

13. Despite the eventual closure of the Hacienda in 1997, both Factory Records and the Hacienda became and remain

as one of the most famous independent labels and clubs in the world. See: http://www.prideofmanchester.com/music/hacienda.htm, http://www.manchester.com/music/features/hacienda.php; and refer to the film about the Hacienda and Factory Records, *24 hrs Party People* (Michael Winterbottom, 2002) http://www.partypeoplemovie.com>.

14. Lee, *Shake, rattle and rain*, p. 2.

15. Jaap Kooijman, 'Turn the beat around: Richard Dyer's '"In defence of disco" revisited' in, *European Journal of Cultural Studies*, 8 (2005), pp. 257–266; Jonathan Bollen, 'Sexing the dance at sleaze ball 1994' in, *The Drama Review*, 40 (1996), pp. 166–191; Richard Dyer, 'In defence of disco' *Gay Left Issue*, 8 (1979), pp. 20–23.

16. Jeffrey Weeks, *Coming out: homosexual politics in Britain from the nineteenth century to the present* (London, 1990), p. 323.

17. David Bell and Jon Binnie, *Sexual citizen: queer politics and beyond* (Cambridge, 2000), p. 87.

18. Sara Cohen, 'Identity, Place, and the "Liverpool Sound"' in, Martin Stokes (ed.), *Ethnicity, identity, and music: the musical construction of place* (Oxford, 1994), p. 133.

19. See more in Alman, *Global sex*.

20. For more on the cultural politics of 'coming out', Diana Fuss 'Introduction' in, Diana Fuss (ed.), *Inside/out: lesbian theories, gay theories* (New York, 1991), p. 4.

21. For more on 'subcultural capital', Sarah Thornton's *Club culture: music, media, and subcultural capital* (Hanover, 1996), p. 203.

22. Refer to Paul Hindle, 'The influence of the Gay Village on migration to central Manchester' in, *Northwest Geography*, 1 (2001), pp. 54–60.

23. Dereka Rushbrook, 'Cities, queer space, and the cosmopolitan tourist', in *GLQ*, 8 (2002), p. 198.

24. Alternative events along the lines of 'Gay Shame' in the US led by students, women of colour, and 'others who don't fit' are now emerging in Manchester as an antidote to Pride: an example being *Kaffequeeria* who organize counter-Pride events 'to poke the

gay conscience with our knitting needles' http://www.kaffequeeria.org.uk. Bell and Binnie, *Sexual citizen*, p. 116.

25. BBC News Website described *QueerUpNorth* as, 'Featuring a staggering array of queer stars, be them local, national, or international, the festival has highlights a-plenty and something for every taste' (2 May 2006).

26. Phillip E. Wegner, *Imaginary communities: utopia, the nation, and the spatial histories of modernity* (Berkeley, 2002); Edward W. Soja, *Thirdspace: journeys to Los Angeles and other real-and-imagined places* (Cambridge, 1996); Benedict Anderson, *Imagined communities: reflections on the origin and spread of nationalism* (London, 1991).

27. I am using the term *queer* to reflect the LGBT community's own transformation during the 1990s, a culture which adopted a politics of consumerism. The city of course had a large part to play in the growth of the 'pink pound'. http://www.visitmanchester.com [updated June 2006]. The BBC have discontinued this page, however they can be found on their archives. For more information, go to: http://www.bbc.co.uk/search/localarchive/manchester#.

28. *CloneZone* is a gay chain store selling everything from show tickets, greeting cards, clubwear and sex toys. It even offer a sauna/tanning service.

29. Jassbir Puar, 'Circuits of queer mobility: tourism, travel and globalization', in *GLQ*, 8 (2002), pp. 101–137; D. Rushbrook, 'Cities, queer space, and the cosmopolitan tourist', in *GLQ*, 8 (2002), pp. 183–206; R. Hennessy, *Profit and pleasure: sexual identities in late capitalism* (New York, 2000); J. Binnie, *The globalization of sexuality* (London, 2004); K. Weston, 'Get thee to a big city: sexual imaginary and the great gay migration', in *GLQ*, 2 (1995).

30. Puar, 'Circuits of queer mobility', p. 104.

31. A UK chart hit (1965) by Sam Cooke.

32. Jed, who became chair in 2005.

33. The former was a UK/US chart hit (1964) written by Tony Hatch and performed

by Petula Clark, the latter, a popular jazz song written by Duke Ellington, Don George, Johnny Hodges, and Harry James (1944).

34. MLGC, minutes from the repertoire meeting, Oct 2005.

35. Frith, *Performing rites*, p. 73.

36. Ken Plummer, 'Symbolic interactionism and the forms of homosexuality' in, Steven Seidman (ed.), *Queer theory/sociology* (Massachusetts, 1996), p. 78.

37. Arlene Stein, 'Crossover dreams: lesbianism and popular music since the 1970s' in, Corey K. Creekmuir and Alexander Doty (eds), *Out in culture: gay, lesbian, and queer essays on popular culture* (Durham, 1995), p. 416.

38. Ibid.

Digging (out) the beat: sources and resources for the study of popular music in the Manchester region   *Dave Russell*

1. This section refers to *physical* archives. *Virtual* ones are dealt with later.

2. Postgraduate theses are not dealt with in this survey, but it should be noted that these collections have supported such work. Phil Eva's, 1996 Manchester University doctoral thesis, 'Popular song and social identity in Victorian Manchester' (unpublished PhD thesis, University of Manchester, 1996) was heavily rooted in the Pearson Collection and Michael Rowland, 'Popular working-class song in industrial Lancashire *c.* 1832–1862 (Unpublished MPhil thesis, University of Central Lancashire, 2007) made much use of Harkness.

3. http://www.nationalarchives.gov.uk/a2a/.

4. http://libweb.lancs.ac.uk/hylton/.

5. http://www.mosi.org.uk/collections.aspx.

6. I am grateful to James McGrath for this reference.

7. Neither, however, is represented by a complete run and the binding policy adopted with *City Life* means that at certain times, it is hard to date the paper.

8. http://www.nwsoundarchive.co.uk/.

9. http://www.manchestermusictours.com.

10. Tara Brabazon and Stephen Mallinder, 'Popping the museum: the cases of Sheffield and Preston', *Museums and Society*, 4 (2006), pp. 96–112.

11. Other useful sites obviously exist but were not approached. Lanky Beat, http://www.lankybeat.com/ is another well sourced site with a strong 1960s focus.

12. http://www.mdmarchive.co.uk/. I am extremely grateful to Abigail Ward and Mat Norman for their help with the provision of illustrations from the Archive for this collection.

13. http://www.manchesterbeat.com/.

14. MacColl's own autobiography, *Journeyman* (London, 1990) is a valuable source on wider aspects of local and regional left-wing politics and culture.

15. See James McGrath's article in this collection for a more detailed historiography and for commentary on the narratives that have grown up around Factory.

Long Reviews

Ann Brooks
A Veritable Eden – The Manchester Botanic Garden, a History (Oxford, 2011) £25.

The plant kingdom globally contains an estimated diversity of 350,000 species. In the UK we can boast only some 1500 native species, a legacy of both our status as a collection of modestly sized, temperate zone islands, and the effect of the last ice age which scoured much of the land surface of its previously established flora. A depauperate flora, combined with plant envy of the botanical riches of other countries, may be one reason why British botanic gardens have been important in cataloguing and describing the world's plant diversity, and in augmenting that flora by cramming our gardens with exotic specimens from overseas.

This long history of plant study and horticulture can be traced back to at least the mid seventeenth century, with the founding of what was to become Oxford Botanic Garden. Since that time, Britain's botanic gardens have played a significant role in the economic development of both the country and its former Empire, and continue to be important in science and education, and in the leisure and recreation of the British people.

Previous work on the history of botanic gardens in Europe has tended to concentrate on the large metropolitan botanic gardens, particularly Kew, with their star botanists and international networks of contacts and collectors* (e.g. Brockway 1979, Endersby 2010, Ollerton et al. 2012). The smaller provincial botanic gardens, in contrast, have been rather neglected by historians, despite the fact that almost every large British city possessed one, and that they have been an important part of local leisure

and education. This is a tradition that stretches from the early nineteenth century and continues through to the more recent founding of the Eden Project and the National Botanic Garden of Wales.

The history and current utility of such spaces is, as their study reveals, a story that extends far beyond the horticultural and botanical realms, into social, political and economic history. In *A Veritable Eden* Ann Brooks introduces us to the "chequered history including national fame and financial disaster" of Manchester Botanic Garden, which existed from 1831 to 1908. This meticulously researched book explores not only the role of the Garden in local social life, but also the local political intrigues, personality clashes and mismanagement that ultimately doomed the garden. This is exemplified in the way that an un-Victorian attitude to financial prudence (commissioning ambitious building works when finances were in poor shape) collided with a very Victorian snobbery: by refusing to allow the paying general public entry to the Garden more one afternoon a week, a funding stream that may have saved the Garden was effectively curtailed. To paraphrase the author, exclusivity was more important than income.

This was not the only policy that appears inexplicable to the modern reader. Early in its history the subscribing, largely middle class membership of the Garden made it clear that pleasurable perambulations around the site were all that they were interested in, and any pretence to education went when "in 1848 science was eliminated and the horticultural garden...was dismantled". In this regard it was undoubtedly the people of Manchester, rather than botanical science per se, who were the principle losers, as the large botanic gardens of European capital cities dominated plant exploration and plant science up to the present day. Nonetheless the policy jars with Victorian notions of self-improvement.

---

* For example Brockway, L.H., *Science and Colonial Expansion: The Role of the British Royal Botanic Garden* (Yale University Press 1979); Endersby, J., *Imperial Nature: Joseph Hooker and the Practices of Victorian Science* (University of Chicago Press 2010); Ollerton, J., Chancellor, G. and van Wyhe, J., 'John Tweedie and Charles Darwin in Buenos Aires', *Notes and Records of the Royal Society* 66, 2012, pp. 115–24.

A Veritable Eden originated as Dr Brooks' PhD thesis and in general it is engagingly written, demonstrating the author's fascination for her subject, and well-illustrated from material from her personal collection and elsewhere. But there are some places where a firmer editorial hand would have made for a better book. It is clear that a few small sections have been replicated from the thesis out of context, for example a paragraph about the role of a "putter-out" on pp. 60–61. On p. 91, to give another example, we read that a Garden report concluded that "the Curator should be charged with 'gross ignorance and mismanagement' and that he should be replaced"; this is repeated, only three lines later, as "a charge of 'gross ignorance and mismanagement' should be brought against [the Curator]". Finally, to anyone with a botanical, as opposed to historical, training the misspelling and misrendering of scientific names for some plants will jar, such as "Dickensonia" for Dicksonia and "Victoria Regia" for Victoria regia (itself an old synonym, the plant is now called Victoria amazonica).

Such editorial oversights detract only a little the telling of the story of Manchester Botanic Garden and could easily be rectified if the book goes to a second edition. Which I hope it does; it's a great contribution both to the local history of the city and to our understanding of the history of provincial botanic gardens.

Professor Jeff Ollerton
Department of Environmental and
Geographical Sciences,
University of Northampton

Short Reviews

Edited by Chris Makepeace

Withington Civic Society, *A walk through the history of Withington* (Withington. 2014). 20pp. Illus. Map. Bibliog. No price given.

Many people pass through Withington on their way to and from work, but how many consider that this former village, stretching along the main road between Manchester and Didsbury has its own history. This guide to Withington is designed to encourage people to walk through the area and discover those buildings and sites that have played a part in the area's history. Each entry has a short account of its importance and in some cases illustrated with a photograph. There is also a map enables the reader to start their walk anywhere in Withington. This is an important contribution to the literature on Withington which should encourage residents and visitors to discover a little about the history and features of Withington.

Miller, I., *Coal, cotton and chemicals: the industrial archaeology of Clayton* (Lancaster, 2013). 49pp. Illus. Maps. Diags. Bibliog. £5. ISBN 978 1 907686 14 6

For many people, Clayton means Clayton Hall and, for many years, the existence of an important chemical works. However, the district has a much more varied industrial history which this publication points out. It was not only chemicals that gave the areas its importance, but also coal mining and textile production. This well-illustrated booklet examines the industrial past of this part of east Manchester using as its basis a series of excavations undertaken in the area between 2010 and 2012. It has brought to the attention of the public the areas rich industrial heritage and adds another chapter to the history of the development of Clayton as well as to Manchester's industrial heritage.

Nevell, M. and George, D., *A guide to the industrial archaeology of Cheshire* (Coalbrookdale, 2014). 76pp. Illus. Map. Bibliog. No price given. ISBN 978 0 9560215 3 5

Prepared for the AIA's annual conference held at Chester University in September 2014, the contents relate only to the modern Cheshire and does not include those areas which became part of Greater Manchester or Merseyside in 1974. The publication consists of a brief introduction about Cheshire's industrial heritage before drawing attention to the various industrial remains that exist in the county, each entry being accompanied by a short description and a grid reference to enable the reader to find the location. Many of the entries are accompanied by colour photographs. This will be a useful guide to those interested in Cheshire's industrial part and a worthy companion to the volumes on Greater Manchester and Lancashire that were published for previous conferences.

Oliver, R.W.A. and Carrier, M., *The library of John Dalton* (Salford. 2006). 37p. Illus. Bibliog. £6. ISBN 1905732104

According to the introduction, it was believed that John Dalton did not have a private library, but this has been proved not to be the case. In 2003, a copy of an auctioneer's catalogue revealed the sale of Dalton's private possessions including his library. As a result, it has been possible to produce a list of the books he possessed although it has not been possible to identify a number of lots at the sale. The books are divided by subject so it is possible to discover what books he had on subjects like chemistry, travel, poetry or religion. There are also short sections examining the periodicals he possessed as well as the items on chemistry. This booklet is an important contribution to the information available on Dalton and the type of material a prominent scientist might have possessed in the early nineteenth century.

Leitch, D., *The Towers Estate and its place in the making of Manchester 1800–2014* (Didsbury. The Author. 3rd edn). 32pp. Illus. Map. Bibliog. £2.50

There are many buildings in Manchester that have played a significant role in the city's history, one of which is the Towers in Didsbury where the meeting was held in June 1882 that ultimately resulted in the construction of the Manchester Ship Canal. This well-illustrated booklet traces the history of the Towers and a property named "Scotscroft", some of the land from which was later added to that of the Towers. Leitch outlines the events leading up to the meeting in 1882 as well as provided a brief account of the life and work of Daniel Adamson. The history of the building did not end with Adamson's death as the author then traces the modern development of the site and building. This publication will be a useful addition to the literature on Didsbury and its buildings.

Hyton, S., *The Little Book of Manchester* (Stroud, 2013). 190pp. Illus. £9.99. ISBN 978 0 7524 7947 7

This book comprises of a series of short facts about Manchester and its history arranged by subject such as "Law and disorder", "Prominent buildings", "Made in Manchester" and "Dirty old town". The contents are similar to those that might appear in a series of newspaper articles on the history of the city similar to those that appeared in the "Manchester City News" at the end of the nineteenth and early in the twentieth centuries under the heading "Notes and Queries" or in "Palatine Notebook". In some respects, it encourages the reader to investigate further to discover more about the subject. This is a useful publication for those who want to discover some of the interesting things about Manchester in the past.

Phythian, G., *Manchester at war 1939–45: the people's story* (Stroud, 2014). 160pp. Illus. Bibliog. £12.99. ISBN 978 0 7524 9102 8

In recent decades, there has been a trend to look at events not only through official reports and newspapers reports, but also through the eyes of those who experienced the event first hand. This is especially the case with World War II where the experiences of those who lived through it, especially the Blitz, have been recorded, providing a more human side to these traumatic events. In this book, Phythian has made use of oral history as well as written accounts such as diaries, to record the experiences of Mancunians during the World War II in Manchester. The information these extracts provides additional information and adds a human touch to the events that would otherwise be lacking. It is unfortunate that the bibliography is not as comprehensive as it might have been with several important works on Manchester in this period omitted. Apart from this, the publication of these interviews and accounts is a valuable contribution to Manchester's history at this time.

Warrender, K., *Bollin Valley: from Macclesfield to the Ship Canal* (Timperley. 2013). 208pp. Illus. Map. Bibliog. £15.95. ISBN 978 0 946361 45 8

Rising in the foothills of the Pennines, the River Bollin wends its way from the Macclesfield Forest to join the River Mersey near Warburton. On its way, it passes through towns, villages, and open country. This book takes the reader on an illustrated walk along the Bollin valley, drawing attention to the many interesting features that can be found there with short accounts of the history of interesting buildings and sites, some of which are no longer extant. The book is lavishly illustrated with coloured photographs of the buildings and sites referred to as well as architectural detail that might otherwise be overlooked. Although some might regard this as a "coffee table" book, it is one which can be used by readers and others to plan an interesting and enjoyable day, either in the country or visiting sites of historic interest.

Hewitt, E.J., *Capital of Discontent: Protest and crime in Manchester's Industrial Revolution* (Stroud. 2014). 167pp. Illus. £12.99. ISBN 978 0 7524 9963 5

This publication looks at Manchester at a time when things were changing very rapidly in the nineteenth century, when people were flooding into the town to find employment, some of whom became involved with demands for change whilst others became involved in criminal activities. The author includes events such as Peterloo, Chartism, the Anti-corn Law League as well as information on the development of Manchester's police force, information on crimes and criminals as well as on punishments inflicted on those found guilty. This publication will be a useful addition to the literature available on nineteenth century Manchester and although there is no bibliography, there are footnotes at the end of each chapter that can be used by those wanting to further investigate the subject.

Rothman, B., *et al*, *The Battle for Kinder Scout including the 1932 Mass Trespass* (Timperley, 2012). 98pp. Illus. Bibliog. Map. £9.95. ISBN 978 0 946361 44 1

Today we take access to the Peak District and the moors around Kinder Scout as a "right", but this was not the case 80 years ago when a group of ramblers from Manchester and Sheffield set out to try and establish the right of working people to have access to the area. This book traces the story of the Kinder Trespass on 1932, an event that has gone down as part of the area's heritage, and what happened afterwards. Rothman's account has been supplemented by material provided by those who have researched the subject in more recent times including an account by the son of one of the gamekeepers involved which provides a different point of view ton the event. This is a well-illustrated and includes copies of reports from newspapers of the trespass itself and the ensuring trials that were held. This book should be read by all those who take the freedom to walk or enjoy the Peak District for granted and a tribute to those who fought for this access as well as

those who were protecting the interests of the landowners.

Hearle, A., *Marple and Mellor: a new history*, Marple Local History Society (Marple, 2012). 68pp. Illus. Maps. Bibliog. £12.50. ISBN 978 0 9540582 2 7

Since the first modern history of Marple was published in 1973 and reprinted with revisions in 1993, research has continued with fresh material becoming available. This new history of Marple is not a revamping of the earlier publication, but a complete rewriting of it incorporating the results of the latest research. Much of the book concentrates on the period from the late eighteenth century when industry began to make its appearance in the area and Marple began its development from a small village into a self-governing area, a status that it retained until 1974 when it was absorbed by Stockport. Although the early history of the area is covered chronologically, as life became more complicated, so the author has adopted a subject approach, bringing together similar subjects. For example in the chapter entitled "Changing surroundings" she included changes in transport, the arrival of gas and electricity, postal services and sanitation, making it easier for the reader to consult those topics in which they are interested. The book is well illustrated and is an important addition to the literature on Marple and Mellor which should be read by all those living in the area.

Hearle, A., *Brabyns Hall and Park*, Marple Local History Society (Marple, 2013). 36pp. Illus. Map. £3. ISBN 978 0 9540582 4 1

This booklet traces the history of one of Marple's most important open spaces, Brabyns Park, close to Marple Bridge and Marple Station. The author has traced the lives of those who owned and lived in the hall and has used a wide range of sources to provide an interesting account of the development of the hall and its surrounding estate from the late seventeenth century up to the twentieth century when it was a military hospital. Although the hall has been demolished, the estate has become a public park to be enjoyed by many whilst one of its features, the Iron Bridge over the River Goyt has been restored and is an important feature of the park. This well-written and informative booklet should be of interest to all those who live in Marple and use the park for recreational activities.

Jones, A., *From fields to flowerbeds: the growth of Marple,* Marple Local History Society (Marple, 2013). Illus. Maps. £3. ISBN 978 0 9540582 6 5

When communities grow, population figures and maps showing where the new housing is located are commonplace, but only rarely is attention paid to the landowners and those who are involved in developing sites for new housing. In this booklet published by Marple Local History Society, Anthony Jones has examined this aspect of the growth of Marple from the late eighteenth century to the twentieth century. His research throws new light onto this area developed, especially in the early twentieth century. His approach is one that is to be welcomed and could benefit the study of other communities that are basically middle class commuter areas. This book is a worthy addition to the literature available on Marple.

Hills, G., *Walks around Marple,* Marple Community Council (Marple, 1998, revised 2009). Single A4 sheet folded. Map. Illus. £2.50

Hill has compiled six walks around Marple in which he provides a detailed map showing the route to take as well as where the walk starts. Various places and points of interest are marked and these are accompanied by brief notes on their history which the walker can follow up at his or her leisure. The distance is given as well as the average length of time it should take. A decade after publication, the Marple Local History Society has issued an up-date to the walks whereby changes have been noted for the benefit of those following the walks. These walks are only available as a pack of six with the up-date and not individually. They provide a very useful and interesting guide to the area and gives an idea of something that can be done in half a day.

Article abstracts and keywords

Dave Russell
Going with the mainstream: Manchester cabaret clubs and popular music in the 1960s

In the 1960s, the Manchester region was at the heart of Britain's 'cabaret' or 'variety' club culture. The products of a propitious economic and legal environment of the late 1950s and early 1960s, they were run by local entrepreneurs seeking to provide late-night entertainment for a mass audience anxious to feel part of the modern consumer environment. Although stand-up comedians played a large role, clubs were, above all, centres for the enjoyment of what historians have often dismissively termed 'mainstream' popular music. While they undoubtedly featured music that was determinedly commercial and often aesthetically conservative, they provided a wide range of musical genres for their audiences, ranging from contemporary pop music to 'standards' and operatic ballads. Although effectively dead as a form by the late 1970s, cabaret clubs made a major contribution to the development of the region's night life and entertainment culture more widely.

Keywords: *Cabaret; consumption; mainstream music; ballads*

Dennis Bourne and Melanie Tebbutt
Shebeens and black music culture in Moss Side, Manchester, in the 1950s and 1960s

Unlicensed drinking clubs, or shebeens, played an important role in in the leisure and musical life of Manchester's black communities from the late 1940s. The arrival of black American servicemen at the Bamber Bridge and Burtonwood air force bases in the 1940s was a critical moment in the emergence of the city's black club culture. Often excluded from public leisure activity as a result of the US military's policy of racial segregation, black servicemen stimulated a distinctive part of the night-time economy through their wages, supplies of alcohol, records and, in some cases, musical skills. In the 1950s, shebeens became a key social focus for the city's growing West Indian (particularly Jamaican) population, seeking both an escape from the rigours of work and an institution that to some degree replicated the social and cultural worlds that they had left behind. Shebeens became a critical centre for the consumption and performance of a variety of black American and Jamaican musical genres and undoubtedly played a role in the popular musical education of a number of white listeners and musicians.

Keywords: *Americanisation; Burtonwood; jazz; Moss Side; segregation*

CP Lee
Bob Dylan, Folk Music and Manchester

This article presents an account of Dylan's first three visits to Manchester during the 1960s and how he influenced and was influenced by the British folk revival which was at its height. It shows how folk stereotypes were created and how progressively the cliché of the folk entertainer was propagated by middle-class media types and eventually replaced by musician and audiences through action, revival and renewal. Using historical record and oral accounts, it connects movements in folk to rock to punk particularly in the Manchester area and demonstrates direct links in performance style and delivery.

Keywords: *Bob Dylan; Manchester; Folk Music Revival*

Bob Dickinson
Audiences in punk and post-punk Manchester Abstract

This essay looks at the importance of audiences during the punk and post-punk period, 1976–1983, in the Manchester area, when the city's creativity became recognized nationally, thanks to the success of bands like the Buzzcocks, The Fall and Joy Division. The essay argues that this creativity was shared by audiences themselves, and was, to an extent, caused by them. This creative phase is widely agreed to have begun with the Sex Pistols' concerts at the Lesser Free Trade Hall in 1976.

The way audiences changed between the initial minority phase of punk, its growing popularity and eventual commercial success is examined using different sources, including photographic evidence and material published in fanzines, as well as personal recollection and interviews. The significance of audience-inclusive organizations like Manchester Musicians' Collective is acknowledged, as well as the role of fanzines and other 'DIY' projects. A picture emerges of the way punk grew audiences that eventually fragmented into factions, often conservative in nature, undermining, in many important aspects, the initial 'spirit' of punk. But the interaction between audiences and performance throughout the period also points to certain vital inventive processes having continued, realized in the importance of processions and audience 'alienation'.

Keywords: *Punk; Post-Punk; Audiences; Fanzines*

James McGrath
'Closer from a distance': The auras of Factory Records in music, place, film, and historiography

Factory Records operated from Manchester as an independent label from 1978 to 1992, when this experimental enterprise met bankruptcy. Factory's history has been narrated in numerous media forms, yet most representations are authored or dominated by individuals who had direct involvement with the label. The following article offers a more detached approach, and is one of the first academic studies to focus specifically on Factory itself. I identify and critique how Factory initially mythologized itself and its artists through notions of distance from the audience, and how these approaches served as alternative promotional techniques. I then highlight how post-1992 narratives concerning Factory continue to stoke the label's mythology, by ostensibly removing (yet still relying upon) the earlier invocations of distance. The article aims to broaden debates concerning Factory itself as a text by offering new perspectives on individual albums, songs, videos, films and historiographies. Outlining new critical approaches to Factory's legacy, I expand on Walter Benjamin's term 'aura' (1936)

to consider how original Factory artefacts both exploited and beautified tensions between mass production and the individual object. In doing so, I hope to demonstrate further directions for interdisciplinary discussions of Factory's legacy and its cultural relevance in the twenty-first century.

Keywords: *Walter Benjamin; aura; Ian Curtis; Joy Division; Martin Hannett; Tony Wilson*

Georgina Gregory
Madchester and the representations of the North-South divide in the 1980s and 1990s

The Madchester music scene of the late 1980s and early 1990s flourished for a short time as a relatively underground subculture. When the music was discovered by the mainstream media, the response drew on long-standing stereotypes of northern identity, thereby reinforcing the hegemony of the south in matters cultural. The origins and manifestations of the divide are explored first before looking more closely at the particular social and political conditions underpinning the emergence of a separate music scene in Manchester. The individual characteristics of Madchester fashion and music are examined to relate elements of style to the traditional stereotypes and discourses surrounding 'northernness'. Examples of contemporary media coverage of the Madchester scene are discussed to show the media mobilized well-worn cultural tropes to portray the artists and the city in a negative light. I also show how, in an era of extreme social division, members of the local creative community sometimes hyperbolized their northern identities as a means of resistance to southern cultural imperialism

Keywords: *Madchester, stereotypes, northern, identity, North-South divide*

Esperanza Miyake
The Manchester Lesbian and Gay Chorus: Manchester, the Gay Village, and local music-making practices

Based on an ethnographical research I carried out in Manchester with the Manchester Lesbian and Gay Chorus (MLGC) between 2003 and 2005, this article examines the relationship between the local music scene in Manchester and the emergence of a more openly gay and lesbian culture between late 1980s throughout the 1990s. I explore Manchester's own urban transformation starting in the early 1990s, and how this consequently opened up new socio-cultural and political opportunities for the local lesbian and gay community. By analyzing the MLGC's everyday life musical activities in the city, this article thus addresses issues relating to Manchester's local music-making practices and gay and lesbian culture in order to understand one aspect of the relationship between music and sexuality.

Keywords: *city; music; everyday life; lesbian and gay; subculture; ethnography*

Contributors' notes

Dennis Bourne graduated from Manchester Metropolitan University in 2012 with an upper second in BA (Hons) History. Born and raised in Manchester, he completed an Access course in International Relations at The Manchester College, before progressing onto Higher Education in 2009. Music has always been a passion of his and, from leaving Abraham Moss High school in 1991, he has been part of the Manchester music scene as singer/songwriter/composer for a number of different bands including Large (1995–98), Brahma (1998–200), Buffalo 66/Hippy Mafia (1999–present day) and Jooks Official (2007–2009). He has featured on a number of releases. Since graduating from university he has continued his research into shebeens and, their impact on the Manchester community and music scene.

Bob Dickinson participated in Manchester's punk and post-punk subcultures during the late 1970s and early 1980s, writing for fanzines like *City Fun* and alternative magazines like *New Manchester Review*, as well as reporting for national publications including *New Musical Express*. He also worked on oral history projects for the Manchester Studies Unit at Manchester Polytechnic, before working at Granada Television, Channel 4 TV, and BBC TV. He now works as a freelance radio producer and presenter for BBC Radio 4, teaches part-time at Huddersfield University, and is a regular contributor to *Art Monthly* magazine.

Georgina Gregory, a Mancunian, is a Senior Lecturer in Media and Film at University of Central Lancashire where she teaches modules on the visual culture of popular music and youth culture. She has published a number of papers on aspects of popular music and her research interests currently include gender and performance, tribute entertainment and posthumous performance. Her latest project is a monograph on boybands and the performance of pop masculinity.

Chris 'CP' Lee is a writer, broadcaster, lecturer and performer who began his singing career in the North West folk and beat clubs of the 1960s before starting the band Alberto y Lost Trios Paranoias. Changing professions in the 1980s, CP is currently a senior lecturer at the University of Salford. As well as his autobiography *When we were thin*, CP has written two books on Bob Dylan, one of which is about Dylan's 1966 concert at Manchester's Free Trade Hall *Like the night (revisited)*, as well as a book on the history of popular music-making in Manchester, *Shake, rattle & rain*. CP is a writer and presenter of documentaries for BBC Radio and TV and he also conducts walks and talks on a variety of subjects. Most importantly – he was there the night Dylan went 'electric'!

James McGrath specializes in interdisciplinary literary studies. He lectures at Leeds Metropolitan University in the departments of History, Music, Media, and Journalism, as well as English. His AHRC-funded PhD (2010) was a first cultural study of Lennon and McCartney's work, and his subsequent research has detailed the previously undocumented ways in which black musicians in Liverpool mentored the young Beatles, and he is a guest lecturer on Liverpool Hope University's MA programme *The Beatles, Popular Music and Society*. James's poems regularly appear in literary periodicals. His current research emphasises the importance of the Arts and Humanities towards understandings of adult autism.

Esperanza Miyake currently teaches Media Studies at Liverpool John Moores University, including the Mass Communications summer programme. Her PhD thesis was on Queer Ethnographies of Music and Sexuality. She has and continues to present, publish and review works on popular culture, music, and race/raciality, particularly in relation to sexuality. She is the co-editor (with Dr Adi Kuntsman) of *Out of Place: Interrogating Silences in Queerness/*

Raciality (Raw Nerve, 2008). She is the author of the award-winning essay, 'My, is that cyborg a little bit queer?' (*Journal of International Women's Studies*, 2004).

Dave Russell taught in schools in Bradford and Leeds, at the University of Central Lancashire and at Leeds Metropolitan University, from where he retired as Professor of History and Northern Studies in 2010. His publications include *Popular music in England, 1840–1914.*

A social history; *Football and the English* and *Looking North. Northern England in the national imagination.*

Melanie Tebbutt is Reader in History in the Department of History, Politics and Philosophy at Manchester Metropolitan University. She has a particular interest in the history of youth and leisure. Her most recent book is *Being Boys: Youth Leisure and Identity in the Inter-war Years* (Manchester: Manchester University Press, 2012).

Manchester Region History Review

Editors
Melanie Tebbutt   Craig Horner   John F. Wilson

Editorial board

Morris Garratt (Libraries)   Paula Moorhouse
Clare Hartwell   Catharine Rew (Museums)
Karen Hunt   Mike Rose
Alan Kidd   Bill Williams
Neville Kirk   Terry Wyke
Brian Maidment   Chris Makepeace (Short Reviews)

Book Reviews editor
Fiona Cosson (f.cosson@mmu.ac.uk)

Corresponding members
Robert Glen, University of New Haven, US
Kazuhiko Kondo, University of Tokyo, Japan

Correspondence
The Editors
Manchester Region History Review
Manchester Centre for Regional History
Manchester Metropolitan University
Geoffrey Manton Building
Rosamond Street West
Manchester M15 6LL
United Kingdom
http://www.mcrh.mmu.ac.uk

For full details of individual and institutional
subscription rates for the UK and overseas,
refer to:
http://www.hssr.mmu.ac.uk/mcrh/mrhr/

Illustrations
We acknowledge the following for permission
in reproducing illustrations or for providing
assistance in the preparation of articles:
Manchester Archives and Local Studies;
Manchester District Music Archive;
Manchester Lesbian and Gay Chorus; Mark
Makin; Esperanza Miyake. Every effort has
been made to contact the copyright holders but
if any have been inadvertently overlooked, the
editors will be pleased to make the necessary
arrangements at the first opportunity.

Notes for contributors
If you would like to contribute to this journal,
please contact the editors before submitting
copy. Authors should consult: http://www.hssr.
mmu.ac.uk/mcrh/mrhr/
Conventional articles should not exceed 8,000
words including footnotes, although they can
be much shorter. We encourage a variety of
contributions and are willing to discuss ideas
and draft articles at an early stage. Intending
contributors to the Libraries, Museums and
Societies sections should consult the editors in
the first instance. Book reviews should be sent
to the Book Reviews editor. All submitted work
should be in Word format.

Advertisements
For details of advertising rates, please contact
the editors.

Indexing
Articles appearing in this journal are
abstracted and indexed in: HISTORICAL
ABSTRACTS and AMERICA: HISTORY
AND LIFE.